The AutoCAD
Programming and Customizing
Quick Reference

DRAW FROM EXPERIENCE!

Also available from Autodesk Press:

Maximizing AutoCAD R13
      by Rusty Gesner
      ISBN 0827379935

Maximizing AutoLISP R13
      by Rusty Gesner
      ISBN 0827379943

Customizing AutoCAD for R13 DOS/Windows
      by Sham Tickoo
      ISBN 0827375018

AutoCAD Productivity Book for R13 Windows
      by James Brittain, George O. Head, A. Ted Schaefer
      ISBN 1566041856

AutoLISP in Plain English: A Practical Guide for Non-programmers for R13 Windows
      by George O. Head
      ISBN 1566041406

AutoLISP: Programming for Productivity for R11 and R12 DOS
      by William Kramer
      ISBN 0827358326

The Illustrated AutoCAD R13 Quick Reference for Windows
      by Ralph Grabowski
      ISBN 0827371497

The Illustrated AutoCAD R13 Quick Reference for DOS
      by Ralph Grabowski
      ISBN 0827366450

Call your local representative for more information and a complete listing of all that Autodesk Press offers the AutoCAD user!

The AutoCAD Programming and Customizing Quick Reference

Ralph Grabowski

Press

 An International Thomson Publishing Company

Albany • Bonn • Boston • Cincinnati • Detroit • London • Madrid
Melbourne • Mexico City • New York • Pacific Grove • Paris • San Francisco
Singapore • Tokyo • Toronto • Washington

NOTICE TO THE READER

Publisher does not warrant or guarantee any of the products described herein or perform any independent analysis in connection with any of the product information contained herein. Publisher does not assume, and expressly disclaims, any obligation to obtain and include information other than that provided to it by the manufacturer.

The reader is expressly warned to consider and adopt all safety precautions that might be indicated by the activities herein and to avoid all potential hazards. By following the instructions contained herein, the reader willingly assumes all risks in connections with such instructions.

The publisher makes no representation or warranties of any kind, including but not limited to, the warranties of fitness for particular purpose or merchantability, nor are any such representations implied with respect to the material set forth herein, and the publisher takes no responsibility with respect to such material. The publisher shall not be liable for any special, consequential, or exemplary damages resulting, in whole or part, from the readers' use of, or reliance upon, this material.

Trademarks
AutoCAD® and the AutoCAD® logo are registered trademarks of Autodesk, Inc.
Windows is a trademark of the Microsoft Corporation.
All other product names are acknowledged as trademarks of their respective owners

Cover art by Robert Seed

COPYRIGHT © 1997
By Delmar Publishers
Autodesk Press imprint
an International Thomson Publishing Company
The ITP logo is a trademark under license

Printed in the United States of America

For more information, contact:

Delmar Publishers
3 Columbia Circle , Box 15015
Albany, New York 12212-5015

International Thomson Publishing Europe
Berkshire House 168-173
High Holborn
London, WC1V7AA
England

Thomas Nelson Australia
102 Dodds Street
South Melbourne, 3205
Victoria, Australia

Nelson Canada
1120 Birchmont Road
Scarborough, Ontario
Canada M1K 5G4

International Thomson Editores
Campos Eliseos 385, Piso 7
Col Polanco
11560 Mexico D F Mexico

International Thomson Publishing Gmb
Königswinterer Strasse 418
53227 Bonn
Germany

International Thomson Publishing Asia
221 Henderson Road
#05 -10 Henderson Building
Singapore 0315

International Thomson Publishing - Japan
Hirakawacho Kyowa Building, 3F
2-2-1 Hirakawacho
Chiyoda-ku, Tokyo 102
Japan

1 2 3 4 5 6 7 8 9 10 XXX 01 00 99 98 97 96

Library of Congress Cataloging-in-Publication Data

Grabowski, Ralph.
    The AutoCAD programming and customizing quick reference / Ralph Grabowski
        p.   cm.
    Includes index.
    ISBN: 0-8273-7991-9
    1. Computer graphics.   2. AutoCAD (Computer file)   I. Title

T385. G6917   1996
 20' .0042'02855369–dc20   96-9930
                                                                                          CIP

Quick Contents

How to Reach Us

To access Autodesk Press on the World Wide Web, point your browser to: ***http://www.autodeskpress.com***

Autodesk Press is an imprint of the International Thomson Publishing
organization: ***http://www.thomson.com***

Table of Contents

AutoLISP and ADS Reference, continued

B

C

D

E

AutoLISP and ADS Reference, continued

L

M

N

AutoLISP and ADS Reference, continued

O

P

Q

R

AutoLISP and ADS Reference, continued

Z

DIESEL

DIESEL, continued

LINETYPES

HATCH PATTERNS

ALIASES

SCRIPTS

TOOLBAR

Dialog Control Language, continued

SYSTEM VARIABLES

INDEX

How to Use This Book

The AutoCAD Programming and Customizing Quick Reference presents concise facts about the most-common programming interfaces found in AutoCAD Release 13 for DOS and Windows.

The clear format of this reference book demonstrates each function on its own page, plus these exclusive features:

- Handy references to AutoCAD many macro commands, control codes, and meta characters.

- Quick Start mini-tutorials that help you get started in customizing AutoCAD right now!

- Hundreds of context-sensitive tips that point out how to better use the programming function.

- All system variables, including those not listed by AutoCAD's **SetVar** command.

- Every function includes a list of related functions to help you find the right function in a hurry!

- Undocumented features and corrections to Autodesk's documentation.

AUTOCAD VERSIONS COVERED

This edition of *The AutoCAD Programming and Customizing Quick Reference* is specific to Release 13 of AutoCAD. However, most functions work with earlier versions, such as Release 10, 11, and 12. Distinction is made between the Release 11/12 and Release 13 versions of the Toolbar.

The DOS version of AutoCAD is capable of everything in the Windows version, with the exception of the Toolbar.

AutoCAD LT for Windows has many fewer programming capabilities than full AutoCAD. Specifically, LT has scripts, menu macros, toolbar macros, and Diesel programming, as well as linetype, hatch pattern, and shape customization.

Autodesk released two versions of ARx (short for AutoCAD Runtime eXtension). The first was a hybrid version that took on most of the function names found in ADS (short for AutoCAD development system); this version is included in the book. The second version is very different from ADS and is not included in this book.

AutoCAD Release 12 and 13 include a programming interface for SQL-based (short for Structure Query Language) external databases. The ASI (short for AutoCAD SQL Interface) functions are not in this book, neither are ASE-specific (short for AutoCAD SQL Extension) AutoLISP and ADS functions.

Each function includes the following information:

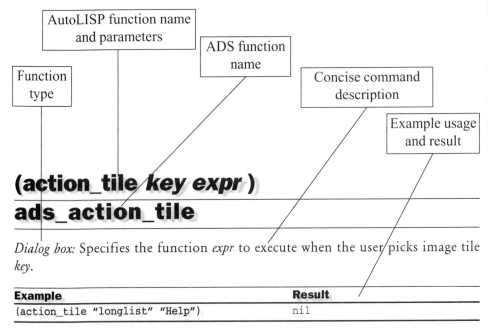

AutoLISP function name and parameters

ADS function name

Function type

Concise command description

Example usage and result

(action_tile key expr)
ads_action_tile

Dialog box: Specifies the function *expr* to execute when the user picks image tile *key*.

Example	Result
(action_tile "longlist" "Help")	nil

The **Help** *button is an example of an image tile; the* **OK** *and* **Cancel** *buttons appear in every dialogue box by default:*

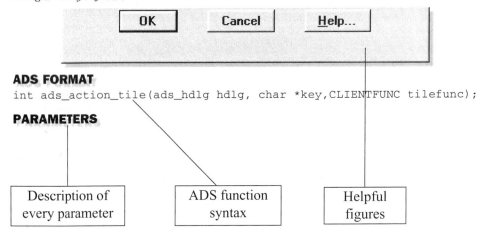

ADS FORMAT
```
int ads_action_tile(ads_hdlg hdlg, char *key,CLIENTFUNC tilefunc);
```

PARAMETERS

Description of every parameter

ADS function syntax

Helpful figures

The AutoCAD Programming and Customizing Quick Reference covers these AutoCAD APIs (short for applications programming interface):

AUTOLISP AND ADS REFERENCE
All of the AutoLISP, ADS, and hybrid ADS-ARx functions found in AutoCAD Release 13 are listed in alphabetical order.

DIESEL

The Direct Interpretively Evaluated String Expression Language — Diesel — is AutoCAD's "other" programming language and is the only programming available in AutoCAD LT. Quick Starts teach you how to use Diesel, followed by an alphabetical listing of Diesel functions.

LINETYPES

Quick Start tutorials teach you how to code linetypes and Release 13's new complex linetypes.

HATCH PATTERNS

Once linetypes are mastered, you are in a good position to use Quick Start tutorials to create two-dimensional hatch patterns.

ALIASES

Command aliases are AutoCAD's simplest customization. They let you get your work done faster by typing less at the keyboard.

SCRIPTS

The script was AutoCAD's first programming interface. The Quick Start tutorial shows you how to create a batch of commands that execute automatically, followed by an alphabetical description of AutoCAD's script-related commands.

TOOLBAR

The Toolbar is AutoCAD's most user-friendly programming capability. Quick Start tutorials show you employ the Toolbar in AutoCAD Release 11/12/LT and Release 13.

MENUS

The menu has become AutoCAD's most important user interface. Quick Start tutorials explain the intricate inner workings of the menu file, along with creating an icon menu.

SHAPES

Shapes are used to create AutoCAD's text fonts and an early version of the block, called the "shape," that uses a cryptic system of hexadecimal codes.

DIALOG CONTROL LANGUAGE

DCL is the way that AutoCAD displays exactly the same dialog boxes, no matter which operating system its running under.

Ralph Grabowski
Abbotsford, British Columbia, Canada
25 July, 1996
email: ralphg@xyzpress.com

■ ■ ■

ads_abort(*prompt*)
acrx_abort(*prompt*)

Error handler: Displays a prompt to the user and terminates the ADS or ARx application.

Example	Result
acrx_abort ("Ending app")	Ending app

ARX FORMAT
```
void acrx_abort (const char * format, ...);
```

ADS FORMAT
```
void ads_abort(const char *str);
```

PARAMETER
■ *prompt*   (*Optional*) Displays a prompt to the user.

TIPS
■ **Ads_abort** and **Acrx_abort** ask AutoLISP to terminate the ADS (or ARx) application, and displays an error message.

■ **Ads_abort** must be used only with ADS applications; **Acrx_abort** must only be used with ARx applications; there is no equivalent in AutoLISP.

■ **Ads_abort** is called by any ADS function when a fatal error occurs.

■ These abort functions should only be used as a last resort.

RELATED ADS FUNCTIONS
■ **ads_alert**   Displays dialog box with a programmer-defined message.

■ **ads_exit**   Exits the ADS application.

■ **ads_fail**   Prints a programmer-defined error message.

(abs *nbr*)

...

Arithmetic function: Absolute value of the number *nbr* (*short for ABSolute*).

Examples	Result
(abs -19.56)	19.56
(abs 815)	815

PARAMETER
- *nbr*   A single integer or real number.

TIPS
- **abs** strips off the negative sign to make the number positive.

- Three system variables accept positive and negative values, **PdMode**, **PsQuality**, and **TreeDepth**, plus all variables that deal with coordinates, such as **ViewCtr** and **VsMax**.

- Negative values are used to define length of spaces in LIN linetype definition files and PAT hatch pattern files.

RELATED AUTOLISP FUNCTIONS
fix   Rounds down a real number and converts it to an integer.

float   Converts an integer to a real number.

minusp   Checks if a number is negative.

(acad_colordlg *clrno [flag]*)

...

Command function: Displays AutoCAD's standard **Select Color** dialog box with *clrno* as the default color; (*an external function defined in AcadApp.Ads*).

Example	Result
(acad_colordlg 250)	250
(acad_colordlg 5 nil)	5
(acad_colordlg 942 T)	94
Cancel	nil

*The **Select Color** dialog box with disabled logical colors (BYLAYER and BYBLOCK) and default color blue (bottom):*

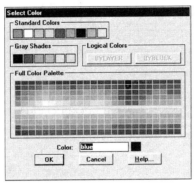

PARAMETERS

■ *clrno* Specifies the default color.

Range: A single integer between 0 and 256 with these special meanings:

Number	Color Name
0	ByBlock
1	Red
2	Yellow
3	Green
4	Cyan
5	Blue
6	Magenta
7	White (or black)
8	Dark grey
9	Light grey
10 - 249	The rainbow of colors
250 - 255	Six shades of grey
256	ByLayer

■ *flag* (*Optional*) When **T**, displays the **ByLayer** and **ByBlock** buttons.

TIPS

- The **DdColor** command also displays the **Select Color** dialog box.
- System variable **CeColor** stores the current color number.
- Use the predefined variable, T, as a non-nil flag.

RELATED AUTOLISP FUNCTIONS

command	Executes any AutoCAD command, such as **DdColor**.
help	Displays the **Help** window.
getvar	Gets the value of a system variable, such as **CeColor**.
setvar	Sets the value of a system variable.

RELATED SYSTEM VARIABLE

CeColor	The value of the current color.

(acad_helpdlg *file topic*)

...

(*Obsolete*): Displays the *file*.Hlp in the **Help** dialog box and related *topic* (*an external function in AcadR13.Lsp*).

Example	Result
(acad_helpdlg "acad.hlp" "line")	"acad.hlp"

The **AutoCAD Help** *window showing topic* **Line:**

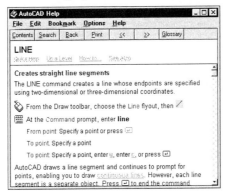

PARAMETERS

- *file*   A string specifying the HLP help filename.

- *topic*   A string specifying the help file topic name.

TIPS

- In Release 13, the **help** function replaces the **acad_helpdlg** function and remains for compatibility reasons only. In fact, **acad_helpdlg** is an AutoLISP function that passes its parameters to the built-in **help** function. It's only purpose is R12 compatibility.

- Since **acad_helpdlg** has been replaced, your code should call **help** instead.

- AutoCAD Release 13 for Windows includes 12 help files.

- You obtain the list of help topic names with the **Help | Search for Help On** command.

*An example of using the Help engine's **Search** function on Acad.Hlp:*

RELATED AUTOLISP FUNCTIONS

help   The new, Release 13 AutoLISP function that loads the HLP file.

command Executes any AutoCAD command, including the **Help** (or ?) command.

(acad_strlsort *list*)

∎ ∎ ∎

List manipulation: Sort a *list* of strings in alphabetial order (*short for STRing List SORT; an external function defined in AcadApp.Ads*).

Example	Result
(acad_strlsort '("st" "hd" "kt"))	("hd" "kt" "st")

PARAMETER
- *list*   The list of strings.

TIP
- The **acad_strlsort** function returns *nil* when the computer lacks memory to perform the sort, or when the list contains invalid strings.

RELATED AUTOLISP FUNCTIONS

list   Creates a list from several expressions.

listp   Checks whether the list is indeed a list.

reverse   Reverses the order of the list.

(action_tile *key expr*)
ads_action_tile

Dialog box: Specifies the function *expr* to execute when the user picks image tile *key*.

Example	Result
(action_tile "longlist" "Help")	nil

*The **Help** button is an example of an image tile; the **OK** and **Cancel** buttons appear in every dialog box by default:*

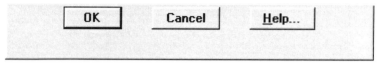

ADS FORMAT
```
int ads_action_tile(ads_hdlg hdlg, char *key,CLIENTFUNC tilefunc);
```

PARAMETERS
- *key*   Name of the tile triggering the action specified by the tile's *key* attribute.
- *expr*   Name of the function executed when the user picks the image tile.

TIPS
- The *key* parameter is case sensitive.
- The *expr* function specified by **(action_tile)** supercedes:
  - The tile's default action as defined by **(new dialog)**.
  - The tile's *action* attribute.
- Expression *expr* is permitted to make the following references:
  - **$value**   Tile's current *value* attribute.
  - **$key**   Tile's name.
  - **$data**   Application specific data set by **(client_data_tile)**.
  - **$reason**   Tile's callback.
  - **$x** *and* **$y**   Image coordinates, if tile is an image button.

RELATED AUTOLISP AND ADS FUNCTIONS
client_data_tile *and* ads_client_data_tile
> Associates application data to a dialog box tile

new_dialog *and* ads_new_dialog
> Intializes and displays the dialog box.

(add_list *str*)
ads_add_list

Dialog box: Changes or adds *str* to a string in a dialog box.

Example	Result
(add_list "List of files")	nil

ADS FORMAT
```
int ads_add_list(char *item);
```

PARAMETER
- *str*   Any string of text.

TIPS
- Use **start_list** to open and initialize the list before using the **add_list** function.
- The **add_list** function either: (1) adds to the list; or (2) replaces the list item, depending on the options specified by the **start_list** function.

RELATED AUTOLISP AND ADS FUNCTIONS
start_list *and* **ads_start_list**

   Starts the processing of a list in a dialog box.

end_list *and* **ads_end_list**

   Ends the processing of a dialog box list.

(ads)
ads_loaded

External apps: Lists the filenames of ADS applications currently loaded in AutoCAD (*short for AutoCAD Development System*).

Example	Result
(ads)	("D:\\ACAD13\\WIN\\acadapp.exe")

ADS FORMAT
```
struct  resbuf  *ads_loaded(void);
```

PARAMETERS
none

TIP
■   The string returned by **ads** might be formatted with \\ (double backslashes) or / (single forward slash), depending on the operating system.

RELATED AUTOLISP AND ADS FUNCTIONS
arxloaded *and* **ads_arxloaded**

> Lists the filenames of ARx applications currently loaded in AutoCAD.

xload *and* **ads_xload**

> Loads an ADS application into AutoCAD.

xunload *and* **ads_xunload**

> Unloads an ADS application from AutoCAD, freeing up memory.

(alert *str*)
ads_alert

Error handler: Displays the alert dialog box with a specified string.

Example	Result
(alert "Do you really want to do this?")	nil

The AutoCAD Message dialog box with user-defined message:

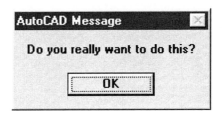

ADS FORMAT
```
int ads_alert(const char *str);
```

PARAMETER
- *str*   Any string of text.

TIPS
- **Alert** attempts to display the string on a single line. If you have a long message, use \n to break the string up into several lines.

- The length of text is limited to 132 characters or what the operating system and display driver can display.

- Use DCL programming to create a customized alert dialog box.

RELATED AUTOLISP AND ADS FUNCTIONS
ads_fail   Prints an error message.

error   Programmer-definable error message.

(alloc *int*)

■■■

Memory management: Sets the memory segment size to the number of nodes specified by *int* and returns the previous segment size (*short for ALLOCate*).

Example	Result
(alloc 512)	1024

PARAMETERS
■ *int*   The number of nodes of required memory (AutoLISP only).

■ *sz*   Array size (ADS only)

TIPS
■ Memory management in AutoLISP is independent of the operating system since AutoCAD acts as the operating system for AutoLISP; this ensures portability between platforms.

■ Each node takes up 12 bytes.

■ Each segment takes up 514 nodes (6,168 bytes).

RELATED AUTOLISP AND ADS FUNCTIONS
expand	Increases node space by segments.
gc	Frees up unused nodes.
ads_free	Releases the memory allocated by **ads_calloc**.
ads_realloc	Changes the size of the memory region set by **ads_calloc**.

(and *expr* ...)

...

Logic function: Returns **T** or **nil** after applying a logical AND to *expr*.

Example	Result
(and 1.2 3.4 5.6)	T

PARAMETER
- *expr*   A list of expressions

TIP
- This function stops evaluating upon finding the first **nil** in its arguments.

RELATED AUTOLISP FUNCTIONS

boole   Bitwise Boolean function.

not   Logical NOT.

or   Logical OR.

(angle *pt1 pt2*)
ads_angle(*pt1, pt2*)

Geometric function: Measures the counterclockwise angle between x-axis and line
with endpoints *pt1* and *pt2*; returned in radians.

Example	Result
(angle pt1 pt2)	0.671228

*The **angle** measured from the x-axis to the line formed by **pt1** and **pt2**:*

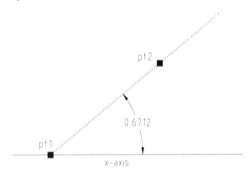

ADS FORMAT
```
ads_real ads_angle(const ads_point pt1, const ads_point pt2);
```

PARAMETERS
- pt1   A 2D or 3D coordinate.
- pt2   Another 2D or 3D coordinate.

TIPS
- The angle is measured in the current UCS.
- The z-coordinate of **pt1** and **pt2** is ignored.
- All angular measurement by AutoLISP and ADS is performed using radians.
- The following function (subroutine) converts degrees to radians:

```
; DtoR.Lsp: Converts degrees to radians
(defun dtor (d)
  (* PI (/ d 180.0)
)
```

RELATED AUTOLISP AND ADS FUNCTIONS
angtof   Converts a string angle to real radians.

angtos   Converts angular radians to a string.

polar *and* **ads_polar**

        Finds a point given a distance and an angle.

(angtof *str [mode]*)
ads_angtof

Conversion: Converts string *str* to an angle as a real number; *mode* determines the format of the angle (*short for ANGle TO Floating point*).

Example	Results
(angtof ang1)	0.6712
(angtof ang1 1)	0.0117146

ADS FUNCTION
```
int ads_angtof(const char str, int mode, ads_real *v);
```

PARAMETERS
- *str*   A string in the format of an angle.

- *mode*   (*Optional*) Specifies the format of the conversion, as follows:

Mode	System	String formatted as
0	Decimal degrees:	00.0000 (default)
1	Degrees	00d00'00.0000"
2	Grad	00.0000g
3	Radian	00.0000r
4	Surveyor's	N00d00.0000E

TIPS
- **Angtof** uses the value stored in system variable **AUnits** when *mode* is omitted.
- Systems of angle measurement:

     Degrees: 360 degrees in a full circle.

     Grad: 400 grads in a full circle.

     Radian: 2*pi (6.2831852) radians in a full circle.

- AutoLISP defines the constant **pi** as 3.1415926

RELATED AUTOLISP AND ADS FUNCTION
angtos *and* ads_angtos

     Converts an angle to a string.

RELATED SYSTEM VARIABLE
AUnits   Mode of angular units as set by the **Units** and **DdUnits** commands; default value = 0.

(angtos *ang [mode [prec]]*)
ads_angtos

Conversion: Converts an angle *ang* to a string; *mode* determines the format of the string and *prec* determines the number of decimal places (*short for ANGle TO String*).

Example	Result
(angtos ang1)	"0.6712"
(angtos ang1 2)	"200g"
(angtos ang1 2 5)	"200.00000g"

ADS FORMAT
```
int ads_angtos(ads_real v, int mode, int prec, char *str);
```

PARAMETERS
- *ang*   An angle in radians.
- *mode*   (*Optional*) Specifies the format of the conversion, as follows:

Mode	System	String format
0	Decimal degrees:	00.0000 (default)
1	Degrees	00d00'00.0000"
2	Grad	00.0000g
3	Radian	00.0000r
4	Surveyor's	N00d00.0000E

- *prec*   (*Optional*) Specifies the number of decimal places:

Prec	Range
Minimum	0
Default	4
Maximum	8

TIPS
- When *mode* and *prec* are missing, **angtos** uses the value stored in **AUnits** and **AuPrec**.
- **Angtos** accepts negative values but always returns positive values.

RELATED AUTOLISP AND ADS FUNCTION
angtof *and* ads_angtof

Converts a string representing an angle into a number in radians format.

RELATED SYSTEM VARIABLES
AUnits   Mode of angular units as set by the **Units** and **DdUnits** commands.

AuPrec   Precision of decimals displayed by angles.

UnitMode   (Toggle)   0 = Adds in spaces in surveyor's units "N 30d E"

                     1 = Does not add spaces: "N30dE"

(append *list* ...)

...

List manipulation: Appends all *list* items into a single list.

Example	Result
(append '(1.2 3.4) '(10.0))	(1.2 3.4 10.0)

PARAMETER
- *list*   A list of elements.

RELATED AUTOLISP FUNCTIONS

acad_strlsort	Sorts a list into alphanumerical order.
length	Determines the length of the list (number of elements).
listp	Verifies that an element is a list.
nth	Returns the nth element of the list.
reverse	Reverses the order of elements in the list.
subst	Substitutes an element in the list.

(apply *func list*)

...

Function handler: Applies the *list* of arguments to AutoLISP and programmer-defined functions *func*.

Example	Result
(apply '+ '(1.2 3.4 10.0))	14.6

PARAMETERS
- *func*   Any function defined by AutoLISP or the programmer.
- *list*   Any list of elements that the function *func* accepts.

RELATED AUTOLISP FUNCTIONS
defun   Creates a programmer-defined function.

lambda   Creates an anonymous, programmer-defined function.

(arx)
ads_arxloaded

External applications: Lists the filenames of ARx applications currently loaded into AutoCAD (*short for Autocad Runtime eXtension*).

Example	Result
(arx)	("D:\\ACAD13\\WIN\\render.arx")

ADS FORMAT
```
struct resbuf *ads_loaded(void);
```

PARAMETERS
none

TIPS
■ The string returned by **ads** might be formatted with \\ (double backslashes) or / (single forward slash), depending on the operating system..

■ If the application is no longer in memory, use **ads_relrb** to release the list that **ads_arxloaded** returns.

RELATED AUTOLISP AND ADS FUNCTIONS
ads *and* ads_loaded
> Reports the filenames of loaded ADS applications.

arxload *and* ads_arxload
> Loads an ARx application.

arxunload *and* ads_arxunload
> Unloads an ARx application to free up memory.

atoms-family   Lists the names of all loaded AutoLISP functions.

(arxload *app [flag]*)
ads_arxload

External applications: Loads ARx application *app* into AutoCAD; if the file cannot be loaded, returns argument *flag*.

Example	Result
(arxload "render.arx")	"render.arx"
(arxload "junk.arx" 2)	2

ADS FORMAT
```
int ads_arxload(const char *app);
```

PARAMETERS
- *app*   Filename (including optional drive designation and subdirectory name) of the ARx application to load.

- *flag*   (*Optional*) Message to display when ARx app cannot be loaded.

RELATED AUTOLISP AND ADS FUNCTIONS
arx *and* arx_loaded

     Reports the filenames of loaded ADS applications.

adsload *and* ads_adsload

     Loads an ADS application.

arxunload *and* ads_arxunload

     Unloads an ARx application to free up memory.

(arxunload *app [flag]*)
ads_arxunload

External applications: Unloads ARx application *app*; if the filename cannot be unloaded, returns arguement *flag*.

Examples	Result
(arxunload "render.arx")	. . .
(arxunload "junk.arx" 2)	2

ADS FORMAT
```
int ads_arxunload(const char *app);
```

PARAMETERS
- *app*   Filename (including optional drive designation and subdirectory name) of the ARx application to unload.

- *flag*   (*Optional*) Message to display when ARx app cannot be unloaded.

TIP
- Use the *flag* to avoid an AutoLISP error when **arxunload** fails.

RELATED AUTOLISP AND ADS FUNCTIONS
arxload *and* ads_arxload

Loads an ARx application.

arx *and* ads_arxloaded

Reports the filenames of ARx applications in memory.

ads *and* ads_loaded

Reports the filenames of loaded ADS applications.

(ascii *str*)

■■■

Conversion function: Converts the first character in string *str* to its ASCII code number (*short for American Standard Code for Information Interchange*).

Example	Result
(ascii "Quick")	81

PARAMETER
■ *str*   Any string of text.

TIPS
■ The ASCII table:

ASCII	Meaning		ASCII	Meaning
0	nul		30	rs
1	soh		31	us
2	stx		32	(Space)
3	etx (Cancel)		33	!
4	eot		34	"
5	enq		35	#
6	ack		36	$
7	bel (Bell)		37	%
8	bs (Backspace)		38	&
9	ht (Tab)		39	'
10	lf (Line feed)		40	(
11	ff (Form feed)		41	)
12	vt (Vertical tab)		42	*
13	cr (Carriage return)		43	+
14	so		44	,
15	si		45	-
16	dle		46	.
17	dc1		47	/
18	dc2		48	0
19	dc3		49	1
20	dc4		50	2
21	nak		51	3
22	syn		52	4
23	etb		53	5
24	can		54	6
25	etx		55	7
26	sub		56	8
27	esc (Escape)		57	9
28	fs		58	:
29	gs		59	;

ASCII	Meaning	ASCII	Meaning	ASCII	Meaning
60	<	83	S	106	j
61	=	84	T	107	k
62	>	85	U	108	l
63	?	86	V	109	m
64	@	87	W	110	n
65	A	88	X	111	o
66	B	89	Y	112	p
67	C	90	Z	113	q
68	D	91	[	114	r
69	E	92	\	115	s
70	F	93	]	116	t
71	G	94	^	117	u
72	H	95	_	118	v
73	I	96	'	119	w
74	J	97	a	120	x
75	K	98	b	121	y
76	L	99	c	122	z
77	M	100	d	123	{
78	N	101	e	124		
79	O	102	f	125	}
80	P	103	g	126	~
81	Q	104	h	127	(Delete)
82	R	105	i		

RELATED AUTOLISP FUNCTIONS

chr   Converts an ASCII code number into the equivalent character string.

atoi   Converts a string to an integer number.

atof   Converts a string to a real number.

angtof   Converts a string to an angle in radians.

(assoc *item list*)

...

List manipulation: Returns the first matching *item* found in the *list* (short for ASSOCiation).

Example	Result
(assoc 'x xyz)	(X 1.2)

PARAMETERS
- *item*   Any element.
- *list*   A list containing items.

TIP
- Use the **assoc** function with the **ent***xx* functions to change entity data.

RELATED AUTOLISP FUNCTIONS

member	Returns the remainder of a list.
length	Determines the length of the list.
mapcar	Executes a function using a list as input.
nth	Returns the nth item of a list.
subst	Searches and replaces items in a list.

(atan *n1 [n2]*)

...

Geometric function: Calculates the arctangent of *n1* in radians; when *n2* is present, calculates the arctangent of $^{n1}/_{n2}$ (*short for ArcTANgent*).

Example	Result
(atan 1)	0.785398
(atan 45 22.5)	0.463648

The arctangent is angle (in radians) of the x- and y-distance:

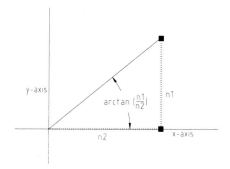

PARAMETERS

- **n1**   When used alone, assumed to be ratio of $^{n1}/_{n2}$, as shown in figure.

- **n2**   (*Optional*) The distance shown in the figure above.

TIPS

- All AutoLISP angular measurement is always in radians, no matter the setting of **Units**.
- The range of values returned by **atan** is between $-^{PI}/_2$ and $^{PI}/_2$.

RELATED AUTOLISP FUNCTIONS

cos   Calculates the cosine of an angle.

sin   Calculates the sine of an angle.

PI   The predefined constant = 3.14172...

(atof *str*)

...

Conversion: Converts string *str* into a real number (*short for Ascii TO Floating-point*).

Example	Result
(atof "8")	8.0
(atof "31.56")	31.56

PARAMETER
■ *str*   Any string in the form of a real number or integer.

RELATED AUTOLISP FUNCTIONS
chr   Converts an ASCII code number into the equivalent character string.

atoi   Converts a string to an integer number.

ascii   Converts the first character of a string to its ASCII number.

angtof   Converts a string to an angle in radians.

(atoi *str*)

Conversion: Converts string *str* into an integer number, rounded down (*short for Ascii TO Integer*).

Example	Result
(atoi "8")	8
(atoi "31.56")	31

PARAMETER

■ *str*   Any string in the format of a real number or integer.

RELATED AUTOLISP FUNCTIONS

chr   Converts an ASCII code number into the equivalent character string.

ascii   Converts the first character of a string to its ASCII number.

atof   Converts a string to a real number.

angtof   Converts a string to an angle in radians.

(atom *item*)

...

Symbol handler: Returns **T** if *item* is an atom; returns **nil** if *item* is a list.

Example	Result
(atom T)	T

PARAMETER
- *item*   Anything.

TIP
- This function returns **T** for anything except a list.

RELATED AUTOLISP FUNCTIONS
type   Determines the type of item.

listp   Checks if the item is a list.

numberp   Checks if an atom is a number.

(atoms-family *flag [list]*)

...

Symbol handler: Displays a list of currently-defined symbols as a list (*flag* = 1) or list of strings (*flag* = 0); or searches for a specific *list* of symbol names and returns **nil** if name does not exist.

Example	Result
(atoms-family 0)	("C:AI_SPHERE" "ALERT" "DEFUN" "LISPED" "C:RENDERUNLOAD" "C:DDRENAME" "GETDIST" ...)
(atoms-family 1)	(C:AI_SPHERE ALERT DEFUN LISPED C:RENDERUNLOAD C:DDRENAME GETDIST ...)
(atoms-family 1 '("getdist"))	("GETDIST")
(atoms-family 1 '("grabowski"))	(nil)

PARAMETERS

- *flag*   Determines whether symbols are displayed as a list or list of strings:

flag	Meaning
0	Display names as a list of strings.
1	Display names as a list.

- *list*   (*Optional*) One or more symbol names.

TIP

- The **atoms-family** function returns **nil** if a function in *list* is not defined.

RELATED AUTOLISP FUNCTIONS

atom   Determines if an item is an atom.

defun   Creates a programmer-defined symbol.

lamda   Creates an anonymous symbol.

(autoarxload *fname list*)

■■■

External applications: Automatically loads the ARx file *fname* when user types a command name defined by *list* (*short for AUTOmatic ARX LOADing; an external function defined in AcadR13.Lsp*).

Example	Result
`(autoarxload "solids" '("solview" "soldraw"))`	`nil`

PARAMETERS

■ *fname*   Filename of the ARx application; optionally includes drive name and subdirectory path; has an extension of .ARX.

■ *list*   The names of commands in the *fname* ARx application.

TIP

■ The first time the user types one of the command names in *list*, the **autoarxload** function automatically loads the associated ARx file.

RELATED AUTOLISP AND ARX FUNCTIONS

arx *and* **ads_arxloaded**

      Reports the filenames of loaded ARx applications.

arxload *and* **ads_arxload**

      Loads an ARx application.

arxunload *and* **ads_arxunload**

      Unloads an ARx application to free up memory.

(autoload *fname list*)

■■■

External applications: Automatically loads the AutoLISP file *fname* when user types a command name defined by *list* (*short for AUTOmatic LOADing*).

Example	Result
(autoload "xplode" '("xp" "xplode"))	nil

PARAMETERS

■ *fname*   Filename of the AutoLISP application; optionally includes drive name and subdirectory path; must have the LSP extension.

■ *list*   The names of commands in the *fname* AutoLISP application.

TIP

■   The first time the user types one of the command names in *list*, the **autoload** function automatically loads the associated AutoLISP file.

RELATED AUTOLISP FUNCTIONS

load   Loads an AutoLISP function from disk.

autoarxload   Automatically loads an ARx application when a function is called.

autoxload   Automatically loads an ADS application when a function is called.

(autoxload *fname list*)

...

External applications: Automatically loads the ADS file *fname* when user types a command name defined by *list* (*short for AUTOmatic ads LOADing*).

Example	Result
(autoxload "geomcal" '("cal" "cal"))	nil

PARAMETERS

- *fname*   Filename of the ADS application; optionally includes drive name and subdirectory path; must have an extension of .ADS.

- *list*   The names of commands in the *fname* ADS application.

TIP

- The first time the user types one of the command names in *list*, the **autoarxload** function automatically loads the associated ADS file.

RELATED AUTOLISP AND ADS FUNCTIONS

ads *and* ads_loaded

> Reports the filenames of loaded ADS applications.

xload *and* ads_xload

> Loads an ARx application.

xunload *and* ads_xunload

> Unloads an ARx application to free up memory.

(boole *func int1 int2*)

...

Logical function: Generalized boolean function for bits (*short for BOOLEan*).

Example	Result
(boole 1 2 3)	2

PARAMETERS

■ *func*   Code number of the boolean function:

func	Boolean operator
1	AND
6	XOR
7	OR
8	NOR

■ *int1, int2*   Two values.

RELATED AUTOLISP FUNCTIONS

and	Logical AND of two expressions.
or	Logical OR of two expressions.

(boundp *sym*)

∎ ∎ ∎

Symbol handler: Returns **T** if a value is bound to a symbol; **nil** otherwise.

Example	Result
(boundp 'a)	nil

PARAMETER
- *sym* Name of a symbol.

TIP
- If *sym* does not exist, AutoLISP creates it and binds it to **nil**.

RELATED AUTOLISP FUNCTIONS
atoms-family Lists the names of all or specific symbols currently loaded into memory.

atom Determines if the item is an atom.

numberp Determines if the item is a number.

type Reports the type of the item.

...

ads_buildlist

Result buffer: Creates a linked list of result buffers.

Example	Result
ads_buildlist(rt1,rt2,rt3)	*point to list*

ADS FORMAT

```
struct resbuf *ads_buildlist(int rtype, ...);
```

TIP

■ When an argument to **ads_buildlist** is a pair, the first identifies the type of the argument following; the second contains the data.

RELATED ADS FUNCTION

ads_relrb   Releases the memory used by **ads_buildlist**.

(car *list*)

■ ■ ■

List manipulation: Returns the first element of a list.

Example	Result
(car '(1.2 3.4 10.0))	1.2
(car '())	nil

PARAMETER
- *list*   A list of any length.

TIPS
- You can nest **car** and **cdr** four levels deep:

    ```
    (car (car (cdr (car a))))
    ```

    which can be abbreviated to:

    ```
    (caadar a)
    ```

- AutoLISP understand the following combinations of **car** and **cdr**:

caar	cddr	cadr	cdar	caddr	caaddr	cadar	cdaadr
caaar	cdddr	caadr	cddar	cadddr	cadaar	caddar	cdaar
caaaar	cddddr	caaadr	cdddar	caadar	cadadr	cdaaar	cdadar
cdaddr	cdadr	cddaar	cddadr				

- The most common combination function is **cadr**, which returns the second item in a list, such as the y-coordinate:

    ```
    (cadr (1.2 3.4 5.6))    ; returns 3.4, the y-coordinate
    (caddr (1.2 3.4 4.6))   ; returns 5.6, the z-coordinate
    ```

RELATED AUTOLISP FUNCTIONS
list	Combines items into a list.
cdr	Returns all but the first item of a list.
append	Creates one list out of many.
cons	Adds an item to the beginning of a list.
last	Returns the last item of a list.
length	Returns the length of the list.
reverse	Reverses the order of items in a list.

(cdr *list*)

∎∎∎

List manipulation: Returns the list with all but the first element.

Example	Return
(cdr '(1.2 3.4 10.0))	(3.4 10.0)

PARAMETER
- *list*   A list of any length.

TIPS
- When *list* is a dotted pair, **cdr** returns the select item (after the dot):

      (cdr '(1 . "LINE") ; returns "LINE"

- See **car** function for the 28 combinations of **car** and **cdr**.

RELATED AUTOLISP FUNCTIONS
list	Combines items into a list.
car	Returns the first item of a list.
append	Creates one list out of many.
cons	Adds an item to the beginning of a list.
last	Returns the last item of a list.
length	Returns the length of the list.
reverse	Reverses the order of items in a list.

(chr *int*)

■ ■ ■

Conversion: Converts integer *int* into the equivalent ASCII character.

Examples	Result
(chr 65)	"A"
(chr 1)	"\001"

PARAMETER
■ *int*   Any integer.

TIPS
■ When the value of *int* becomes higher than 255, the result "loops around" (a similar effect to modulus 256 = 0).

■ The **ascii** function for the table of ASCII values.

RELATED AUTOLISP FUNCTION
ascii   Converts the first character to its ASCII code.

(client_data_tile *key data*)
ads_client_data_tile

Dialog box: Associate a dialog box tile with data managed by an application.

Example	Result
(client_data_tile "just" "trivial")	

PARAMETERS
- *key*   Specifies the name of the tile.
- *data*   Application-managed data associated with a dialog box tile.

TIPS
- The *key* parameter is case sensitive.
- The string in *data* can be referred to by another function as **$data**.

RELATED AUTOLISP FUNCTIONS
All other tile-related functions.

(close *filed*)

...

File function: Closes the open file.

Example	Result
(close data)	nil

PARAMETER
- *filed* The operating-system assigned file descriptor assigned to a filename.

TIP
- The file descriptor remains after the file is closed but isn't valid.

RELATED AUTOLISP FUNCTION
open Opens a file for reading, writing, or appending.

...

ads_cmd

External apps: Execute an AutoCAD command with a result buffer list.

Example	Result
(ads_cmd *ptr1)	RTNORM

ADS FORMAT
```
int ads_cmd(struct resbuf *rbp);
```

PARAMETER
- **rbp*   A pointer to a result-buffer list; each buffer in the list is a data item passed to AutoCAD, just as if a user were typing commands at the 'Command:' prompt.

TIPS
- The advantage of **ads_cmd** over **ads_command** is that the command list can be modified at runtime rather than fixed at compile time.

- The disadvantage of **ads_cmd** over **ads_command** is that it takes longer to execute.

- **Ads_cmd** cannot invoke AutoLISP functions nor other ADS applications; use **ads_invoke** for ADS apps.

- **Ads_cmd** cannot invoke commands that directly access peripheral devices, such as **DText**, **Sketch**, and **Plot**.

- This function returns:

Returns	Meaning
RTNORM	Normal return.
RTCAN	User pressed [Ctrl]+C or [Ctrl]+[Break]
RTERROR *or* RTREJ	Failure of undefined origin.

- This function can be called only in an ARx program when AutoCAD sends the message **kInvkSubrMsg** to the application.

RELATED ADS FUNCTION
ads_command Executes one or more AutoCAD commands and options.

(command *cmd [arg ...]*)
ads_command

External apps: Executes the AutoCAD command *cmd* and its options *arg* as if they were typed at the 'Command:' prompt.

Example	Result
(command "circle" 2.2 4)	nil
(command "redraw")	nil

PARAMETERS

■ *cmd*   Name of any AutoCAD command.

■ *arg*   (*Optional*) Name of command options, input values, etc.

TIPS

■ The **get***xxx* functions and the **DText** and **Sketch** commands cannot be used inside **command** function.

■ The **Script** command should be the last command in the AutoLISP routine, since it exits the LISP routine.

■ The **command** function send the following data as:

Data	Sent As	Example
Command name	String	"LINE"
Command option	String	"C"
2D points	Two reals	1.2 3.4
3D points	Three reals	1.2 3.4 5.6

■ Special cases:

Special Case		Meaning	Sample Code
Null string ""		[Enter]	(command "")
No argument		[Ctrl]+C	(command)
Pause for user input		\	(command \)
Pause for user input		PAUSE	(command PAUSE)
Foreign language		_line	(command "_line")
Redefined command		.line	(command ".line")

■ This is the AutoLISP function that makes it impossible to fully clone AutoLISP in another CAD package because it requires that *every* AutoCAD command be simulated.

RELATED AUTOLISP AND ADS FUNCTIONS

ads_cmd   Executes one or more AutoCAD commands via a pointer to a result buffer.

help *and* ads_help

      Executes the AutoCAD or operating system's help facility.

RELATED SYSTEM VARIABLES

CmdEcho   Toggles commands echo:

CmdEcho	Meaning
0	Commands are not echoed.
1	Command text is echoed (default).

CmdActive   Type of command currently active (a read-only variable):

CmdActive	Meaning
1	Regular command.
2	Transparent command.
3	Script file.
4	Dialog box.

TextEval   Toggles how \ (the pause-for-user-input symbol) is interpreted by commands expecting text input:

TextEval	Meaning
0	Read \ as literal text.
1	Pause for user input.

(cond (*test result*) ...)

. . .

Conditional: Tests a condition and executes the result if true.

Example	Result
(cond ((= inp "Y") 1))	nil

PARAMETERS
- *test*   A test statement, usually involving a conditional.
- *result*   The function to execute when the test is true.

TIPS
- The **cond** function executes the *result* following the first true *test* it comes across.
- The last *test* should always be true (the escape clause).

RELATED AUTOLISP FUNCTIONS

if   Tests a single expression if it is true.

repeat   Repeat an expression a specific number of times.

while   Repeats an expression while it is true.

(cons *element list*)

■■■

List manipulation: Adds an element to the beginning of a list.

Example	Result
(cons '1.2 '(3.4 10.0))	(1.2 3.4 10.0)

PARAMETERS
■ *element*   The element to be added to a list.

■ *list*   A list of any length.

TIP
■   Use **cons** to create dotted pairs:

```
(cons '1 "LINE")  ; returns (1 . "LINE")
```

RELATED AUTOLISP FUNCTIONS
append   Creates one list out of several.

length   Reports the length of the list.

member   Searches for an element in a list.

(cos ang)

...

Geometric function: Returns the cosine in radians of an angle (*short for COSine*).

Example	Result
(cos 1)	0.540302

The cosine of an angle is R divided by X:

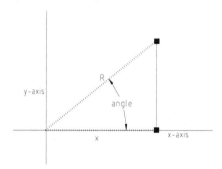

PARAMETER
- *ang*   An angle in radians format.

TIP
- All angular measurement in AutoLISP is performed in radians.

RELATED AUTOLISP FUNCTIONS
sin   Returns the sine of an angle.

arctan   Returns the arctangent of a distance.

(cvunit *value from to*)
ads_cvunit

Conversion function: Converts a value from one unit of measurement to another.

Example	Result
(cvunit 20 "meter" "feet")	65.6168

ADS FORMAT
```
int ads_cvunit(ads_real value, const char *oldunit, const char
*newunit, ads_real *result);
```

PARAMETERS
- *value* Value to be converted.
- *from* Unit to convert from.
- *to* Unit to convert to.

TIPS
- *Value* can be a single value or a list of 2 or 3 points.
- The *from* and *to* parameters can only be those listed in the Acad.Unt file.

RELATED AUTOCAD FILE
acad.unt List of many conversion factors (found in \acadr13\com\support):

Basic SI units
```
*meter(s),metre(s),m  -1,0,1,0,-1,4.1214856408e11,0
*kilogram(s),kg  0,0,0,0,1,1.0977481015e30,0
*second(s),sec  -2,0,1,0,-1,1.235590484e20,0
*ampere(s),amp(s)  2,1,-1,0,1,0.050513907838,0
*kelvin,k  2,0,0,-1,1,1.6863043358e-10,0
*candela,cd  4,0,-1,0,2,9.885226216e-8,0
```

Derived SI units
```
*celsius,centigrade,c  2,0,0,-1,1,1.6863043358e-10,4.6061402932e-8
*rankine  2,0,0,-1,1,9.3683574212e-11,0
*fahrenheit  2,0,0,-1,1,9.3683574212e-11,4.30635285578e-8
*gram(s),gm,g=kg  0.001
*newton(s),n=meter kilogram / second^2
*pascal,pa=newton/meter^2
*joule(s)=newton meter
```

Exponent synonyms
```
*square,sq  ^2
*cubic,cu    ^3
```

Units of time

```
*centur(y.ies)  =  100 year
*day(s)  =  86400 second
*decade(s)  =  10 year
*fortnight(s)  =  14 day
*hour(s),hr  =  3600 second
*milleni(um.a)  =  1000 year
*minute(s),min  =  60 second
*sidereal_year(s)  =  365.25636 day
*tropical_year(s)  =  365.24220 day
*week(s),wk  =  604800 second
*year(s),yr  =  365 day
```

Units of length

```
*Angstrom(s)  =  meter 1E-10
*astronomical_unit(s),au  =  meter 149597870000
*bolt(s)  =  meter 36.576
*cable(s)  =  meter 219.456                    ; U.S. cable length
*caliber  =  meter 0.000254
*centimeter(s),centimetre(s),cm(s)  =  meter 0.01
*chain(s)  =  meter 20.1168              ; Gunther's chain length
*cubit(s)  =  meter 0.4572
*decimeter(s),decimetre(s),dm  =  meter 0.1
*dekameter(s),dekametre(s),dam  =  meter 10
*fathom(s),fath  =  meter 1.8288
*f(oot.eet),ft,'  =  meter 0.3048
*furlong(s),fur  =  meter 201.168
*gigameter(s),gigametre(s)  =  meter 1E9
*hand(s)  =  meter 0.1016
*hectometer(s),hectometre(s),hm  =  meter 100
*inch(es),in(s),"  =  meter 2.54E-2
*kilometer(s),kilometre(s),km  =  meter 1000
*league_nautical  =  meter 5556
*league_statute  =  meter 4828.032
*light_year(s)  =  meter 9.46053E15
*link(s)  =  meter 0.201168               ; Gunther's link length
*micron(s)  =  meter 1E-6
*mil(s)  =  meter 2.54E-5
*mile_nautical,inm  =  meter 1852      ; International Nautical Mile
*mile_statute,mile(s),mi  =  meter 1609.344
*millimeter(s),millimetre(s),mm(s)  =  meter 0.001
*millimicron(s)  =  meter 1E-9
*pace(s)  =  meter 0.762
*palm(s)  =  meter 0.0762
*parsec(s)  =  meter 3.085677E16
*perch(es)  =  meter 5.0292
*pica(s)  =  meter 0.0042175176
*point(s)  =  meter 0.0003514598
*rod(s),pole(s)  =  meter 5.0292
```

```
*rope(s)  = meter 6.096
*skein(s) = meter 109.728
*span(s)  = meter 0.2286
*survey_f(oot.eet) = 0.3048006096 meter
*yard(s),yd = meter 0.9144
```

Units of area

```
*acre(s)  = 4046.85642 meter^2
*are(s)  = 100 meter^2
*barn(s)  = 1.0E-28 meter^2
*centare(s)  = 1 meter^2
*hectare(s)  = 10000 meter^2
*rood(s)  = 1011.7141 meter^2
*section(s)  = 2589988.096 meter^2
*township(s)  = 93239571.456 meter^2
```

Units of volume

```
*barrel(s),bbl = 0.1589873 meter^3       ; Int'l Petroleum barrel
*board_f(oot.eet),fbm  = 144 inch^3
*bushel(s),bu = 0.03523907 meter^3              ; U.S. dry bushel
*centiliter(s),cl  = 0.01 liter
*cord(s)  = 3.6245734 meter^3
*cc = 1e-6 meter^3
*decistere(s)  = 0.1 meter^3
*dekaliter(s),dal  = 10 liter
*dekastere(s)  = 10 meter^3
*dram(s) = 3.6967162 cc                      ; U.S. fluid dram
*dry_pint(s)  = 0.551 liter
*dry_quart(s)  = 1.101 liter
*firkin(s)  = 34.06775 liter
*gallon(s),gal = 0.0037854118 meter^3       ; U.S. fluid gallon
*gill(s)  = 118.29412 cc
*hectoliter(s)  = 100 liter
*hogshead(s),hhd = 0.23848094 meter^3
*kilderkin(s)  = 0.08182957 meter^3
*kiloliter(s)  = 1.000028 meter^3
*liter(s) =0.001 meter^3    ; Redefined from 0.001000028m^3 in 1964
*milliliter(s),ml = 0.001 liter
*minim(s)  = 6.160979e-5 liter
*fluid_ounce(s)  = 2.9573730e-5 meter^3
*peck(s)  = 8.809521 liter
*pint(s),fluid_pint(s)  = 0.4731632 liter
*pottle(s)  = 2.272980 liter
*puncheon(s)  = 0.31797510 meter^3
*quart(s),qt,fluid_quart(s)  = 0.9463264 liter
*register_ton(s)  = 2.8316847 meter^3
*seam(s)  = 290.9414 liter
*stere(s)  = 1 meter^3
*tun(s) = 252 gallon
```

Units of mass

```
*dalton(s) = 1.66053e-27 kg
*dyne(s) = kg/980665
*grain(s) = kg/15432.358
*hundredweight(s),cwt = 45.359337 kg
*long_ton(s) = 1016.0469088 kg
*ounce_weight,ounce(s),oz = kg/35.273962
*ounce_troy = kg/32.150737
*pennyweight(s),dwt,pwt = kg/643.01493
*poundal(s) = kg/70.931635
*pound(s),lb = 0.45359237 kg
*scruple(s) = kg/771.61792
*slug(s) = 14.5939 kg
*stone = 14 pound
*ton(s) = 907.18474 kg
*tonn(e.es) = 1000 kg
```

Unit of frequency

```
*hertz,hz = 1/second
```

Electromagnetic units

```
*coulomb(s) = ampere second
*farad(s) = coulomb/volt
*henr(y.ies) = ohm second
*ohm(s) = volt/ampere
*siemens = 1/ohm
*tesla(s) = weber/meter^2
*volt(s),v = watt/ampere
*watt(s),w = joule/second
*weber(s) = volt second
```

Circular measure

```
*circle(s) 0,0,0,0,0,1,0
*radian(s) = circle/6.28318530717958648
*degree(s) = circle/360
*grad(s) = circle/400
*quadrant(s) = circle/4
```

Solid measure

```
*sphere(s) 0,0,0,0,0,1,0
*hemisphere(s) = sphere/2
*steradian(s) = sphere/12.566371
```

Dimensionless prefixes
Multiples

```
*deca 0,0,0,0,0,10,0
*hecto 0,0,0,0,0,100,0
*kilo 0,0,0,0,0,1000,0
*mega 0,0,0,0,0,1e6,0
```

```
*giga   0,0,0,0,0,1e9,0
*tera   0,0,0,0,0,1e12,0
*peta   0,0,0,0,0,1e15,0
*exa    0,0,0,0,0,1e18,0
```

Fractions
```
*deci   0,0,0,0,0,0.1,0
*centi  0,0,0,0,0,0,0.01,0
*milli  0,0,0,0,0,0.001,0
*micro  0,0,0,0,0,1e-6,0
*nano   0,0,0,0,0,1e-9,0
*pico   0,0,0,0,0,1e-12,0
*femto  0,0,0,0,0,1e-15,0
*atto   0,0,0,0,0,1e-18,0
```

Reference: CRC Handbook, 68th edition ('87-'88). Dimensions of common units in terms of fundamental constants:

Measurement	C	E	H	K	M	Notes
Length	-1	1		-1		
Mass					1	
Time	-2	1		-1		time / C
Current	2	1	-1	1		E / time
Temperature	2		-1	1		H / (K time)
Luminous intensity	4	-1			2	Units of power over solid angle, a dimensionless value.

(defun [c:] *name* (*[arg] / [lvars]*) *expr*)
ads_defun

Function handler: Defines the name of the AutoLISP function; in ADS, defines an external function (*short for DEfine FUNction*).

Example	Result
(defun label () ...)	nil
(defun c:label () ...)	nil
(defun c:label (/ x y z) ...)	nil
(defun c:label (a b / x y z) ...)	nil

ADS FORMAT
```
int ads_defun(const char *sname, short funcno);
```

PARAMETERS
- **c:** (*Optional*) Makes the function an AutoCAD command.
- *name* The name of the programmer-defined function.
- *arg* (*Optional*) Specifies the names of the aguments required by the function.
- *lvars* (*Optional*) Makes variables local.
- *expr* A list of expressions to be executed by the function.

TIPS
- This is arguably the most important function in AutoLISP since it allows programmer-definable functions.

- The **C:** prefix make the function appear as an AutoCAD command.

- Local functions (as in **xyz** below) are undefined outside of the function, which saves memory and isolates variables from different subroutines.

- The semicolon allows you to include comments in AutoLISP programs:
```
; LABEL.LSP labels 3D points.
(defun c:label (/ xyz)
    (setq xyz (getpoint "Pick point: "))
    (command "text" xyz 0.2 0 xyz)
)
```

RELATED AUTOLISP AND ADS FUNCTIONS
command *and* ads_command

        Executes any AutoCAD command.

atom_family   Lists all currently loaded AutoLISP functions.

ads *and* ads_loaded

        List the names of all currently loaded ADS programs.

(dictadd *ename sym obj*)

■ ■ ■

Object handler: Adds object *obj* and keyname *sym* (a nongraphical object) to the
ename dictionary.

Example	Result
(dictadd en1 "ACAD_GROUP" "ISO")	

PARAMETERS

■ *ename*   Name of the dictionary attached to an entity name.

■ *sym*   Keyname to be added to dictionary.

■ *obj*   Name of the object.

RELATED AUTOLISP AND ADS FUNCTIONS

dictdel   Delete an object from the dictionary.

dictnext *and* ads_dictnext

　　　　　Find the next object in the dictionary.

dictrename   Rename an object in the dictionary.

dictsearch *and* ads_dictsearch

　　　　　Search for an object in the dictionary.

(dictdel *ename sym*)
ads_dictdel

Object handler: Deletes symbol *sym* from dictioanry *ename*.

Example	Result
(dictdel en1 "ACAD_GROUP")	

ADS FORMAT
```
struct resbuf* ads_dictnext(ads_name dict, char *sym, int rewind);
```

PARAMETERS
- *ename*   Name of the dictionary attached to an entity name.
- *sym*   Keyname to be removed from the dictionary.

RELATED AUTOLISP AND ADS FUNCTIONS

dictadd   Add an object to the dictionary.

dictnext *and* **ads_dictnext**

    Find the next object in the dictionary.

dictrename   Rename an object in the dictionary.

dictsearch *and* **ads_dictsearch**

    Search for an object in the dictionary.

(dictnext *ename sym [flag]*)
ads_dictnext

Object handler: Finds the next *sym* symbol within dictionary *ename*; the *flag* is a rewind option that returns the search to the beginning of the dictionary when *flag* is non-**nil**.

Example	Results
`(dictnext en acad_group)`	`((-1 . <Entity name: 2000468>)`
	`(0 . "DICTIONARY") (5 . "D")`
	`(102 . "{ACAD_REACTORS")`
	`(330 . <Entity name: 2000460>) (102 . "}")`
	`(100 . "AcDbDictionary"))`

ADS FORMAT
`struct resbuf* ads_dictnext(ads_name dict, char *sym, int flag);`

PARAMETERS
- *ename*   Name of the dictionary attached to an entity name.
- *sym*   Keyname to be added to dictionary.
- *flag*   (*Optional*) When **T**, returns the search to the beginning of the dictionary.

TIP
- **Dictnext** returns data as a list of DXF-format dotted pairs.

RELATED AUTOLISP AND ADS FUNCTIONS
dictadd   Add an object to the dictionary.

dictdel   Delete an object from the dictionary.

dictrename   Rename an object in the dictionary.

dictsearch *and* **ads_dictsearch**

            Search for an object in the dictionary.

(dictrename *ename old new*)
ads_dictrename

Object handler: Renames dictionary *ename* key from *old* to *new*.

Example	Result
(dictrename en1 ACAD_GROUP ACAD_MLINESTYLE)	

PARAMETERS
- *ename*   Name of the dictionary attached to an entity name.
- *old*   Current symbol name.
- *new*   New symbol name.

TIP
- To obtain the master entity name, call **nameobjdict** or **ads_nameobjdict**.

RELATED AUTOLISP AND ADS FUNCTIONS
dictadd   Add an object to the dictionary.

dictdel   Delete an object from the dictionary.

dictnext *and* ads_dictnext

            Find the next object in the dictionary.

dictsearch *and* ads_dictsearch

            Search for an object in the dictionary.

(dictsearch *ename sym [flag]*)
ads_dictsearch

Object handler: Searches the dictionary.

Example	Result
(dictsearch en "D")	nil

ADS FORMAT
```
struct resbuf* ads_dictsearch(ads_name dict, char *sym, int flag);
```

PARAMETERS
- *ename*   Name of the dictionary attached to an entity name.
- *sym*   Keyname to be added to dictionary.
- *flag*   When **T** the next **dictnext** call returns the entry following the current **dictsearch** call.

RELATED AUTOLISP AND ADS FUNCTIONS
dictadd   Add an object to the dictionary.

dictdel   Delete an object from the dictionary.

dictnext *and* ads_dictnext

    Find the next object in the dictionary.

dictrename   Rename an object in the dictionary.

(dimx_tile *key*) *and* (dimy_tile *key*)
ads_dimensions_tile

Dialog box: Returns the dimensions of a specified tile for use by other dialog box functions.

Example	Result
(dimx_tile "pickbox_image")	
(dimy_tile "pickbox_image")	

*The **DdPoint** dialog box displaying 20 tiles*

x-1, y-1

0,0

ADS FORMAT
int ads_dimensions_tile(ads_hdlg hdlg, char *key, short *cx, short *cy);

PARAMETER
- *key*   Specifies the name of the tile.

TIPS
- The coordinates returned are used by other dialog box functions.
- The coordinates start at 0,0.
- *Key* is case sensitive.

RELATED AUTOLISP AND ADS FUNCTIONS
fill_image *and* **ads_fillimage**

        Fills an image rectangle with color.

slide_image *and* **ads_slideimage**

        Displays an AutoCAD SLD image.

vector_image *and* **ads_vectorimage**

        Draws a vector image.

(distance *pt1 pt2*)
ads_distance

Geometric function: Returns the 2D or 3D distance between two points.

Examples	Result
(distance a b)	2.98765
(distance '(1.2 3.4) '(5.6 10))	7.93221

*The **distance** between two points:*

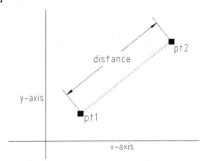

ADS FORMAT
ads_real ads_distance(const ads_point pt1, const ads_point pt2);

PARAMETERS
- *pt1*   A 2D (x,y) or 3D (x,y,z) coordinate.
- *pt2*   A second 2D (x,y) or 3D (x,y,z) coordinate.

TIPS
- **Dist** returns the 3D distance only when both *pt1* and *pt2* are in 3D.
- **Dist** returns the 2D distance when one of *pt1* and *pt2* are in 2D projected onto the current construction plane.

RELATED AUTOLISP AND ADS FUNCTIONS
angle *and* ads_angle

     Calculates the angle in radians between the x-axis and the line.

polar *and* ads_polar

     Calculates a point from a distance and an angle.

inters *and* ads_inters

     Calculates the point of intersection of two lines.

(distof *str [mode]*)
ads_distof

Conversion functions: Converts a string *str* into a real number, based on the format specified by *mode* (*short for DIStance TO Floating point*).

Examples	Result
(distof "31.856")	31.856
(distof "31.856" 3)	31.856

ADS FORMAT
```
int ads_distof(const char *str, int mode, ads_real *v);
```

PARAMETERS

■ *str*   A string of text in the format of a real number.

■ *mode*   (*Optional*) Specifies the units in which the string was formatted:

Mode	Format	String Formatted As
1	Scientific	"0.0000E+01"
2	Decimal (default)	"0.0000"
3	Engineering	"0-0.0000"
4	Architectural	"0-0/64"
5	Fractional	"0 0/64"

TIPS

■ When *mode* is left out, **distof** uses the value stored in system variable **LUnits**.

■ *Str* must be in a format that **distof** can deal with.

RELATED AUTOLISP AND ADS FUNCTIONS
rtos *and* **ads_rtos**

> Converts a number into a string.

angtof *and* **ads_angtof**

> Converts an angle in string format to an angle in radians.

atof *and* **ads_atof**

> Converts a string to a real number.

atoi *and* **ads_atoi**

> Converts a string to an integer.

RELATED SYSTEM VARIABLE
LUnits   Units of linear measurement (default = 2, decimal).

(done_dialog [flag])
ads_done_dialog

Dialog box: Terminates the dialog box and returns **0** if the user clicked **[Cancel]** and **1** if **[OK]** clicked. *flag* has a value greater than 1; if present, this value is returned by **start_dialog**.

Examples	Result
(done_dialog)	(10 20)
(done_dialog 2)	(10 20)

Almost every dialog box has the **OK** *and* **Cancel** *buttons:*

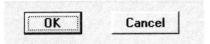

ADS FORMAT
ads_done_dialog(ads_hdlg hdlg, int flag);

PARAMETER
- *flag*   *(Optional)* Alternative return code.

TIPS
- **Done_dialog** returns the x,y-coordinates of the dialog box as a 2D list.
- **Start_dialog** returns the following values:

Returns	Meaning
0	User pressed [Cancel]
1	User pressed [OK]
flag	Value of *flag* in **done_dialog**.

RELATED AUTOLISP AND ADS FUNCTIONS
ads_done_positioned_dialog

        Returns x,y-coordinates of dialog box before termination.

new_dialog *and* ads_newdialog

        Initializes and displays a new dialog box.

start_dialog *and* ads_start_dialog

        Accept user input to the dialog box.

action_tile *and* ads_action_tile

        Associates tiles with callback functions.

...

ads_done_positioned_dialog

Dialog box: Returns the x,y-position of the dialog box, then terminates it.

Example	Result
(ads_done_positioned_dialog st *xr *yr)	RTNORM

ADS FORMAT
```
int ads_done_positioned_dialog(ads_hdlg hdlg, int status, int
*x_result, int *y_result);
```

PARAMETERS
- **status**   Status code of how the dialog box terminated.

- **x_result**   X-coordinate of dialog box before it closed.

- **y_result**   Y-coordinate of dialog box before it closed.

RELATED AUTOLISP AND ADS FUNCTIONS
done_dialog *and* ads_done_dialog

       Terminates the dialog box.

new_dialog *and* ads_newdialog

       Initializes and displays a new dialog box.

start_dialog *and* ads_start_dialog

       Accept user input to the dialog box.

action_tile *and* ads_action_tile

       Associates tiles with callback functions.

...

ads_draggen

User interface: Prompt use to modify selection set by dragging objects (*short for DRAG Graphical ENtities*).

Example	Result
ads_draggen(ss,*pmt,curs,*scnf(pt,mt),p)	RTNORM

ADS FORMAT
```
int ads_draggen(const ads_name ss, const char *pmt, int cursor,
int (*scnf), (ads_point pt, ads_matrix mt), ads_point p);
```

PARAMETERS
- *ss*   Selection set obtained from **ads_ssget** or **ads_ssadd**.

- *pmt*   (*Optional*) Prompt string displayed before pausing for user input.

- *cursor*   Form of cursor to display while user drags the selection set:

Value	Cursor type
0	Displays the normal crosshair cursor.
1	No cursor (no crosshair).
2	Displays entity-select (square) cursor.

- *scnf*   Pointer to a function called by **ads_draggen** when user moves cursor; function must have the following format:

  ```
  int sample_fcn(ads_point pt, ads_matrix mt);
  ```

- *p*   Cursor's final location when user stops dragging.

TIPS
- Ads_draggen does not select nongraphical objects or objects in block definitions.
- This function regenerates the selection set as the user moves the cursor.

RELATED AUTOLISP AND ADS FUNCTION
ssget *and* **ads_ssget**

      Prompt the user to get a selection set.

(end_image)
ads_end_image

Dialog box: Signals the end of the creation of the current dialog box image.

Example	Result
(end_image)	nil

ADS FORMAT
```
int  ads_end_image(void);
```

PARAMETERS
none

TIP
■ Use the **start_image** function as the start of image definition; end it with **end_image.**

RELATED AUOTLISP AND ADS FUNCTION
start_image *and* ads_start_image

> Signals the start of an image specifcation.

(end_list)
(ads_end_list)

Dialog box: Signals the end of processing the current dialog box list.

Example	Result
(end_list)	nil

ADS FORMAT
int ads_end_list(void);

PARAMETERS
none

TIP
- Use **start_list** to start the dialog box list; use **end_list** to end the list.

RELATED AUTOLISP AND ADS FUNCTION
start_list and ads_start_list

Signals the start of processing of a list in a dialog box.

(entdel *ename*)
ads_entdel

Object handler: Deletes object *ename* from the drawing database; if the object is already deleted, undeletes (restores) *ename* (*short for ENTity DELete*).

Example	Result
(entdel en1)	<Entity name: 2000500>

ADS FORMAT
```
int ads_entdel(const ads_name ename);
```

PARAMETER
- *ename*   Entity name of an object, in the format of **<Entity name: 2000500>**.

TIPS
- **Entdel** cannot remove child objects and attributes from the parent block, or polyline vertices from the parent polyline objects.

- To delete attributes and polyline vertices, use the **command** function with the **AttEdit** and **PEdit** commands.

- To delete portions of a block, use **entmake** to redefine the block (without the objects to be deleted).

- Do not use symbol tables and symbol table entries with **entdel**.

- Use **entdel** to restore a deleted object.

- Deleted objects are removed from the drawing when the user exits the drawing; you can no longer use **entdel** to restore the deleted object.

RELATED AUTOLISP AND ADS FUNCTIONS
entmake *and* **ads_entmake**
>   Redefine objects, including complex objects.

entmod *and* **ads_entmod**
>   Modifies an object.

entsel *and* **ads_entsel**
>   Prompt the user to select an object and return its entity number.

(entget *ename [applist]*)
ads_entget

Object handler: Returns the definition data of object *ename*; also returns extended data associated with *applist*.

Example	Result
(entget en)	((-1 . <Entity name: 2000500>) (0 . "POLYLINE") (5 . "28") (100 . "AcDbEntity") (67 . 0) (8 . "0") (100 . "AcDb2dPolyline") (66 . 1) (10 0.0 0.0 0.0) (70 . 1) (40 . 0.0) (41 . 0.0) (210 0.0 0.0 1.0) (71 . 0) (72 . 0) (73 . 0) (74 . 0) (75 . 0))

ADS FORMAT
```
struct resbuf *ads_entget(const ads_name ent);
```

PARAMETERS
- ***ename***   Entity name of an object, in the format of **<Entity name: 2000500>**.

- ***applist***   (*Optional*) List of registered application names.

TIPS
- **Entget** returns entity the following header items when their values differ from the default, as with DXF: color, linetype, thickness, attributes-follow flag, and entity handle.

- This function always returns the optional entity definition fields, unlike DXF.

- **Entget** returns x,y,z-coordinates as a single value, not as separate x (10), y (20), and z (30) groups as does DXF.

- Use the **assoc** and **cdr** functions to extract the data from each dotted pair.

RELATED AUTOLISP AND ADS FUNCTIONS
assoc   Lets you extract items from the definition data.

cdr   Lets you extract data from a dotted pair.

entsel *and* ads_entsel

         Prompts the user to select an object, and returns *ename*.

...

ads_entgetx

Object handler: Returns entity and extended entity data registered to an application.

Example	Result
(ads_entgetx en1 *app1)	*returns xdata*

ADS FORMAT
```
struct resbuf *ads_entgetx(const ads_name ent, const struct resbuf *apps);
```

PARAMETERS
- *ent*   Entity name of an object, in the format of **<Entity name: 2000500>**.

- **apps*   *(optional)* List of registered application names; if missing, **ads_entgetx** acts the same as **ads_enget**.

TIP
- Use the **ads_regapp** function to place the application name in the drawing's APPID symbol table before using **ads_entgetx**.

RELATED AUTOLISP AND ADS FUNCTION
entsel *and* ads_entsel

Prompts the user to select an object, and returns *ename*.

(entlast)
ads_entlast

Object handler: Returns the entity name of the last object added to the drawing.

Example	Result
(entlat)	<Entity name: 2002270>

ADS FORMAT
```
int ads_entlast(ads_name result);
```

PARAMETERS
none

TIPS
■ **Entlast** is useful for getting the object just created with the **command** function.

■ Use **entnext** with no arguments to find the first object in the database:

```
(entnext)
```

■ Unlike the "LAST" selection mode, the last object need not be visible in the viewport or be on an unfrozen layer.

RELATED AUTOLISP AND ADS FUNCTIONS
entsel *and* ads_entsel

> Prompts the user to select an object, and returns *ename.*

entnext *and* ads_entnext

> Returns the entity name of the next object in the drawing.

(entmake *[elist]*)
ads_entmake

Object handler: Adds one or more new objects (using dotted pair format in *elist*) to the drawing database.

Examples	Result
(entmake)	nil
(entmake '((0 . "CIRCLE")(62 . 5) (10 1.2 3.4 10.0)(40 . 5.6)))	...

ADS FORMAT
int ads_entmake(const struct resbuf *elist);

PARAMETER
■ *elist* (*Optional*) List of object definition data in dotted pair format.

TIPS
■   Possibly the most powerful function in AutoLISP, since **entmake** allows you to add new objects in the drawing. The sole exception is the viewport object, which **entmake** cannot make.

■   Block definitions cannot be nested or self-referencing; new blocks are automatically added to the symbol table.

■   A new block overwrites an existing bock of the same name without warning; use **tblsearch** to check for existing block names.

■   To create data in a drawing inaccessable to the user, make an anonymous block as follows:

   1. Start the block name with *

   2. Set the low-order bit of group 70 (block flag type) to 1.

AutoCAD assigns a numbered name starting with *U, such as *U001 and ignores any name you might give it.

■   The **entmake** function with no arguments cancels the making of a complex object, such as blocks and polylines.

■   The *elist* must be correct otherwise **entmake** returns **nil** and does not make the object. **Entmake** checks for the valid values in every object:

   ■   Layer name.

   ■   Linetype name.

   ■   Color name or number.

Entmake checks for valid names if required:

- Block name.
- Dimension stlye name.
- Text style name.
- Shape name.

■ When optional information is left out, **entmake** fills in the default value.

■ When a new "LAYER" name is provided, **entmake** creates the new layer.

■ The **command** function is an easier alternative to the **entmake** function.

RELATED AUTOLISP AND ADS FUNCTIONS

entupd *and* **ads_entupd**

> Updates the screen image of the object.

entmode *and* **ads_entmod**

> Modifies an existing object.

entdel *and* **ads_entdel**

> Removes an object from the drawing.

command, ads_cmd, *and* **ads_command**

> Executes every AutoCAD command, including those that create new objects.

(entmakex [elist])

■■■

Object handler: Adds a new object (as defined by *elist*) to the drawing database without assigning an owner to prevent the object from being saved in a DWG or DXF file.

Example	Result
(entmakex)	nil
(entmakex '((0 . "CIRCLE")(62 . 5) (10 1.2 3.4 10.0)(40 . 5.6)))	. . .

PARAMETER
■ *elist*   (*Optional*) List of object definition data in dotted pair format.

TIPS
■ **Entmakex** operates identically to **entmake**.

■ Since **entmakex** does not assign an owner, objects made with this function are not saved in a DWG and DXF file; use **dictadd** to assign ownership to the object.

RELATED AUTOLISP FUNCTIONS
entmake *and* ads_entmake
> Creates a new object in the drawing.

entupd *and* ads_entupd
> Updates the screen image of the object.

entmode *and* ads_entmod
> Modifies an existing object.

entdel *and* ads_entdel
> Removes an object from the drawing.

(entmod *elist*)
ads_entmod

Object handler: Modifies the definition data of the objects in *elist*.

Example	Result
(entmod en)	. . .

ADS FORMAT
```
int ads_entmod(const struct resbuf *elist);
```

PARAMETER
- **elist**   List of object definition data in dotted pair format.

TIPS
- **Entmod** cannot change an object's type and handle, or modify a viewport.
- The **command** function is an alternative approach to modifying objects.
- The *elist* must be correct otherwise **entmod** returns **nil** and does not modify the object. **Entmod** checks for the valid values in every object:
  - Layer name.
  - Linetype name.
  - Color name or number.

Entmod checks for valid names if required:
  - Block name.
  - Dimension stlye name.
  - Text style name.
  - Shape name.
- When optional information is left out, **entmod** fills in the default value.
- When a new "LAYER" name is provided, **entmod** creates the new layer.
- **Entmod** converts integer values into reals and trucates real value to integer, as required.

RELATED AUTOLISP AND ADS FUNCTIONS
entget *and* **ads_entget**
> Gets the entity data of an object in the drawing.

entmake *and* **ads_entmake**
> Creates a new object.

command, ads_cmd, *and* **ads_command**
> Executes every AutoCAD command, including those that create new objects.

(entnext *[ename]*)
ads_entnext

Object handler: When called with argument *ename*, returns the first nondeleted object *following* the *ename*.

Example	Results
(entnext)	<Entity name: 2000500>
(entnext en)	<Entity name: 2000508>

ADS FORMAT
```
int ads_entnext(const ads_name ent, ads_name result);
```

PARAMETERS
- *ename*   (*Optional*) Entity name of an object, in the format of **<Entity name: 2000500>**.

TIPS
- When **entnext** is used with no argument, it returns the first object in the drawing.
- Use **entlast** to get the last object in the drawing.
- **Entnext** returns **nil** when it reaches the end of the drawing database.

RELATED AUTOLISP AND ADS FUNCTIONS
entlast *and* **ads_entlast**

>   Gets the last object in the drawing database.

entsel *and* **ads_entsel**

>   Prompts the user to select an object.

(entsel *[prompt]*)
ads_entsel

Object handler: Selects an object by prompting the user with *prompt*; returns the entity name and pick coordinates.

Example	Results
(entsel)	Select object:
	(<Entity name: 2002270> (40.8277 3.00518 0.0))
(entsel "Pick object: ")	Pick object:
	(<Entity name: 2002270> (40.8277 3.00518 0.0))

ADS FORMAT
```
int ads_entsel(const char *str, ads_name entres, ads_point ptres);
```

PARAMETER
- *prompt*   (*Optional*) A customized prompt for the user; otherwise, **entsel** prompts, "Select object: ".

TIP
- The pick coordinates returned are in the current UCS (user coordinate system).

RELATED AUTOLISP AND ADS FUNCTIONS
entlast *and* ads_entlast

> Gets the *ename* of the last object added to the drawing.

entnext *and* ads_entnext

> Gets the next object in the drawing.

entget *and* ads_entget

> Gets the definition data belonging to an object.

(entupd *ename*)
ads_entupd

Object handler: Updates the screen image of the *ename* object (*short for ENTity UPDate*).

Example	Result
(entupd en1)	<Entity name: 2000508>

ADS FORMAT
```
int ads_entupd(const ads_name ename);
```

PARAMETER
- *ename*   Entity name of an object, in the format of **<Entity name: 2000500>**.

TIPS
- **Entupd** does what **entmod** cannot: change objects nested in a block (such as attributes) and polyline vertices; however, **entupd** can be used for all other objects, as well.

- Autodesk recommends using the **Regen** command to ensure all objects appear updated, since **entupd** might not update the display of objects in blocks and nested blocks.

RELATED AUTOLISP AND ADS FUNCTIONS
entget *and* **ads_entget**

   Prompt the user to select an object.

endmod *and* **ads_endmod**

   Modifies an object.

(eq *expr1 expr2*)

■ ■ ■

Symbol handler: Returns **T** if expressions *expr1* and *expr2* are bound to the same object; otherwise, returns **nil**.

Example	Result
(eq x y)	T

PARAMETERS
- *expr1*   An expression.
- *expr2*   Another expression.

RELATED AUTOLISP FUNCTIONS
=   Returns **T** if the numbers are equal.

equal   Returns **T** if the two expressions are equal within a fuzz factor.

(equal *expr1 expr2 [fuzz]*)

■ ■ ■

Symbol handler: Returns **T** if expressions *expr1* and *expr2* are the same; returns **T** when two real numbers are within the *fuzz* factor; returns **nil** otherwise.

Examples	Result
(equal 1.2 1.201)	nil
(equal 1.2 1.201 0.1)	T

PARAMETERS

■ *expr1*   An expression.

■ *expr2*   Another expression.

■ *fuzz*   (*Optional*) A value representing the fudge factor.

TIPS

■   The *fuzz* factor is useful because computers cannot accuately calculate repeating decimals and irrational numbers (such as pi). A simple example is 3 * ($^1/_3$) = 0.999999, instead of 1.0.

RELATED AUTOLISP FUNCTIONS

=   Returns **T** if the numbers are equal.

eq   Returns **T** if the two expressions are identical.

(*error* *str*)
ads_fail

Error handler: The built-in AutoLISP error handler; can be replaced by a programmer-definable error handler.

Example	Result
(*error* "No negative values.")	No negative values.

PARAMETER
- *str*   A string that tells the user an error occurred.

TIP
- Redefine *error* to create a custom error handler, such as:

```
(defun *error* (message)
  . . .
)
```

RELATED AUTOLISP FUNCTIONS
command   Calling (command) without an argument cancels the current command, as if the user pressed [Ctrl]+C.

altert *and* ads_alert
            Displays a dialog box with a programmer-definable message.

trace   Sort of helps out in debugging.

untrace   Turns of debugging.

exit, quit, ads_exit, *and* ads_quit
            Forces the applicaiton to terminate.

(eval *expr*)

■ ■ ■

Function handler: Evaluates an AutoLISP expression.

Example	Result
(eval (+ 1.2 3.4 10.0))	14.6

PARAMETER
■ *expr*   Any expression.

RELATED AUTOLISP FUNCTIONS
apply   Passes arguments to a function.

progn   Evaluates each expression sequentially.

(exit)
ads_exit

Error handler: Terminates the application.

Example	Result
(exit)	error: quit / exit abort
	(EXIT)
	Cancel

PARAMETERS
none

TIP
■ Termines the AutoLISP routine and returns to the 'Command:' prompt.

RELATED AUTOLISP AND ADS FUNCTIONS
altert *and* ads_alert

    Displays a dialog box with a programmer-definable message.

error   Programmer-definable error handler.

trace   Sort of helps out in debugging.

untrace   Turns of debugging.

quit *and* ads_quit

    Forces the application to terminate.

(exp *num*)

■ ■ ■

Math function: Exponent (natural antilog): e^{num}, where e = 2.71828.

Examples	Result
(exp 1)	2.71828
(exp 10.0)	22026.5

PARAMETER
■ *num*   Any real or integer number.

RELATED AUTOLISP FUNCTIONS
expt   Number raised to a power.

log   Natural log of a number.

sqrt   Square root of a number.

(expand *int*)

■■■

Memory management: Allocates node space (memory) by *int* number of segments.

Example	Result
(expand 10)	10

PARAMETER
- *int*   An integer number of segments.

TIPS
- One segment = 514 nodes (6,168 bytes).
- 1 node = 12 bytes.

RELATED AUTOLISP FUNCTIONS
mem   Returns the current state of AutoLISP memory.

alloc   Sets the segment size to a given number of nodes.

E

■■■

ads_fail

Error handler: Prints an error message.

Example	Result
ads_fail("Try again.")	Try again.

ADS FORMAT
void ads_fail(const char *str);

PARAMETER
■ *status*   Set to 0 for normal termination.

TIP
■ This function is for use with recoverable errors.

RELATED ADS FUNCTIONS
ads_alert   Displays a dialog box with a programmer-specified message.

ads_exit   Ends the ADS application.

(fill_image *x y wid ht clr*)
ads_fill_image

Dialog box: Draws a rectangle filled with a color in the current dialog box.

Example	Return
(fill_image x y 20 27 -2)	nil

The Select Color dialog box with menu filled image tiles:

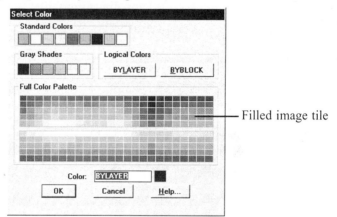

— Filled image tile

ADS FORMAT
```
int ads_fill_image(short x, short y, short wid, short hgt, short clr);
```

PARAMETERS

- *x*   Starting x-coordinate of the image tile.

- *y*   Starting y-coordinate of the image tile.

- *wid*   Width of the image tile in x-direction.

- *ht*   Heightof the image tile in x-direction.

- *clr*   Color of the image tile:

Color Number	Mnemonic	Meaning
1 to 255	...	Standard 255 ADI colors
-2	BGLCOLOR	Current graphics screen background
-15	DBGLCOLOR	Dialog box background color
-16	DFGLCOLOR	Dialog box test foreground color
-18	LINELCOLOR	Dialog box line color

RELATED AUTOLISP AND ADS FUNCTIONS

slide_image *and* ads_slideimage

>Displays an AutoCAD SLD image.

vector_image *and* ads_vectorimage

>Draws a vector image.

(dimx_tile *key*), (dimy_tile *key*), *and* ads_dimensions_tile

>Returns the dimensions of a tile.

(findfile *fname*)
ads_findfile

File function: Searches for filename *fname*.

Example	Result
(findfile "ddcolor.lsp")	"d:\\acad13\\com\\SUPPORT\\ddcolor.lsp"

ADS FORMAT
```
int ads_findfile(const char *fname, char *result);
```

PARAMETER
- *fname*   The name of a file.

TIPS
- The maximum length of *fname* depends on the operating system:

fname	Operating System
78 characters	Restricted length (e.g. DOS)
511 characters	Unrestricted length (e.g. Unix)

- When *fname* includes the drive and/or subdirectory, **findfile** only searches there.
- When *fname* is just the filename, **findfile** seaches the current AutoCAD library path:
    1. Current directory.
    2. Directory with the current drawing file.
    3. Directories named by the ACAD environment variable.
    4. Directory with the AutoCAD program files.

RELATED AUTOLISP AND ADS FUNCTIONS
load   Loads the found AutoLISP file.

xload *and* ads_xload

        Loads the found ADS application.

arxload *and* ads_arxload

        Loads the found ARx application.

startapp   Starts the found Windows application.

open   Opens the found file for reading, writing, or appending.

RELATED SYSTEM VARIABLE
acad   The pathnames specified by the ACAD environment variable.

(fix *num*)

■ ■ ■

Conversion: Truncates real number *num* to the nearest smaller integer.

Examples	Return
(fix 250)	250
(fix 1.2)	1
(fix 3.9)	3

PARAMETERS
■ *num*   Any real or integer number.

TIPS
■ The **fix** function always rounds down.

■ On 32-bit operating systems:

Integer	Value
Largest within AutoLISP	2,147,483,647
Largest between AutoLISP and AutoCAD	65,536
Smallest between AutoLISP and AutoCAD	-65,535
Smallest within AutoLISP	-2,147,483,648

When the *num* is larger than the values shown in the table above, the **fix** function returns a real number.

RELATED AUTOLISP FUNCTIONS
float   Converts an integer number into a real number.

itoa   Converts an integer to a string.

itos   Converts a real number to a string.

atof   Converts a string to a real number.

atoi   Converts a string to an integer.

(float *num*)

■ ■ ■

Conversion: Converts number *num* to a real number.

Examples	Result
(float 250)	250.0
(float 1.2)	1.2

PARAMETER
- *num*   Any integer or real number.

RELATED AUTOLISP FUNCTIONS
fix   Converts a real number into an integer number.

itoa   Converts an integer to a string.

itos   Converts a real number to a string.

atof   Converts a string to a real number.

atoi   Converts a string to an integer.

(foreach *name list expr* ...)

■ ■ ■

Function handler: Applies expression *expr* to every item in the *list*.

Example	Result
(foreach n '(x y z) (+ n 2))	4

PARAMETERS

- *name*　　Name of a variable.
- *list*　　A list of values.
- *expr*　　A list of expressions.

RELATED AUTOLISP FUNCTION

mapcar　　Applies a function to a list of values.

...

ads_free

Memory management: Frees memory allocated by **ads_malloc**, **ads_realloc**, and **ads_calloc**.

Example	Result
ads_free	

ADS FORMAT
```
void ads_free(void *buff);
```

PARAMETER
- **buff*   The memory pointer assigned by **ads_calloc**, **ads_malloc**, and **ads_realloc**.

RELATED ADS FUNCTIONS
ads_calloc   Allocates memory to hold an array.

ads_malloc   Allocates memory to hold the size returned by **ads_msize**.

ads_realloc.   Changes the size of allocated memory.

(gc)

■■■

Memory management: Frees up memory by freeing nodes no longer being used (*short for Garbage Collection*).

Example	Return
(gc)	nil

PARAMETERS
none

TIPS
■ Automatic garbage collection occurs when when there are too few nodes in AutoLISP memory.

■ There is no need to use **gc** since AutoLISP carries it out automatically.

RELATED AUTOLISP FUNCTIONS

mem   Reports on the amount of memory used by AutoLISP memory.

alloc   Allocates more memory for AutoLISP.

expand   Expands the memory used by AutoLISP.

(gcd *int1 int2*)

■■■

Math function: Returns the greatest common denominator of integers *int1* and *int2* (*short for Greatest Common Denominator*).

Examples	Result
(gcd 1024 15)	1
(gcd 1024 16)	16

PARAMETERS
- *int1*   A single integer number.
- *int2*   Another single integer number.

TIP
- *Int1* and *int2* must be integers 1 or larger.

RELATED AUTOLISP FUNCTIONS
rem   Returns the remainder after a division.

min   Returns the smallest number from a list.

max   Returns the largest number from a list.

(getangle *[pt] [prompt]*)
ads_getangle

Geometric function: Prompts the user to specify an angle.

Examples	Result
(getangle)	Second point: 0.669946
(getangle pt1)	0.669946
(getangle pt1 "Pick other point:")	Pick other point: 0.669946

GetAngle measures radians from the x-axis to an imaginary line between ***pt1*** *and* ***pt2:***

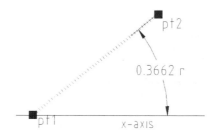

ADS FORMAT
int ads_getangle(const ads_point pt, const char *prompt,ads_real *result);

PARAMETERS
- *pt*   (*Optional*) The first 2D point of a line; user need only select one other point; the z-coordinate is ignored.

- *prompt*   (*Optional*) A programmer-definable prompt string.

TIPS
- The angle is always returned in radians in the current UCS measured counterclockwise; the user can enter an angle in any legitimate AutoCAD format.

- The angle is measured from the x-axis, as defined by system variable **AngBase** in the direction specified by **AngDir**.

- To measure the angle from the absolute x-axis, use the **getorient** function instead.

RELATED AUTOLISP AND ADS FUNCTIONS
getorient *and* ads_getorient
> Get user input for an angle.

getdist *and* ads_getdist
> Get two points that specify a distance.

getpoint *and* ads_getpoint
> Get the 3D coordinates of a point.

■■■

ads_getappname

External applications: Returns the name of the current ARx application.

Example	Result
ads_getappname()	name of ARx app

ADS FORMAT
char * ads_getappname();

PARAMETERS
none

RELATED AUTOLISP FUNCTION
.arxloaded   Names of currently loaded ARx applications.

RELATED GLOBAL VARIABLE
ads_appname Stores the name of the current ARx app, which **ads_getappname** references.

G

■■■
ads_getargs

External applications: Returns the arguments to the requested external function.

Example	Result
ads_getargs()	*linked list of args*

ADS FORMAT
```
struct resbuf *ads_getargs();
```

PARAMETERS
none

RELATED AUTOLISP AND ADS FUNCTIONS
none

(get_attr *key attr*)
ads_get_attr

Dialog box: Returns the DCL value of the dialog box attribute.

Example	Return
(get_attr "pdsize_label" "Units")	"Units"

ADS FORMAT
```
int ads_get_attr(ads_hdlg hdlg, char *key, char *attr, char *value, int len);
```

PARAMETERS
- *key*   Specifies the tile.

- *attr*   Name of the attribute.

TIP
- The DCL value returned is not constant but changes due to user input and calls made by **set_tile** function.

RELATED AUTOLISP AND ADS FUNCTIONS
ads_get_attr_string

> Gets the DCL value of the specified attribute using the tile handle.

get_tile *and* ads_get_tile

> Gets the run-time value of a tile.

set_tile *and* ads_set_tile

> Sets the run-time value of a tile.

...

ads_get_attr_string

Dialog box: Returns the DCL value of the dialog box attribute, using the tile handle passed to the callback function.

Example	Result
`ads_get_attr_string("pdsize_label","Units")`	RTNORM

ADS FORMAT
```
int ads_get_attr_string(ads_htile tile, char *attr, char *value, int len);
```

PARAMETERS
- *attr*   Name of the attribute.
- *len*   Length of the function.

RELATED AUTOLISP AND ADS FUNCTIONS
get_attr *and* ads_get_attr

    Gets the DCL value of the specified attribute.

get_tile *and* ads_get_tile

    Gets the run-time value of a tile.

set_tile *and* ads_set_tile

    Sets the run-time value of a tile.

(getcfg *cfg*)

. . .

External applications: Returns application data from the **AppData** section of the **Acad.Cfg** file. The *cfg* string must include the application name, the section name, and the parameter name (*short for GET ConFiGuration*).

Example	Result
(getcfg "appdata/appname/parameter")	8

PARAMETER

- *cfg*   A string that describes:

    1. The application name

    2. The section name

    3. The parameter name, as in

       "appdata/appname/parameter"

RELATED AUTOLISP FUNCTIONS

setcfg   Changes the value of application data in Acad.Cfg.

getvar   Returns the value of a system variable.

getenv   Returns the value of a variable in the Acad.Ini file.

(getcname *cname*)
ads_getcname

External apps: Returns localized name of the command *cname* (*short for GET Command NAME*).

Examples	Return
(getcname "zoom")	"_ZOOM"
(getcname "_zoom")	"ZOOM"

ADS FORMAT
```
int ads_getcorner(const ads_point pt, const char *prompt, ads_point result);
```

PARAMETER
- *cname*   Name of the command.

TIPS
- Command *cname* must be less than 65 characters long.
- The underscore "internationalizes" the command name as follows:

Underscore	Returns	Example
Present	Localized name	(getcname "_ZOOM")
Missing	English name	(getcname "LINE")

RELATED AUTOLISP AND ADS FUNCTION
command *and* ads_command

> Executes an AutoCAD command.

(getcorner *pt [prompt]*)
ads_getcorner

User input: Prompts user to select a rectangle's second corner point (*pt* is the first corner), displaying the optional *prompt* (*short for GET CORNER*).

Examples	Result
(getcorner pt1)	(58.7599 -1.17375 0.0)
(getcorner pt1 "Pick other corner: ")	Pick other corner: (58.7599 -1.17375 0.0)

GetAngle drags the rectangular outline from **pt** *to the current cursor location:*

ADS FORMAT
int ads_getcorner(const ads_point pt, const char *prompt, ads_point result);

PARAMETERS
- *pt* The coordinates of the first corner of the rectangle.
- *prompt* (*Optional*) A programmer-definable prompt string.

TIPS
- The first point is required; get with **getpoint** or another function.
- The z-coordinate is ignored; instead the current elevation (stored in system variable **Elevation**) is used as the z-coordinate.

RELATED AUTOLISP AND ADS FUNCTIONS
getangle *and* ads_angle
　　　　Get user input for an angle.
getdist *and* ads_getdist
　　　　Get two points that specify a distance.
getpoint *and* ads_getpoint
　　　　Get the 3D coordinates of a point.

RELATED SYSTEM VARIABLE
Elevation　Stores the current elevation, as set by the **Elev** command.

(getdist *[pt] [prompt]*)
ads_getdist

User input: Prompts the user to pick two points indicating a distance, displaying an optional *prompt*. When the first point *pt* is provided, the user is prompted for the second point (*short for GET DISTance*).

Examples	Result
(getdist)	Second point: 3.44039
(getdist pt1)	3.44039
(getdist pt1 "Pick point: ")	Pick point: 3.44039

GetDist prompts for one or two points:

ADS FORMAT
int ads_getdist(const ads_point pt, const char *prompt, ads_real *result);

PARAMETERS
- *pt*   (*Optional*) The coordinates of the first end of the distance.
- *prompt*   (*Optional*) A programmer-definable prompt string.

TIPS
- If *pt* has a z-coordinate, the 3D distance is returned.
- Returns the 2D distance when bit 64 of **initget** is set.

RELATED AUTOLISP AND ADS FUNCTIONS
getangle *and* **ads_getangle**
> Get user input for an angle.

getcorner *and* **ads_getcorner**
> Get the coordiantes of the second corner of a rectangle.

getpoint *and* **ads_getpoint**
> Get the 3D coordinates of a point.

initget *and* **ads_initget**
> Controls the input to the getdist function.

(getenv *var*)

■ ■ ■

External applicationss: Returns the value (as a string) assigned to the environment variable *var* found in the operating system (*short for GET ENVironment*).

Example	Result
(getenv "prototypedwg")	"acad.dwg"

PARAMETER
■ *var*   The name of variable found in the operating system environment.

TIPS
■ **Getenv** returns **nil** when *var* does not exist.

■ *Var* is case sensitive in operating systems that are case sensitive (such as Unix).

RELATED AUTOLISP FUNCTIONS

setenv   Sets the value of an environment variable.

getcfg   Gets the value of application data in Acad.Cfg.

getvar   Returns the value of a system variable.

(getfiled *title default ext [flag]*)
ads_getfiled

Dialog box: Displays the **Select File** *title* dialog box and waits for the user to select a filename (*short for GET FILE Dialog box*).

Example	Result
(getfiled "Drop Everything" "Pickup" "LSP" 4) nil	

*The **File Select** dialog box customized by the **GetFileD** function:*

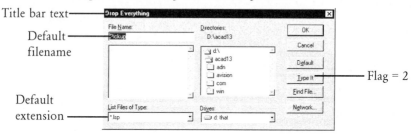

Title bar text —
Default filename —
Default extension —
Flag = 2

ADS FORMAT
```
int ads_getfiled(const char *title, const char *default, const char *ext, int flags, struct resbuf *result);
```

PARAMETERS

- ■ *title*   String specifying the wording for the title bar.
- ■ *default*   String specifying the default filename.
- ■ *ext*   The default filetype extension.
- ■ *flag*   Behaviour of the dialog box:

Flag	Meaning
1	New filename is being created.
2	Disables the 'Type It' button.
4	Allow any extension, including none.
8	Searches for the filename.
16	Second argument is a path or directory.
32	Inhibits display of the alert box.

RELATED AUTOLISP AND ADS FUNCTIONS
alert *and* ads_alert

        Displays a warning dialog box with custom message.

All DCL-related functions

...

ads_getfuncode

External applications: Returns the code number of a requested external function.

Example	Results
ads_getfuncode()	*function code*

ADS FORMAT
int ads_getfuncode(void);

PARAMETERS
none

RELATED ADS FUNCTIONS
none

...

ads_getinput

User input: Returns the keyword passed to a user-input function.,

Example	Result
ads_getinput(*str1)	*user keyboard data*

ADS FORMAT
```
int ads_getinput(char *str);
```

PARAMETER

- **str*   Stores the keyword, a pointer to a character buffer large enough to hold the keyword entered by the user.

RELATED ADS FUNCTIONS

ads_get*xxx*   Get geometric input from the user.

ads_entsel   Selects an object.

ads_nentselp   Selects and object and returns nested information.

ads_nentsel   Returns nested information in a 4x3 matrix.

ads_draggen   Select objects by dragging the cursor.

(getint *[prompt]*)
ads_getint

User input: Prompts the user to input an integer number.

Example	Result
(getint)	4
(getint "Enter number: ")	Enter number:
	4

ADS FORMAT
```
int ads_getint(const char *prompt, int *result);
```

PARAMETER
- *prompt*   (*Optional*) Programmer-definable prompt string.

TIP
- Valid range of integer is 32,768 to -32,767.

RELATED AUTOLISP AND ADS FUNCTIONS
getreal *and* **ads_getreal**

         Get a real number from the user.

getstring *and* **ads_getstring**

         Get a string from the user.

getkword *and* **ads_getkword**

         Get a keyword from the user.

(getkword [prompt])
ads_getkword

User input: Prompts the user for a keyword; must be used in conjunction with initget.

Example	Result
(getkword)	...
(getkword "Continue <Yes, No>: ")	...

```
int ads_getkword(const char *prompt, char *result);
```

PARAMETER
- *prompt* (*Optional*) Programmer-definable prompt string.

TIP
- AutoCAD keeps repeating the **getkword** function until the user enters the correct response.

RELATED AUTOLISP AND ADS FUNCTIONS
initget *and* ads_iniget

        Specifies valid user input.

getstring *and* ads_getstring

        Gets a string from the user.

ads_getinput Gets a keyword for use with other than **ads_getkword**.

usrbrk *and* ads_usrbrk

        Determines whether the user has pressed **[Ctrl]+C** or **[Esc]**.

(getorient *[pt] [prompt]*)
ads_getorient

User input: Prompts the user for angle; unaffected by system settings.

Examples	Result
(getorient)	Second point: 0.669946
(getorient pt1)	0.669946
(getorient pt1 "Pick point: ")	Pick point: 0.669946

*GetOrient returns the angle (in radians) from the x-axis to the imaginary line between **pt1** and **pt2**:*

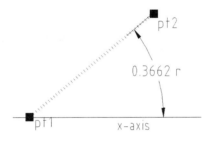

ADS FORMAT
int ads_getorient(const ads_point pt, const char *prompt, ads_real *result);

PARAMETERS
- **pt**   (*Optional*) Starting point of the line.
- **prompt**   (*Optional*) Programmer-definable prompt string.

TIPS
- The angle returned is always measured in radians counterclockwise from the x-axis.
- **Getorient** is unaffected by the settings of system variables **AngDir** and **AngBase**.
- Use **getangle** to input an angle based on **AngDir** and **AngBase**.

RELATED AUTOLISP AND ADS FUNCTIONS
getangle *and* ads_getangle

       Gets an angle from the user.

getdist *and* ads_getdist

       Gets a distance from the user.

(getpoint *[pt]* *[prompt]*)
ads_getpoint

User input: Prompts the user to pick a point; when *pt* is present, draws a drag line.

Example	Result
(getpoint)	(80.743 0.990388 0.0)
(getpoint pt1)	(80.743 0.990388 0.0)
(getpoint pt1 "Pick point: ")	Pick point:
	(80.743 0.990388 0.0)

ADS FORMAT
int ads_getpoint(const ads_point pt, const char *prompt, ads_point result);

PARAMETERS
- *pt*   (*Optional*) Starting point of the line.

- *prompt*   (*Optional*) Programmer-definable prompt string.

TIPS
- Argument *pt* can be 2D or 3D; the value returned in 3D.

- When *pt* is present, **getpoint** displays a rubberband line.

RELATED AUTOLISP AND ADS FUNCTIONS
inters *and* ads_inters

      Returns the 3D coordiantes of the intersection of two lines.

getint *and* ads_getint

      Get an integer from the user.

getreal *and* ads_getreal

      Get a real number from the user.

(getreal *[prompt]*)
ads_getreal

User input: Prompts the user to input a real number.

Example	Result
(getreal)	1.2
(getreal "Enter value: ")	Enter value: 1.2

ADS FORMAT
```
int ads_getreal(const char *prompt, ads_real *result);
```

PARAMETER
- *prompt*   (*Optional*) Programmer-definable prompt string.

RELATED AUTOLISP AND ADS FUNCTIONS
getint *and* ads_getint

>   Get a real number from the user.

getstring *and* ads_getstring

>   Get a string from the user.

getkpoint *and* ads_getpoint

>   Get a point from the user.

(getstring *[flag] [prompt]*)
ads_getstring

User input: Prompts the user to input a string.

Example	Result
(getsting)	"String"
(getstring T)	"String is long"
(getstring T "Enter text: ")	Enter text:
	"String is long"

ADS FORMAT
int ads_getstring(int cronly, char *prompt, char *result);

PARAMETERS
- *flag*   (*Optional*) If T, allows spaces in input text; when **nil**, a space terminates text input.

- *prompt*   (*Optional*) Programmer-definable prompt string.

TIPS
- AutoLISP truncates a string longer than 132 characters; some older versions of AutoCAD have lower limits for the maximum string size.

- When *flag* is **nil**, the input is terminated when the user presses the spacebar or [Enter]; when *flag* is **T**, spaces are allowed.

RELATED AUTOLISP AND ADS FUNCTIONS
getkword *and* ads_getkword

Get a keyword from the user.

usrbrk *and* ads_usrbrk

Checks for the user having pressed **[Ctrl]+C**.

■■■

ads_getsym

Symbol handler: Returns the value of a bound AutoLISP symbol

Example	Result
ads_getsym(*sn1,**val1)	RTNORM

ADS FORMAT
```
int ads_getsym(const char *sname, struct resbuf **value);
```

PARAMETERS
- **sname* The AutoLISP symbol name.
- ***value* A pointer in a result-buffer list containing the value of the symbol; note additional level of indirection.

TIP
- This function can only be used in an ARx program. AutoCAD sends the message **kInvkSubrMsg** to the application.

RELATED ADS FUNCTIONS
ads_putsym Sets the values of an AutoLISP symbol.

ads_getappname Gets the name of the current ARx application.

ads_getcname Gets the localized version of a command name.

ads_vports Gets information on the current viewport.

(get_tile *key*)
ads_get_tile

Dialog box: Returns the runtime value of the current dialog box tile.

Example	Result
(get_tile "pdsize_r")	"pdsize_r"

ADS FORMAT

```
int ads_get_tile(ads_hdlg hdlg, char *key, char *value, int maxlen);
```

PARAMETER

■ *key*   Specifies the tile name.

RELATED AUTOLISP AND ADS FUNCTIONS

set_tile *and* ads_set_tile

      Sets the runtime value of a tile.

get_attr *and* ads_get_attr

      Gets the DCL value of a specific attribute.

(getvar *var*)
ads_getvar

External applications: Returns the value of system variable *var*.

Example	Result
(getvar "gripsize")	3

ADS FORMAT
```
int ads_getvar(const char *var, struct resbuf *result);
```

PARAMETER
- *var*   Name of any system variable.

RELATED AUTOLISP AND ADS FUNCTIONS
setvar *and* ads_setvar

        Changes the value of a system variable.

setenv   Sets the value of an environment variable in Acad.Ini.

getcfg   Gets the value of application data in Acad.Cfg.

(graphscr)
ads_graphscr

Display control: Forces the display of the AutoCAD graphics window.

Example	Result
(graphscr)	nil

The AutoCAD graphics window under Windows 95:

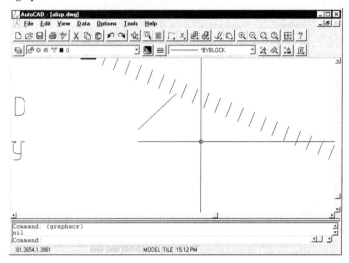

ADS FORMAT
int ads_graphscr();

PARAMETERS
none

RELATED AUTOLISP AND ADS FUNCTIONS
textscr *and* ads_textscr

> Forces the display of the AutoCAD Text window.

grclear *and* ads_grclear

> Clears the current viewport of the graphics display.

(grclear)
ads_grclear

Display control: Clears the current viewport of all objects.

Example	Result
(grclear)	nil

*The viewport cleared of all objects by **GrClear**:*

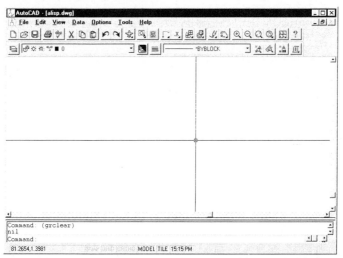

ADS FORMAT
int ads_grclear();

PARAMETERS
none

TIPS
■ Restore the screen display with the **Redraw** command.

■ The **grclear** function does not affect the menu, command, and status areas.

RELATED AUTOLISP AND ADS FUNCTIONS
grdraw *and* **ads_grdraw**

> Draws a vector.

redraw *and* **ads_redraw**

> Redraws the graphics screen.

(grdraw *pt1 pt2 clr [highlite]*)
ads_grdraw

Display control: Draws a single vector from *pt1* to *pt2* in color *clr* with optional highlighting (typically dashed).

Example	Result
(grdraw pt1 pt2 3)	nil
(grdraw pt1 pt2 3 1)	nil

A vector drawn by **GrDraw:**

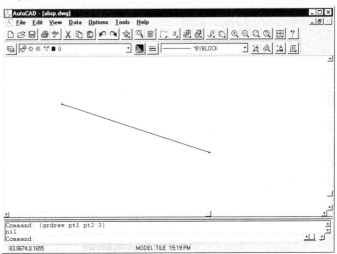

ADS FORMAT
int ads_grdraw(const ads_point from, const ads_point to, int color, int hl);

PARAMETERS
- *pt1*   The starting 2D or 3D point.
- *pt2*   The ending 2D or 3D point.
- *clr*   The color of the vector:

Clr	Color
-1	XOR ink
1 -to 255	Standard AutoCAD colors

- *highlite*   (*Optional*) The starting 2D or 3D point.

TIPS

- *Pt1* and *pt2* can be 2D or 3D coordinates.

- The vector is automatically clipped to fit the viewport.

RELATED AUTOLISP AND ADS FUNCTIONS

grvecs *and* ads_grvecs

Draws a series of vectors.

grclear *and* ads_grclear

Clears the current viewport.

(grread *[flag]* *[keys [cursor]]*)
ads_grread

User input: Reads values from all AutoCAD input devices.

Examples	Result
(grread)	(2 13)
(grread 1)	(5 (83.7535 2.09966 0.0))

ADS FORMAT
```
int ads_grread(int track, int *type, struct resbuf *result);
```

PARAMETERS

■ *flag* (*Optional*) If T, returns all coordinates from moving pointing device.

■ *keys* (*Optional*) Controls the type of data returned:

Keys	Meaning
1	Returns drag mode coordinates.
2	Returns all pressed key values; does not move cursor when arrow keys pressed.
4	Use value passed by *cursor* argument.
8	Don't display "Error: console break" when user presses [Ctrl]+C.

■ *cursor* (*Optional*) Specifies the type of cursor display; only in effect when *keys* is set to **2**:

Cursor	Meaning
0	Display default crosshair cursor.
1	Display no cursor.
2	Display object selection box cursor.

TIPS

■ Autodesk advises that the other **get***xx* functions should be used before **grread**.

■ **Grread** gives the programmer complete control over all input devices with one exception: when *key* allows the user to press [**Esc**].

■ All coordinate data being generated by an input device is returned when *track* is T; this can overwhelm a poorly written routine.

- Return values from **grread** and **ads_grread**:

Type Value	Type of input	Result Value	Meaning
2	Keyboard	Varies	Character code
3	Select	3D point	Point coordinates
4	Menu item	0 to 999	Screen menu box #
	(from pointing device)	1001 - 1999	POP1 menu box #
		2001 - 2999	POP2 menu box #
		3001 - 3999	POP2 menu box #
		... etc ...	
		16001 - 16999	POP16 menu box #
5	Pointing device	3D point	Drag mode coordinate
	(returned only if tracking is enabled)		
6	BUTTONS menu	0 - 999	BUTTONS1 menu button #
		1000 - 1999	BUTTONS2 menu button #
		2000 - 2999	BUTTONS3 menu button #
		3000 - 3999	BUTTONS4 menu button #
7	TABLET1 menu	0 - 32767	Digitized box number
8	TABLET2 menu	0 - 32767	Digitized box number
9	TABLET3 menu	0 - 32767	Digitized box number
10	TABLET4 menu	0 - 32767	Digitized box number
11	AUX menu	0 - 999	AUX1 menu button #
		1000 - 1999	AUX2 menu button #
		2000 - 2999	AUX3 menu button #
		3000 - 3999	AUX4 menu button #
12	Pointer button	3D point	Point coordinates
	(follows a type 6 or type 11 return)		

RELATED AUTOLISP AND ADS FUNCTIONS
all **getxxx** *functions*

(grtext [box txt [highlite]])
ads_grtext

Display control: Types text in the status line and side screen menu area.

Example	Results
(grtext)	nil
(grtext -1 "Quick Ref")	"Quick Ref"
(grtext 5 "Quick Ref" 1)	"Quick Ref"

The GrText function writes "Quick Ref" to the status area:

ADS FORMAT

```
int ads_grtext(int box, const char *text, int hl);
```

PARAMETERS

■ *box* (*Optional*) Writes text the following screen location:

Box	Meaning
0	Screen menu box #1.
1	Screen menu box #2.
	. . .
n-1	Screen menu box *n*.
-1	Mode status area.
-2	Coordinate display area.

■ *text* (*Optional*) String to be written; truncated to fit available space.

■ *highlite* (*Optional*) Highlights the screen menu box:

Highlite	Meaning
1	Highlights the current screen menu box.
0	Dehighlights the box.
-1	Ignored.

TIPS

■ Restore the text areas by using **grtext** with no arguments.

■ Use DIESEL as an alternative method of writing to the status and coordinate areas.

RELATED AUTOLISP AND ADS FUNCTIONS

grdraw *and* ads_grdraw

Draws a vector on the graphics screen.

(grvecs *list [trans]*)
ads_grvecs

Display control: Draws one or more vectors specified in *list* on the screen, with an optional transformation specified by matrix *trans*.

Example	Result
(grvecs '(1(1.2 3.4) (5.6 10)	
(10 12) (11 13)))	nil

ADS FORMAT
```
int ads_grvecs(const struct resbuf *list, ads_matrix trans);
```

PARAMETERS
■ *list* A list of vectors in the format of an optional color followed by two endpoints in the current UCS:

([*clr*] *pt1 pt2* [*clr*] *pt3 pt4* ...)

The *clr* has the following values:

Clr	Meaning
0 - 255	Standard AutoCAD colors.
256	XOR ink.
-1	Highlighted.

■ *trans* (*Optional*) A 4x4 transformation matrix to scale and move the vectors in list format. For example, to apply a scale factor of 1.0 and move the vectors by 2,2,0, use the following list:

```
'( (1.0  0.0  0.0  2.0)
   (0.0  1.0  0.0  2.0)
   (1.0  0.0  1.0  0.0)
   (1.0  0.0  0.0  1.0))
```

TIPS
■ The color value holds true for all vectors until changed.
■ Color values greater than 255 are drawn in XOR ink.
■ The points can be 2D or 3D but must be provided in pairs.
■ The vectors are clipped to fit the viewport.

RELATED AUTOLISP AND ADS FUNCTIONS
grdraw *and* ads_grdraw

Draws a single vector.

grclear *and* ads_grclear

Clears the current viewport.

(handent *handle*)
ads_handent

Object handler: Returns the entity name attached to its *handle* name (*short for HANDle ENTity*).

Example	Result
(handent "5")	<Entity name: 2000428>

ADS FORMAT
```
int ads_handent(const char *handle, ads_name entres);
```

PARAMETER
■ *handle*   An objet's entity handle string.

TIPS
■ The **handent** function returns the entity name of deleted objects, which can then be undeleted with the **entdel** function.

■ The handle of an object is its permanent name in the drawing database.

■ The entity name of an object changes each time the drawing is loaded into AutoCAD.

■ As of Release 13, users can no longer turn off handles with the **Handles** command.

■ The **handent** function returns **nil** when the handle number does not exist.

RELATED AUTOLISP AND ADS FUNCTION
entget *and* ads_entget

   Get the entity data associated with an entity name.

(help [hlpfile [topic [flag]]])
ads_help

Dialog box: Displays the *hlpfile* HLP (or AHP) help file with the given *topic.*

Example	Result
(help)	*" "*

Help window displayed by the **Help** *function in Windows 95:*

ADS FORMAT
```
int ads_help(char *filename, char *topic, int command);
```

PARAMETERS
- *hlpfile* (*Optional*) Name of the help file in Windows HLP or Autodesk AHP format; when missing or "" (empty string), **help** uses the AHP file.

- *topic* (*Optional*) Name of the help file topic; when "" (empty string), **help** displays the Contents page.

- *flag* (*Optional*) Specifies the state of the **Help** window:

Flag	Meaning
HELP_CONTENTS	Display the first Help topic, usually the contnets.
HELP_HELPONKEY	Display help on using Help.
HELP_PARTIALKEY	Display the Search dialog box, with *topic* as the search string.

TIPS
- The **help** function is able to use both the Windows HLP file format (using the Windows help engine) and the Autodesk AHP file format (using the AutoCAD help viewer).
- This function is a replacement for the **acad_helpdlg** function.

(if *test then [else]*)

■ ■ ■

Conditional: Evaluation of *test* expression.

Example	Result
(if (> x 0) (setq ht 10.0) (setq ht 0.0))	10

PARAMETER

■ *test*   A test expression.

■ *then*   An expression that is executed when *text* is not **nil**.

■ *else*   (*Optional*) An expression that is executed when *text* is **nil**.

TIPS

■ Use the **if** function to test one of two conditions.

■ While you can nest the **if** function to test more than two conditions, it is more efficient to use the **cond** function to test more than two conditions.

■ The **if** function normally only allows a simple statement for the *then* and *else* tests; to get around this limitation, use the **progn** function, as follows:

```
(if (> x 0)
  (progn (
    (setq ht 10.0 wd 5.0 t 1.0)
    (grdraw a b clr)
    (grtext -1 "Step")
    ) ; end progn
  ) ; end then
) ; end if
```

RELATED AUTOLISP FUNCTIONS

progn   Allows the use of complex *then* and *else* statements.

cond   Branches to the first expression after the first non-**nil** expression.

repeat   Repeats an expression a specific number of times.

while   Executes an experssion until the text experssion is **nil**.

...

ads_init

External apps: Initializes the ADS interface to AutoLISP.

Example	Result
ads_init(arg1,*arg2[])	*any value*

ADS FORMAT

int ads_init(int argc, char *argv[]);

PARAMETERS

- *argc*   The same **argc** passed to the **main()** function of the ADS application.

- **argv[ ]*   The same **argv** passed to the **main()** function of the ADS application.

RELATED ADS FUNCTIONS

all

(initget *[flag]* *[str ...]*)
ads_initget

User input: Establishes keyword(s) *str* via *flag* for the functions that recognize keywords: **get***xxx*, **entsel**, **nentsel**, and **nentselp** (*short for INITialize GET*).

Example	Result
(initget)	nil
(initget 4)	nil
(initget 4 "LType", "LtScale")	nil
(initget 4 "LTYPE","LT")	nil

ADS FORMAT
```
int ads_initget(int val, const char *kwl);
```

PARAMETER
■ *flag*   (*Optional*) Controls the type of user input:

flag	Meaning
1	User cannot press [Enter].
2	User cannot enter 0 (zero).
4	User cannot enter negative value.
8	User can pick point outside limits.
16	*not used*
32	Uses highlight for rubber-banding.
64	User cannot enter z-coordinate.
128	Allows any input.

■ *str*   (*Optional*) One or more keywords consisting of alphanumeric characters and the - (hyphen) character; separate more than one keyword with a space, such as "Yes No"; upper-case characters indicate required input.

TIPS
■ The **getstring** function does not make use of key words.

■ When the user input does not match the keyword, AutoCAD keeps asking until the input is correct.

■ Flag bits can be combined to create complex conditions. For example, flag = 6 (2 + 4) means the user cannot enter 0 or negative numbers.

RELATED AUTOLISP AND ADS FUNCTIONS

all get*xxx and* ads_get*xxx functions*

entsel	Select an object.
nentsel	Select an object and provide complex data.
nentselp	Select an object and provide complex data.

RELATED SYSTEM VARIABLES

LimMin *and* LimMax

> The lower-left and upper-right coordinates of the drawing limits.

Popups   Determines whether display driver supports AUI (*short for Advanced User Interface*):

Popups	Meaning
0	AUI not supported.
1	AUI supported (default).

(inters *pt1 pt2 pt3 pt4 [flag]*)
ads_inters

Geometric function: Returns the 3D coordinates of the intsersection of two lines defined by *pt1*, *pt2* and *pt3*, *pt4*; when *flag* is **nil**, the two lines are considered infinite in length.

Example	Result
(inters pt1 pt2 pt3 pt4)	nil
(inters pt1 pt2 pt3 pt4 T)	(1.2 3.4)

The **nil** *flag ensures an answer, even when the two lines do not intersect:*

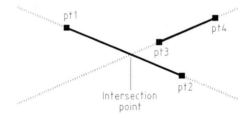

ADS FORMAT
```
int ads_inters(const ads_point from1, const ads_point to1, const ads_point from2, const ads_point to2, int teston, ads_point result);
```

PARAMETERS
- *pt1 and pt2* The starting and ending 2D or 3D coordinates of the first line.

- *pt3 and pt4* The starting and ending 2D or 3D coordinates of the second line.

- *flag*   (*Optional*) If **T**, returns the intersection point when beyond line endpoints.

TIP
- The **inters** function only returns a 3D point when all four input points are 3D.

RELATED AUTOLISP FUNCTIONS
osnap *and* ads_osnap

> Finds a point via one of the object snap modes.

getpoint *and* ads_getpoint

> Prompts the user to select a single 2D or 3D point.

...

ads_invoke

External apps: Calls a function defined in another ADS application.

Example	Result
ads_invoke(*arg1,**rslt1)	*external functions return values*

ADS FORMAT
```
int ads_invoke(const struct resbuf *args, struct resbuf **result);
```

PARAMETERS
- *args*   Result-buffer list that specifies the external function call.
- *result*   Address of a result-buffer pointer.

RELATED ADS FUNCTION
ads_init   Initializes the interface between the ADS application and AutoLISP.

...

ads_isalnum

Error handler: Checks whether the character is alphnumeric.

Example	Result
ads_isalnum(c1)	TRUE

ADS FORMAT
```
int ads_isalnum(int c);
```

PARAMETER
- *c*   The character being tested.

RELATED ADS FUNCTIONS

ads_isalpha   Tests whether the character is alphabetical.

ads_iscntrl   Tests whether the character is a control character.

ads_isdigit   Tests whether the character is a digit.

ads_isgraph   Tests whether the character is a graphical character.

ads_islower   Tests whether the character is a lowercase character.

ads_isprint   Tests whether the character is a printable character.

ads_ispunct   Tests whether the character is punctuation.

ads_isspace   Tests whether the character is whitespace.

ads_isupper   Tests whether the character is an uppercase character.

ads_isxdigit   Tests whether the character is a hexadeciamal number.

...

ads_isalpha

Error handler: Checks whether the character is alphabetical.

Example	Result
ads_isalpha(c1)	TRUE

ADS FORMAT
```
int ads_isalpha(int c);
```

PARAMETER
- *c*   The character being tested.

RELATED ADS FUNCTIONS

ads_isalnum Tests whether the character is alphanumeric.

ads_iscntrl Tests whether the character is a control character.

ads_isdigit Tests whether the character is a digit.

ads_isgraph Tests whether the character is a graphical character.

ads_islower Tests whether the character is a lowercase character.

ads_isprint Tests whether the character is a printable character.

ads_ispunct Tests whether the character is punctuation.

ads_isspace Tests whether the character is whitespace.

ads_isupper Tests whether the character is an uppercase character.

ads_isxdigit Tests whether the character is a hexadeciamal number.

...

ads_iscntrl

Error handler: Checks whether the character is a control character.

Example	Result
ads_isctrl(c1)	TRUE

ADS FORMAT
```
int ads_iscntrl(int c);
```

PARAMETER
■ *c*   The character being tested.

RELATED ADS FUNCTIONS

ads_isalnum   Tests whether the character is alphanumeric.

ads_isalpha   Tests whether the character is alphabetical.

adads_isdigit   Tests whether the character is a digit.

ads_isgraph   Tests whether the character is a graphical character.

ads_islower   Tests whether the character is a lowercase character.

ads_isprint   Tests whether the character is a printable character.

ads_ispunct   Tests whether the character is punctuation.

ads_isspace   Tests whether the character is whitespace.

ads_isupper   Tests whether the character is an uppercase character.

ads_isxdigit   Tests whether the character is a hexadeciamal number.

...

ads_isdigit

Error handler: Checks whether the character is a digit.

Example	Results
ads_isdigit(c1)	TRUE

ADS FORMAT
```
int ads_isdigit(int c);
```

PARAMETER
- *c* The character being tested.

RELATED ADS FUNCTIONS

ads_isalnum	Tests whether the character is alphanumeric.
ads_isalpha	Tests whether the character is alphabetical.
ads_iscntrl	Tests whether the character is a control character.
ads_isgraph	Tests whether the character is a graphical character.
ads_islower	Tests whether the character is a lowercase character.
ads_isprint	Tests whether the character is a printable character.
ads_ispunct	Tests whether the character is punctuation.
ads_isspace	Tests whether the character is whitespace.
ads_isupper	Tests whether the character is an uppercase character.
ads_isxdigit	Tests whether the character is a hexadeciamal number.

...

ads_isgraph

Error handler: Checks whether the character is graphical.

Example	Results
ads_isgraph(c1)	TRUE

ADS FORMAT
```
int ads_isgraph(int c);
```

PARAMETER
- *c*   The character being tested.

RELATED ADS FUNCTIONS

ads_isalnum	Tests whether the character is alphanumeric.
ads_isalpha	Tests whether the character is alphabetical.
ads_iscntrl	Tests whether the character is a control character.
ads_isdigit	Tests whether the character is a digit.
ads_islower	Tests whether the character is a lowercase character.
ads_isprint	Tests whether the character is a printable character.
ads_ispunct	Tests whether the character is punctuation.
ads_isspace	Tests whether the character is whitespace.
ads_isupper	Tests whether the character is an uppercase character.
ads_isxdigit	Tests whether the character is a hexadeciamal number.

...

ads_islower

Error handler: Checks whether the character is a lowercase character.

Example	Results
ads_islower(c1)	TRUE

ADS FORMAT
```
int ads_islower(int c);
```

PARAMETER
- *c*   The character being tested.

RELATED ADS FUNCTIONS

ads_isalnum	Tests whether the character is alphanumeric.
ads_isalpha	Tests whether the character is alphabetical.
ads_iscntrl	Tests whether the character is a control character.
ads_isdigit	Tests whether the character is a digit.
ads_isgraph	Tests whether the character is a graphical character.
ads_isprint	Tests whether the character is a printable character.
ads_ispunct	Tests whether the character is punctuation.
ads_isspace	Tests whether the character is whitespace.
ads_isupper	Tests whether the character is an uppercase character.
ads_isxdigit	Tests whether the character is a hexadeciamal number.

■■■

ads_isprint

Error handler: Checks whether the character is a printable character.

Example	Results
ads_isprint(c1)	TRUE

ADS FORMAT

```
int ads_isprint(int c);
```

PARAMETER

■ *c*   The character being tested.

RELATED ADS FUNCTIONS

ads_isalnum   Tests whether the character is alphanumeric.

ads_isalpha   Tests whether the character is alphabetical.

ads_iscntrl   Tests whether the character is a control character.

ads_isdigit   Tests whether the character is a digit.

ads_isgraph   Tests whether the character is a graphical character.

ads_islower   Tests whether the character is a lowercase character.

ads_ispunct   Tests whether the character is punctuation.

ads_isspace   Tests whether the character is whitespace.

ads_isupper   Tests whether the character is an uppercase character.

ads_isxdigit   Tests whether the character is a hexadeciamal number.

...

ads_ispunct

Error handler: Checks whether the character is a punctuation character.

Example	Results
ads_ispunct(c1)	TRUE

ADS FORMAT
```
int ads_ispunct(int c);
```

PARAMETER
- *c*   The character being tested.

RELATED ADS FUNCTIONS

ads_isalnum   Tests whether the character is alphanumeric.

ads_isalpha   Tests whether the character is alphabetical.

ads_iscntrl   Tests whether the character is a control character.

ads_isdigit   Tests whether the character is a digit.

ads_isgraph   Tests whether the character is a graphical character.

ads_islower   Tests whether the character is a lowercase character.

ads_isprint   Tests whether the character is a printable character.

ads_isspace   Tests whether the character is whitespace.

ads_isupper   Tests whether the character is an uppercase character.

ads_isxdigit   Tests whether the character is a hexadeciamal number.

...

ads_isspace

Error handler: Checks whether the character is a whitespace character (such as a space or a tab).

Example	Results
ads_isspace(c1)	TRUE

ADS FORMAT
```
int ads_isspace(int c);
```

PARAMETER
- *c*   The character being tested.

RELATED ADS FUNCTIONS

ads_isalnum   Tests whether the character is alphanumeric.

ads_isalpha   Tests whether the character is alphabetical.

ads_iscntrl   Tests whether the character is a control character.

ads_isdigit   Tests whether the character is a digit.

ads_isgraph   Tests whether the character is a graphical character.

ads_islower   Tests whether the character is a lowercase character.

ads_isprint   Tests whether the character is a printable character.

ads_ispunct   Tests whether the character is punctuation.

ads_isupper   Tests whether the character is an uppercase character.

ads_isxdigit   Tests whether the character is a hexadeciamal number.

...

ads_isupper

Error handler: Checks whether the character is an uppercase character.

Example	Results
ads_isupper(c1)	TRUE

ADS FORMAT
```
int ads_isupper(int c);
```

PARAMETER
- *c*   The character being tested.

RELATED ADS FUNCTIONS

ads_isalnum	Tests whether the character is alphanumeric.
ads_isalpha	Tests whether the character is alphabetical.
ads_iscntrl	Tests whether the character is a control character.
ads_isdigit	Tests whether the character is a digit.
ads_isgraph	Tests whether the character is a graphical character.
ads_islower	Tests whether the character is a lowercase character.
ads_isprint	Tests whether the character is a printable character.
ads_ispunct	Tests whether the character is punctuation.
ads_isspace	Tests whether the character is whitespace.
ads_isxdigit	Tests whether the character is a hexadeciamal number.

...

ads_isxdigit

Error handler: Checks whether the character is a hexadecimal digit.

Example	Results
ads_isxdigit(c1)	TRUE

ADS FORMAT

```
int ads_isxdigit(int c);
```

PARAMETER

- *c*   The character being tested.

RELATED ADS FUNCTIONS

ads_isalnum	Tests whether the character is alphanumeric.
ads_isalpha	Tests whether the character is alphabetical.
ads_iscntrl	Tests whether the character is a control character.
ads_isdigit	Tests whether the character is a digit.
ads_isgraph	Tests whether the character is a graphical character.
ads_islower	Tests whether the character is a lowercase character.
ads_isprint	Tests whether the character is a printable character.
ads_ispunct	Tests whether the character is punctuation.
ads_isspace	Tests whether the character is whitespace.
ads_isupper	Tests whether the character is an uppercase character.

(itoa *int*)

. . .

Conversion: Converts integer *int* into a string.

Example	Result
(itoa 2)	"2"

PARAMETER
■ *int*   Any integer number.

TIP
■ The argument must be an integer.

RELATED AUTOLISP FUNCTIONS
atoi   Converts a string representing an integer number into an integer.

ascii   Converts the first character of a string to its ASCII number.

(lambda *arg expr*)

...

Function handler: Creates an unnamed function consisting of *expr* and taking arguments *arg*.

Example	Result
(lambda (a b) (+ a b))	((A B) (+ A B))

PARAMETERS
- *arg*   A list of arguments used by the expression.
- *expr*   The expression.

TIP
- Using **lambda** uses less overhead than **defun**.

RELATED AUTOLISP FUNCTION
defun   Defines a function with a name.

(last *list*)

■ ■ ■

List manipulation: Returns the last element of the list *list*.

Examples	Result
(last '(1.2 3.4 5.6 10.0))	10.0
(last '(x y (z t)))	(z t)

PARAMETER
■ *list*   A list of items.

TIP
■ **Last** returns the y-coordinate of a 2D point and the z-coordinate of a 3D point.

RELATED AUTOLISP FUNCTIONS

car	Returns the first item of a list.
cdr	Returns all but the first item of the list.
nth	Returns the nth item in a list.
length	Returns the length of a list.
reverse	Reverses the items in a list.

(length *list*)

■■■

List manipulation: Returns the number of elements in *list*.

Examples	Result
(length '(1.2 3.4 5.6 10.0))	4
(last '(x y (z t)))	3

PARAMETER
■ *list*   A list of items.

RELATED AUTOLISP FUNCTIONS
car   Returns the first item of a list.

cdr   Returns all but the first item of the list.

nth   Returns the nth item in a list.

last   Returns the last item of a list.

reverse   Reverses the items in a list.

...

ads_link

External applications: Signals AutoLISP the ADS application is ready.

Example	Result
ads_link(c2)	*return request code*

ADS FORMAT
int ads_link(int cbc);

PARAMETER
■ *cbc*   Must be **RSRSLT, RSERR, -RSRSLT,** or **-RSERR.**

RELATED ADS FUNCTION
ads_init   Initializes the ADS application with AutoLISP.

(list *expr* ...)

■ ■ ■

List manipulation: Converts expressions *expr* into a list.

Examples	Result
(list 1.2 3.4 5.6 10.0)	(1.2 3.4 5.6 10.0)
(list 'x 'y '(z t))	(x y (z t))

PARAMETER
■ *expr*   A series of items.

RELATED AUTOLISP FUNCTIONS
cons   Adds an item to the beginning of a list.

length   Returns the length of the list.

listp   Determines if the item is a list.

(listp *item*)

■■■

List manipulation: Checks if the item *item* is a list.

Examples	Result
(listp '(x y (z t)))	T
(listp 1.2)	nil

PARAMETER
■ *item*   An item.

RELATED AUTOLISP FUNCTIONS
list   Creates a list from several expressions.

reverse   Reverses the order of the list.

(load *fname* *[flag]*)

∎ ∎ ∎

External applications: Loads AutoLISP file *fname*; returns *flag* if unable to load.

Examples	Result
(load "ddptype.lsp")	DDPTYPE loaded
(load "ddptype")	DDPTYPE loaded
(load "heckler.lsp" "failed")	"failed"

PARAMETERS
∎ *fname*   Name of the AutoLISP filename; the LSP extension is optional.

∎ *flag*   (*Optional*) A string that is displayed when the load fails.

TIPS
∎ Don't confuse the AutoLISP **load** function (which loads AutoLISP files) with the AutoCAD **Load** command, which loads SHX shape files.

∎ When the file being loaded is not a command (**defun** does not include the *c:* parameter), then the function runs immediately upon being loaded.

∎ You can use / (single forward slash) or \\ (double backslash) to separate subdirectory names.

RELATED AUTOLISP AND ADS FUNCTIONS
atoms-family   Lists the names of all AutoLISP functions in memory.

load_dialog *and* ads_load_dialog

        Loads a DCL (dialog control language) file into memory.

xload *and* ads_xload

        Loads an ADS application into AutoCAD memory.

arxload *and* ads_arxload

        Loads an ARx application into memory.

(load_dialog *dcl*)
ads_load_dialog

Dialog box: Loads dialog control file *dcl*.

Example	Result
(load_dialog "base.dcl")	5

*A portion of the **Base.Dcl** dialog control language file displayed by Notepad text editor:*

ADS FORMAT
```
int ads_load_dialog(char *dclfile, int *dcl_id);
```

PARAMETER
- *dcl*   Name of the DCL (short for dialog control language) file to load; the DCL file extension is not required.

TIP
- This function searches the AutoCAD paths for the DCL file and returns a negative number if the file cannot be found.

RELATED AUTOLISP AND ADS FUNCTIONS
load   Loads an AutoLISP file into memory.

xload *and* ads_xload

     Loads an ADS application into AutoCAD memory.

arxload *and* ads_arxload

     Loads an ARx application into memory.

...

ads_loaded

External applications: Returns the names of loaded ADS and ARx applications.

Example	Results
ads_loaded()	*pointer to list of loaded ADS apps*

ADS FORMAT
struct resbuf *ads_loaded(void);

PARAMETERS
none

RELATED AUTOLISP AND ADS FUNCTIONS
arxloaded *and* ads_arxloaded

> List of ARx applications loaded.

atoms-family   List of AutoLISP functions in memory.

xload *and* ads_load

> Loads an ADS application into memory.

(log *num*)

■■■

Math function: Returns the natural log of *num* as a real number.

Examples	Result
(log 10)	2.30259
(log 1)	0.0
(log pi)	1.14473

PARAMETER
- *num*   Any real or integer number.

RELATED AUTOLISP FUNCTION
exp   The natural exponent raised to a number (natural anti-log).

(logand *int1 int2 ...*)

■ ■ ■

Logical function: Returns the logical bitwise AND of integers *int1, int2, ...*

Examples	Result
(logand 1 2 3)	0
(logand 1)	1

PARAMETERS
- *int1*   The first integer.
- *int2*   The second integer.

RELATED AUTOLISP FUNCTIONS

logior   Logical bitwise OR of integers.

lsh   Logical bitwise shift of integers.

and   Logical AND of a list of expressions.

or   Logical OR of a list of expressions.

(logior *int1 int2 ...*)

■■■

Logical function: Returns the logical bitwise inclusive OR of integers *int1, int2, ...*

Examples	Result
(logior 1 2 3)	3
(logior 1)	1

PARAMETERS
■ *int1*   The first integer.

■ *int2*   The second integer.

RELATED AUTOLISP FUNCTIONS
logiand   Logical bitwise AND of integers.

lsh   Logical bitwise shift of integers.

and   Logical AND of a list of expressions.

or   Logical OR of a list of expressions.

(lsh *int bits*)

■ ■ ■

Logical function: Returns the logical bitwise shift of integer *int* by the number of *bits* specified.

Examples	Results
(lsh 1 2)	4
(lsh 1 2)	8

PARAMETERS

■ *int*   The integer.

■ *bits*   Number of bits to shift by:

bits	Shifted
negative	Left.
positive	Right.
zero	In.
dicarded	Out.

RELATED AUTOLISP FUNCTIONS

logiand   Logical bitwise AND of integers.

logior   Logical bitwise OR of integers.

and   Logical AND of a list of expressions.

or   Logical OR of a list of expressions.

ads_malloc

Memory management: Allocates memory large enough to hold an object specified by **ads_msize** (*short for Memory ALLOCation*).

Example	Result
ads_malloc(sz1)	*pointer to memory*

ADS FORMAT
void *ads_malloc(int sz);

PARAMETER
- *sz*   The amount of memory to allocate.

RELATED ADS FUNCTIONS

ads_free   Frees up memory allocated by **ads_calloc, ads_malloc,** and **ads_realloc.**

ads_msize   Returns the size of a buffer.

ads_calloc   Allocates memory to hold an array.

ads_realloc   Changes the size of a memory allocation.

(mapcar *func list* ...)

■■■

Function handler: Applies function *func* to either (1) the individual elements of *list*; or (2) each list; and returns the result as a list.

Example	Result
(mapcar '1+ a)	(2.2 4.4 6.6)

PARAMETERS
■ *func*   An AutoLISP function.

■ *list*   A list of elements; the number of lists must match the number of arguments expected by *func*.

RELATED AUTOLISP FUNCTIONS
apply   Passes a list of arguments to a function.

defun   Defines a programmer-definable function.

eval   Returns the result of evaluating expressions.

(max *num1 num2* ...)

List manipulation: Returns the maximum value of *num1, num2, ...*

Example	Result
(max 1.2 3.4 5.6 10.0)	10.0

PARAMETER
■ *num1*   A single integer or real number.

RELATED AUTOLISP FUNCTIONS
min   Returns the minimum number of a list.

fix   Rounds down a real number and converts it to an integer.

float   Converts an integer to a real number.

(mem)

■■■

Memory management: Displays the number of nodes, free nodes, segments, allocation, and collections of the AutoLISP memory space.

Example	Result	
(mem)	Nodes:	33934
	Free nodes:	1744
	Segments:	40
	Allocate:	514
	Collections:	24
	nil	

PARAMETERS
none

TIPS
■ Reports the following data:

mem	Meaning
Nodes	Total number of nodes allocated.
Free nodes	Nodes freed by garbage collection.
Segments	Number of segments allocated.
Allocate	Size of the segment.
Collections	Number of garbage collections.

RELATED AUTOLISP FUNCTIONS
gc   Cleans memory of unused nodes.

alloc   Expands memory by allocating additional nodes.

(member *item list*)

■ ■ ■

List management: Determines if item *item* is a member of *list*; if so, returns the remainder of the list.

Example	Result
(member 'z '(x y z t))	(Z T)

PARAMETERS

■ *item*   An AutoLISP item of any sort.

■ *list*   A list that may (or might not) contain *item*.

RELATED AUTOLISP FUNCTIONS

listp   Determines whether an item is a list.

length   Determines the length of a list.

list   Creates a list.

(menucmd *str*)
ads_menucmd

Display control: Executes a menu command; sets and retrieves menu status (*short for MENU CoMmanD*).

Example	Result
(menucmd "PO=export")	...

ADS FORMAT
```
int ads_menucmd(const char *str);
```

PARAMETER
- *str*   A string in the form of a menu command, *"menu_area=value"* as shown below:

Menu_Area	Value
A1 - A4	AUX menus 1 thru 4.
B1 - B4	BUTTONS menus 1 thru 4.
I	Image tile menu.
M	Diesel string expression.
P0 - P16	POP menus 0 thru 16.
S	SCREEN menu.
T1 - T4	TABLET menus 1 thru 4.

TIP
- Diesel expressions can be used with the **menucmd** function.

RELATED AUTOLISP AND ADS FUNCTIONS
none

(min *num1 num2* ...)

...

List manipulation: Determines the minimum value of *num1, num2, ...*

Example	Result
(min 1.2 3.4 5.6 10.0)	1.2

PARAMETER
- *num1*   A single integer or real number.

RELATED AUTOLISP FUNCTIONS
max   Returns the maximum number of a list.

fix   Rounds down a real number and converts it to an integer.

float   Converts an integer to a real number.

(minusp *num*)

■■■

Symbol handler: Checks if the number *num* is negative.

Examples	Result
(minusp 2)	nil
(minusp -2)	T

PARAMETER
■ *num*   Any real or integer number.

RELATED AUTOLISP FUNCTION
numberp   Determines if the element is a number.

(mode_tile *key mode*)
ads_mode_tile

Dialog box: Sets the mode *mode* of tile *key*.

Example	Result
(mode_tile pt1 2)	

ADS FORMAT
```
int ads_mode_tile(ads_hdlg hdlg, char *key, short mode);
```

PARAMETERS
- *key* — Specifies the tile.
- *mode* — An integer number describing the mode of the tile:

Mode	ADS Symbol	Meaning
0	MODE_ENABLE	Enable tile.
1	MODE_DISABLE	Disable tile.
2	MODE_SETFOCUS	Set focus to tile.
3	MODE_SETSEL	Select edit box contents.
4	MODE_FLIP	Toggle image highlight.

RELATED AUTOLISP AND ADS FUNCTIONS
get_attr *and* ads_get_attr

Get the DCL value of an attribute.

get_tile *and* ads_get_tile

Get the runtime value of a tile.

...

ads_msize

Memory management: Returns the size of the specified buffer.

Example	Results
ads_msize(*b1)	*size in bytes*

ADS FORMAT
```
int ads_msize(void *buff);
```

PARAMETER
■ *buff*   A pointer to a buffer.

RELATED ADS FUNCTIONS

ads_malloc   Allocates memory based on the size returned by **ads_msize**.

ads_free   Frees up memory allocated by **ads_calloc, ads_malloc,** and **ads_realloc**.

ads_calloc   Allocates memory to hold an array.

ads_realloc   Changes the size of a memory allocation.

(namedobjdict)
ads_namedobjdict

Entity access: Returns the entity name of the drawing's named object dictionary, which is the starting point for all nongraphical objects in the current drawing (*short for NAME of Drawing OBJect DICTionary*).

Example	Result
(namedobjdict)	<Entity name: 2000460>

ADS FORMAT
int ads_namedobjdict(ads_name result);

PARAMETERS
none

TIP
■ This function accesses nongraphical objects when used with **dictsearch** and **dictnext**.

RELATED AUTOLISP AND ADS FUNCTIONS
dictsearch *and* **ads_dictsearch**

> Moves the program pointer to the next entry in the dictionary.

dictnext *and* **ads_dictnext**

> Searches the dictionary for an object.

(nentsel *[prompt]*)
ads_nentsel

Entity access (Obsolete): Prompts the user to pick a point, returns definition data in a 4x3 matrix *(short for Nested ENTity SELection).*

Example	Result
(nentsel)	Select object:
	(<Entity name: 2001ba0> (91.814 3.03939 0.0)
	((1.0 0.0 0.0) (0.0 1.0 0.0) (0.0 0.0 1.0)
	(93.9477 5.19489 0.0)) (<Entity name: 2002620>))
(nentsel "Pick object: ")	Pick object:
	(<Entity name: 2001ba0> (91.814 3.03939 0.0)
	((1.0 0.0 0.0) (0.0 1.0 0.0) (0.0 0.0 1.0)
	(93.9477 5.19489 0.0)) (<Entity name: 2002620>))

ADS FORMAT
```
int ads_nentsel(const char *str, ads_name entres, ads_point ptres,
ads_point xformres[4], struct resbuf **refstkres);
```

PARAMETER
■ *prompt*   *(Optional)* A programmer-definable prompt string.

TIPS
■ The **nentsel** function acts the same as the **entsel** function when the selected object contains no complex data.

■ This function does not return the **Seqend** subobject of polylines.

■ This function returns the following block information:

Element	Meaning
First	Selecteted entity name.
Second	Pick point coordinates.
Third	Model-to-world transformation.
Fourth	Block's entity name.

RELATED AUTOLISP AND ADS FUNCTIONS
entsel *and* ads_entsel

      Prompts the user to select an object.

nentselp *and* ads_nentselp

      Includes nested data.

initget *and* ads_initget

      Provides keywords for use with this function.

(nentselp [prompt] [pt])
ads_nentselp

Entity access: Returns a 4x4 transformation matrix with an optional user-specified point *pt*.

Example	Result
(nentselp)	(<Entity name: 2001ba0>
	(91.8481 3.00526 0.0)
	((1.0 0.0 0.0 93.9477)
	(0.0 1.0 0.0 5.19489)
	(0.0 0.0 1.0 0.0)
	(0.0 0.0 0.0 1.0))
	(<Entity name: 2002620>))

ADS FORMAT
```
int ads_nentselp(const char *str, ads_name entres, ads_point ptres,
int pickflag, ads_matrix xformres, struct resbuf **refstkres);
```

PARAMETERS
- *prompt*   (*Optional*) A programmer-definable prompt string.

- *pt*   (*Optional*) First point.

TIP
- The matrix returned by this function is a 4x4 matrix: the first three columns are for rotation and scaling; the fourth column is for translation.

RELATED AUTOLISP AND ADS FUNCTIONS
entsel *and* ads_entsel

> Prompt the user to select an object.

nentsel *and* ads_nentsel

> Includes nested data.

initget *and* ads_initget

> Provides keywords for use with this function.

(new_dialog *dlg dcl_id func [pt]*)
ads_new_dialog

Dialog box: Initializes a new dialog box named *dlg* with *dcl_id* DCL file, executes AutoLISP routine *func* as the default action, and displays the dialog box at *pt* as the coordinates of the upper-left corner.

Example	Result
(new_dialog "ddptype" dcl_id)	T

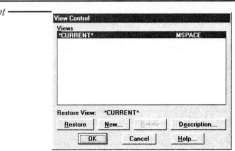

ADS FORMAT
```
int ads_new_dialog(char *dlgname, int dcl_id, CLIENTFUNC
def_callback, ads_hdlg *hdlg);
```

PARAMETERS
- *dlg*   String that specifies the dialog box.

- *dcl_id*   The DCL file identifier returned by **load_dialog**.

- *func*   A string specifying the name of an AutoLISP function; use "" an empty string □.if no function is to be executed.

- *pt*   (*Optional*) A 2D point list indicating the x,y-coordinates of the upper-left corner of the dialog box; to place the dialog box in the center of the AutoCAD screen, use '(-1 -1) .

TIP
- This function must proceed the **start_dialog** function.

RELATED AUTOLISP AND ADS FUNCTION
load_dialog *and* ads_load_dialog

Returns the DCL id number for the DCL filename.

■■■
ads_new_positioned_dialog

Dialog box: Initializes a new dialog box at a specified screen location.

Example	Result
ads_new_positioned_dialog(20,30,*hd1)	RTNORM

ADS FORMAT
```
int ads_new_positioned_dialog(char *dlgname, int dcl_id, CLIENTFUNC
def_callback, int x, int y, ads_hdlg *hdlg);
```

PARAMETERS
- *x*   The x-coordinate of the upper-left corner of the dialog box.

- *y*   The y-coordinate of the upper-left corner of the dialog box.

RELATED ADS FUNCTION
ads_done_positioned_dialog

Returns the position of the dialog box.

ads_newrb

Result buffer: Creates a new result buffer.

Example	Result
ads_newrb ???	pointer to allocated result buffer

ADS FORMAT
```
struct resbuf *ads_newrb(int v);
```

PARAMETER
- *v*   Result type code defined in file adscodes.h or a valid DXF group code.

RELATED ADS FUNCTION
ads_relrb   Releases the memory created by **ads_newrb**.

(not *item*)

■■■

Symbol handler: Checks whether *item* evaluates to **nil**.

Examples	Result
(not a)	T
(not pi)	nil

PARAMETER
- *item*   Any AutoLISP item.

TIP
- Use this function for non-lists; use the **null** function for lists.

RELATED AUTOLISP FUNCTIONS

null   Checks if an item is *bound* to nil.

numberp   Checks if an item is a real or integer number.

type   Returns the type of item.

(nth *n list*)

...

List manipulation: Returns element *n* of *list*, where for the first item *n* = 0.

Examples	Result
(nth 3 ' (1.2 3.4 5.6 10.0))	10.0
(nth 0 ' (x y z t))	X

PARAMETERS
- *n*   An integer number.
- *list*   The list of items.

TIP
- The first element is no #1 but #0.

RELATED AUTOLISP FUNCTIONS

car   Returns the first item of a list.

last   Returns the last item of a list.

cdr   Returns all but the first item of a list.

length   Returns the length of a list.

reverse   Reverses the order of items in a list.

(null *item*)

...

Symbol handler: Checks if *item* is bound to **nil**.

Example	Result
(null a)	T
(null pi)	nil

PARAMETER
- *item*   Any AutoLISP item.

TIP
- Use this function for lists; use the **not** function for non-lists.

RELATED AUTOLISP FUNCTIONS

not   Checks that an item *evaluates* to nil.

numberp   Checks is an item is a real or integer number.

type   Returns the ty pe of item.

(numberp *item*)

■■■

Symbol handler: Returns **T** if *item* is a real or integer number; if not, returns **nil**.

Examples	Result
(numberp 4)	T
(numberp "Quick")	nil
(numberp 1.2)	T

PARAMETER
- *item*   Any AutoLISP item.

RELATED AUTOLISP FUNCTIONS
not   Checks that an item *evaluates* to nil.

null   Checks that an item is *bound* to nil.

type   Returns the type of item.

(open *fname mode*)

■ ■ ■

File function: Open filename *fname* in one of three *modes*.

Examples	Result
(open "data.txt" "r")	<File #859>
(open "/subdir/data.txt" "r")	<File #859>

PARAMETERS
- *fname* A string containing the drive, subdirectory, and filename to be opened.
- *mode* One of three file manipulation modes:

Mode	Meaning
"a"	Append data to an existing file.
"r"	Open file for reading.
"w"	Open file for writing.

TIPS
- The *mode* must be in lowercase.

- The append mode creates a new file if it does not exist; data is appended to the end of the file.

- The write mode creates a new file if it does not exist; existing data is overwritten.

RELATED AUTOLISP FUNCTIONS
close   Closes an open file.

read-line   Reads a line of data from a file.

write-line Writes a line of data to a file.

(or *expr* ...)

∎∎∎

Logical function: Returns **nil** if *expr* contains all nil expressions; returns **T** if *expr* contains at least one non-nil expression.

Example	Result
(or a nil)	nil
(or pi 1.2 nil)	T

PARAMETER
∎ *expr*   Two or more expressions.

RELATED AUTOLISP FUNCTIONS
and   The logical AND of a list of expressions.

equal   Determines whether two expressions are identical.

(osnap *pt mode*)
ads_osnap

Geometric function: Returns a 3D point after applying object snap *mode* at point *pt* (*short for Object SNAP*).

Example	Result
(osnap pt1 "mid")	(94.6049 2.11175 0.0)

ADS FORMAT
```
int ads_menucmd(const char *str);
```

PARAMETERS
- *pt*   A 2D or 3D point where the object snap should be applied.
- *mode*   One of the object snap modes separated by commas:

Mode	Meaning
non	none (turn osnap off)
end	endpoint
mid	midpoint of line
cen	center of circle or arc
nod	node (point)
qua	quadrant (0,90,180,and 270 of a circle)
int	intersection of two objects
ins	insertion point of text or block
per	perpendicular
tan	tangent to a circle or arc
nea	nearest point on the object
qui	quick mode
app	apparent intersection

TIP
- You can specify several object snap modes separated by a comma: "mid,cen".

RELATED AUTOLISP AND ADS FUNCTIONS
inters   Returns the intersection of two lines.

getpoint   Prompts the user to pick a point.

RELATED SYSTEM VARIABLE
Aperture   Controls the area searched by the **osnap** function.

Osmode   Hold the current value of object snap mode.

(polar *pt ang dist*)
ads_polar

Geometric function: Returns 3D point at *angle* (in radians) and *dist* from point *pt*.

Example	Result
(polar pt1 0.2 10.0)	(88.3785 4.10532 0.0)

*The **Polar** function measures the angle from the x-axis and must be in radians:*

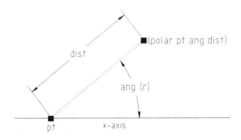

ADS FORMAT
```
void ads_polar(const ads_point pt, ads_real angle, ads_real
dist, ads_point result)
```

PARAMETERS

- *pt*   The 2D or 3D coordinates of the starting point.

- *ang*   The angle in radians, counterclockwise from the x-axis in the current UCS.

- *dist*   The distance from point *pt*.

TIP
- This function always works with radians, no matter the setting of the **AUnits** system variables.

RELATED AUTOLISP AND ADS FUNCTIONS
angle *and* ads_angle

    Finds the angle between the x-axis and a line.

distance *and* ads_distance

    Finds the distance between two points.

(prin1 *[expr [filed]]*)

...

Output function: Prints expressions *expr* to the 'Command:' prompt area or to the file attached to file descriptor *filed*; control characters are treated literal.

Example	Result
(prin1)	*(blank line)*
(prin1 "Quick \n Ref")	"Quick \n Ref" "Quick \n Ref"
(prin1 "Quick \n Ref" fil)	"Quick \n Ref"

PARAMETERS

- *expr*   (*Optional*) Any expression, string, or variable.

- *filed*   (*Optional*) The system-assigned descripter for the open file.

TIP

- Use this function without arguments — as in **(prin1)** — to suppress the display of **nil** when a function finishes running.

RELATED AUTOLISP FUNCTIONS

princ	Prints as prin1 but control characters are retained.
print	Prints a newline before *expr* and a space following.
prompt	Displays a string at the 'Command:' prompt area.
terpri	Prints only a newline (\n) to the 'Command:' prompt area.

(princ *[expr [filed]]*)

■ ■ ■

Output function: Prints expressions *expr* to the 'Command:' prompt area or to the file attached to file descriptor *filed*; control characters are acted upon.

Example	Result
(princ)	*(blank line)*
(princ "Quick \n Ref")	Quick
	Ref "Quick \n Ref"
(princ "Quick \n Ref" fil)	"Quick \n Ref"

PARAMETERS

■ *expr*   (*Optional*) Any expression, string or variable.

■ *filed*   (*Optional*) The system-assigned descripter for the open file.

TIP

■ Control characters recognized by AutoLISP:

Character	Meaning
\\	\ backslash character
\"	" quote character
\e	Escape character
\n	Newline character
\r	Return character
\t	Tab character
\nnn	Octal code nnn
\U+nnn	Unicode nnn
\M+Nnnn	Unicode nnn

RELATED AUTOLISP AND ADS FUNCTIONS

prin1   Prints as princ but control characters are literal.

print   Prints a newline before *expr* and a space following.

prompt   Displays a string at the 'Command:' prompt area.

terpri   Prints only a newline (\n) to the 'Command:' prompt area.

(print *[expr [filed]]*)

■■■

Output function: Prints expressions *expr* to the 'Command:' prompt area or to the file attached to file descriptor *filed*; control characters are treated literal; prints \n before *expr* and a space after.

Example	Result
(print)	*(blank line)*
(print "Quick \n Ref")	"Quick \n Ref" "Quick \n Ref"
(print "Quick \n Ref" fil)	"Quick \n Ref"

PARAMETERS

■ *expr*   (*Optional*) Any expression, string or variable.

■ *filed*   (*Optional*) The system-assigned descripter for the open file.

RELATED AUTOLISP FUNCTIONS

prin1   Prints as princ but control characters are literal.

princ   Prints as princ but control characters are retained.

prompt   Displays a string at the 'Command:' prompt area.

terpri   Prints only a newline (\n) to the 'Command:' prompt area.

...

ads_printf

Output function: Prints the message on AutoCAD's Text window.

Example	Result
ads_printf("Keep trying!")	RTNORM

ADS FORMAT
```
int ads_printf(const char *format, ...);
```

PARAMETER
- *format*   The string to be sent to the Text window.

TIP
- This function mimics the standard C **printf** function but ensures output to the AutoCAD Text window.

RELATED AUTOLISP FUNCTIONS

print	Prints a newline before *expr* and a space following.
prin1	Prints as princ but control characters are literal.
princ	Prints as princ but control characters are retained.
prompt	Displays a string at the 'Command:' prompt area.
terpri	Prints only a newline (\n) to the 'Command:' prompt area.

(progn [expr] ...)

■ ■ ■

Function handler: Evaluates each expression *expr* in order; used when a function expects only one expression but you need to use more than one; returns the value of the last expression.

Example	Result
(progn (1+ a b) (- a c))	...

PARAMETER
■ *expr*   AutoLISP expressions

TIP
■ Use this function inside other functions, such as **if**, that allow only a single expression.

RELATED AUTOLISP FUNCTIONS
apply   Passes a list of arguments to a function.

defun   Defines a new programmer-definable function.

(prompt *str*)
ads_prompt

Output function: Prints message *str* at the 'Command:' prompt area.

Example	Result
(prompt "Time to wake up.")	Time to wake up.nil

ADS FORMAT
int ads_prompt(const char *str);

PARAMETER
■ *str*   Any text string.

RELATED AUTOLISP FUNCTIONS

princ   Prints as prin1 but control characters are retained.

print   Prints a newline before *expr* and a space following.

prin1   Prints as princ but control characters are literal.

terpri   Prints only a newline (\n) to the 'Command:' prompt area.

...

ads_putsym

External applications: Sets the value of an AutoLISP symbol.

Example	Result
ads_putsym(*sn1,*v)	RTNORM

ADS FORMAT
```
int ads_putsym(const char *sname, struct resbuf *value);
```

PARAMETERS
- *sname*   Specifies the name of an AutoLISP symbol.
- *value*   Value of the symbol.

RELATED ADS FUNCTION
ads_getsym   Gets the value associated with an AutoLISP symbol.

(quit)

■ ■ ■

Error handler: Quits the AutoLISP routine and returns to the AutoCAD 'Command:' prompt.

Example	Results
(quit)	error: quit / exit abort
	(QUIT)
	Cancel

PARAMETERS
none

RELATED AUTOLISP FUNCTION
exit   Forces the application to end.

(quote *expr*) *or* '*expr*

■■■

Symbol handler: Returns *expr* without evaluating it.

Examples	Result
'(x y z t)	(X Y Z T)
(quote (x y z t))	(X Y Z T)

PARAMETER
■ *expr*   An expression.

TIP
■ The ' (quote) symbol is the only AutoLISP symbol that cannot be used at the 'Command:' prompt.

RELATED AUTOLISP FUNCTIONS
type   Determines the type of item.

lambda   Creates an unnamed function.

(read *[str]*)

∎∎∎

List manipulation: Returns the first list or atom in string *str*.

Example	Result
(read "Quick Ref")	QUICK
(read "1.2 3.4 10.0")	1.2

PARAMETER

∎ *str*   (*Optional*) A string or text or numbers or lists.

RELATED AUTOLISP FUNCTIONS

last   Returns the last item of a list.

car   Returns the first item in a list.

cdr   Returns all but the first item of a list.

(read-char [filed])

∎∎∎

File function: Reads a single character from the keyboard buffer (or from the file attached to file descriptor *filed*) and returns the ASCII code; returns **nil** when end-of-file is reached.

Example	Result
(read-char)	*10*
(read-char fn)	*62*

PARAMETER
∎ *filed*   (*Optional*) The system-assigned descriptor of the filename; when missing, this function waits for the user to press a key on the keyboard.

TIPS
∎ Using this function with no arguments — such as **(read-char)** — is an excellent way to pause for user reaction.

∎ This function accepts both the DOS and Unix conventions for end-of-line:

OS	EOL	ASCII
DOS	CR-LF	13 10
Unix	LF	10

RELATED AUTOLISP FUNCTIONS
write-char   Writes a single ASCII character to file.

read-line   Returns a string read from file.

(read-line [filed])

■■■

File function: Reads a string from the keyboard or from the file attached to file descriptor *filed*.

Example	Returns
(read-line)	"This is a test."
(read-line fn)	"This is a test."

PARAMETER
■ *filed*   (*Optional*) The system-assigned descriptor of the filename.

TIP
■ When this function reaches EOF (end of file), it returns **nil**.

RELATED AUTOLISP AND ADS FUNCTIONS
write-line   Writes a string to file.

read-char   Returns the ASCII code of the character read from file.

...

ads_realloc

Memory management: Changes the size of allocated memory while preserving contents.

Example	Result
ads_realloc(*ptr1,sz1)	*pointer to memory region*

ADS FORMAT
char * realloc(char *ptr, int sz);

PARAMETERS
- *ptr*   Pointer to memory.

- *sz*   Requested size of memory.

RELATED ADS FUNCTIONS
ads_free   Free up allocated memory.

ads_calloc   Allocate memory to hold an array.

ads_malloc   Allocate memory.

(redraw *[ename [mode]]*)
ads_redraw

Display control: Redraws the current viewport or just object *ename* with *mode* action.

Example	Results
(redraw)	nil
(redraw en)	nil
(redraw en 3)	nil

ADS FORMAT
```
int ads_redraw(const ads_name ent, int mode);
```

PARAMETERS

- *ename*   (*Optional*) Entity name of the object; when missing, redraws all objects in the current viewport.

- *mode*   (*Optional*) Type of redraw action:

Mode	Meaning
1	Redraw object.
2	Undraw object (blank out).
3	Highlight object.
4	Unhighlight object.
positive	Redraw all parts of a complex object.
negative	Redraw only the head of a complex object.

RELATED AUTOLISP AND ADS FUNCTIONS
grdraw *and* ads_grdraw

    Draws a vector in the graphics window.

grclear *and* ads_grclear

    Clears the current viewport.

graphscr *and* ads_graphscr

    Switches to the graphics window.

(regapp *appname*)
ads_regapp

External applications: Registers application name *appname* with the current AutoCAD drawing.

Example	Result
(regapp "SuperApp")	"SUPERAPP"

ADS FORMAT
```
int ads_regapp(const char *appname);
```

PARAMETER
- *appname*   The name of the application as a sting; maximum 31 characters.

TIPS
- When this function is successful, the *appname* is added to the APPID table; when unsuccessful, this function returns **nil**.

- Autodesk recommends using a unique name for your *appname*, choosing your company name, phone number, or the current data and time. Include the product name and version number, such as:

```
(regapp "DESIGNER-v2.1-8599597")
```

RELATED AUTOLISP AND ADS FUNCTIONS
ads *and* ads_loaded

> Lists the names of loaded ADS applications.

xload *and* ads_xload

> Loads an ADS application.

setfunhelp *and* ads_setfunhelp

> Registers help for ADS applications.

...

ads_regfunc

External applications: Registers an external ADS function and calls it directly, bypassing the dispatch loop (*short for REGister FUNCtion*).

Example	Result
ads_regfunc(*fh1,	

ADS FORMAT
```
int ads_regfunc(int (*fhdl) (), int fcode);
```

PARAMETERS
- **fhdl*   Pointer to function handler.
- *fcode*   Integer code that identifies the function when defined by **ads_defun**.

RELATED AUTOLISP AND ADS FUNCTIONS
ads_undef   Undefines an external function.

ads_defun   Defines and external function.

ads *and* ads_loaded
            Lists the names of loaded ADS applications.

xload *and* ads_xload
            Loads an ADS application.

■■■

ads_relrb

Result buffer: Releases memory allocated to the result buffer (*short for RELease Result Buffer*).

Example	Result
ads_relrb(*rb1)	RTNOTM

ADS FORMAT

int ads_putsym(const char *sname, struct resbuf *value);

PARAMETER

■ *rb*   Pointer to the result buffer.

RELATED ADS FUNCTION

ads_newrb   Creates a new result buffer.

R

(rem *num1 num2* ...)

■ ■ ■

Math function: Returns the remainder after dividing *num1* by *num2* (*short for* REMainder).

Examples	Result
(rem 10 5)	0
(rem 10.1 3)	1.1
(rem 10.1 3 5)	1.1

PARAMETERS

■ *num1*   Any real or integer number.

■ *num2*   Any real or integer number.

RELATED AUTOLISP FUNCTIONS

/   Divides two or more numbers.

fix   Converts a number into the nearest smaller integer.

(repeat *int expr* ...)

■■■

Conditional: Repeatedly evaluates *expr* by *int* number of times.

Example	Result
(repeat 4 (setq a (1+ a)))	4

PARAMETERS
- *int*   Any positive integer number.
- *expr*   An expression.

TIP
- Use this function to repeat an action a specific number of times.

RELATED AUTOLISP FUNCTIONS

cond	Conditional evaluation.
if	If conditional.
while	Repeat conditional while a condition remains T.

R

···

ads_retint

External applications: Returns an integer (*short for RETurn INTeger*).

Example	Results
ads_retint(i)	RTNORM

ADS FORMAT
```
int ads_retint(int ival);
```

PARAMETER
- *ival*   An integer number.

RELATED AUTOLISP AND ADS FUNCTIONS
getint *and* ads_getint
        Prompt user to enter an integer.
ads_isdigit   Determines whether character is a digit.
numberp   Determines whether item is a number.

···

ads_retlist

External applications: Returns a list (*short for RETurn LIST*).

Example	Results
ads_retlist (*rb1)	RTNORM

ADS FORMAT
int ads_retlist(const struct resbuf *rbuf);

PARAMETER
- *rbuf*   A pointer to a result buffer list.

RELATED AUTOLISP FUNCTION
listp   Determines if the item is a list.

...

ads_retname

External applications: Returns an entity or selection set name (*short for RETurn NAME*).

Example	Results
ads_retname (an1,type1)	RTNORM

ADS FORMAT
```
int ads_retname(const ads_name aname, int type);
```

PARAMETERS
- *aname*   A selection set or entity name.

- *type*   Determines the meaning of *aname*:

type	Meaning
RTPICKS	*aname* specifies a selection set.
RTENAME	*aname* specifies an entity.

RELATED AUTOLISP AND ADS FUNCTIONS
entsel *and* ads_entsel
        Get the entity name of an object.

ssget *and* ads_ssget
        Gets a selection set and assigns it a name.

...

ads_retnil

External applications: Returns a **nil**.

Example	Results
ads_renil ()	RTNORM

ADS FORMAT
```
int ads_retnil();
```

PARAMETERS
none

RELATED AUTOLISP FUNCTIONS
not   Determines if an item evaluates to **nil**.

nil   Determines if an item is bound to **nil**.

...

ads_retpoint

External applications: Returns a point.

Example	Results
ads_retpoint (pt1)	RTNORM

ADS FORMAT
```
int ads_retpoint(const ads_point pt);
```

PARAMETER
- *pt*   A 2D or 3D point.

RELATED AUTOLISP AND ADS FUNCTION
getpoint *and* ads_getpoint
                Prompts user to pick a point.

...

ads_retreal

External applications: Returns a real number.

Example	Results
ads_retreal (rv1)	RTNORM

ADS FORMAT
```
int ads_retreal(ads_real rval);
```

PARAMETER
- *rval*   A real number.

RELATED AUTOLISP AND ADS FUNCTIONS
getreal *and* ads_getreal
         Prompts the user to input a real number.

ads_isdigit   Determines whether character is a digit.

numberp   Determines whether item is a number.

...

ads_retstr

External applications: Returns a string.

Example	Results
ads_retstr (*s1)	RTNORM

ADS FORMAT
int ads_retstr(const char *s);

PARAMETER
■ *s*   A pointer to a string.

RELATED AUTOLISP AND ADS FUNCTIONS
getstr *and* ads_getstr
     Prompt user to enter a string.
ads_isalnum Determines that the character is alphanumeric.

···

ads_rett

External applications: Returns **T** (true).

Example	Results
ads_rett()	RTNORM

ADS FORMAT

int ads_rett();

PARAMETERS

none

RELATED AUTOLISP AND ADS FUNCTIONS

none

...

ads_retval

External applications: Returns the value in the result buffer.

Example	Results
ads_retval (*rb1)	RTNORM

ADS FORMAT
```
int ads_retval(const struct resbuf *rbuf);
```

PARAMETER
- **rbug*   A pointer to the result buffer.

RELATED AUTOLISP AND ADS FUNCTIONS
none

...

ads_retvoid

External applications: Returns void, which is not displayed.

Example	Results
ads_retvoid ()	RTNORM

ADS FORMAT
```
int ads_retvoid();
```

PARAMETERS
none

RELATED AUTOLISP AND ADS FUNCTIONS
none

(reverse *list*)

...

List manipulation: Reverse the order of the elements in a list.

Example	Result
(reverse '(x y (z t)))	((Z T) Y X)

PARAMETER
- *list*   A list.

RELATED AUTOLISP AND ADS FUNCTIONS
acad_strlsort   Sorts a list of strings in alphabetical order.

length   Returns the length of the list.

listp   Determines if the item is a list.

last   Returns the last item in a list.

(rtos *num [mode [prec]]*)
ads_rtos

Conversion: Converts a number *num* into a string in format *mode* using precision *prec*.

Examples	Result
(rtos 31.856)	"31.8560"
(rtos 31.856 2)	"3.1856E+01"
(rtos 31.856 1 2)	"3.19E+01"

ADS FORMAT
```
int ads_rtos(ads_real val, int unit, int prec, char *str);
```

PARAMETERS

- *num*   A real or integer number.

- *mode*   (*Optional*) Conversion format; when missing, uses the value stored in LUnits:

mode	Meaning
1	Scientific
2	Decimal (default)
3	Engineering
4	Architectural
5	Fractional

- *prec*   (*Optional*) Number of decimal places (range 0 to 8); when missing, uses the value stored in system variable **LuPrec** (default = 4).

RELATED AUTOLISP FUNCTION
atos   Converts a string into a real number.

RELATED SYSTEM VARIABLES
LUnits   Linear units mode (default = 2).

LuPrec   Linear units precision (default = 4).

UnitMode   Units display (default = 0).

UnitMode	Meaning
0	As set by **Units** command.
1	As input by user.

DimZin   Supression of 0 in feet-inches dimensioning (default = 0):

DimZin	Meaning
0	Suppress 0 feet and 0 inches.
1	Suppress neither.
2	Supress 0 inches.
3	Suppress 0 feet.

(set 'sym expr)

■■■

Function handler: Sets the value of quoted symbol *'sym* to expression *expr*.

Example	Result
(set 'x 25.0)	25.0

PARAMETERS
- *sym*   Name of a symbol (or variable).
- *expr*   An expression.

TIP
- This function is useful for setting a value indirectly without using the quote character.

RELATED AUTOLISP FUNCTIONS
quote   Returns a list without evaluating it.

setq   Sets a value equal to a variable.

(setcfg *cfg val*)

■■■

External applications: Sets *val* of variable *cfg* in the **AppData** section of the **Acad.Cfg** file (*short for SET ConFiGuration*).

Example	Result
(setcfg "AppData/SuperApp/StairM/Rise" "8")	"8"

PARAMETERS

■ *cfg*　　Name of a variable in the Acad.Cfg file using the following format:

　　　　"**AppData**/*app_name*/*section_name*/*parameter_name*"

■ *val*　　The value of the variable.

RELATED AUTOLISP FUNCTIONS

getcfg　　Gets the value of a variable in the Acad.Cfg file.

setvar　　Sets the value of an AutoCAD system variable.

setenv　　Sets the value in the environment.

(setfunhelp c:*fname* [*hlpfile* [*topic* [*cmd* *]]])

ads_setfunhelp

External applications: Registers a user-defined command with the help facility.

Example	Result
(setfunhelp "c:superapp" "help.hlp" "grab")	"c:superapp"

ADS FORMAT

int ads_set_tile(ads_hdlg hdlg, char *key, char *value);

PARAMETERS

- c:*fname*   Filename of the function; the c: prefix must be used..

- *hlpfile*   (*Optional*) Filename of the help file.

- *topic*   (*Optional*) Name of the topic in the help file.

- *cmd*   (*Optional*) Name of the command or function in the file.

TIPS

- The **c:** prefix is required.

- This function must be called after a **defun,** since **defun** removes the name registered with **setfunhelp.**

RELATED AUTOLISP AND ADS FUNCTION

help *and* ads_help
        Access the help facility.

S

(setq *symb1 expr1 [symb2 expr2 ...]*)

■ ■ ■

Function handler: Sets symbol *symb1* to the value of expression *expr1*.

Example	Result
(setq a 1)	1
(setq x 1.2 y 3.4 z 10.0)	10.0

PARAMETERS

- *sumb1*   A symbol (variable).
- *expr1*   An expression.

TIPS

- The optimal length of a variable name in AutoLISP is six characters.
- AutoLISP allows you to set several expressions in one statement, such as:

```
(setq
  x 1.2
  y 3.4
  z 5.6
  t 10.0
)
```

RELATED AUTOLISP FUNCTION

defun   Defines a programmer-defined function.

(set_tile *key val*)
ads_set_tile

Dialog box: Sets the value of a dialog box tile *key*.

Example	Result
(set_tile pt1 "Seven")	"Seven"

ADS FORMAT
```
int ads_setfunhelp(char *sname, char *filename, char *topic, int command);
```

PARAMETERS
- *key*   A string that specifies the tile.

- *val*   A string that assigns a new value.

RELATED AUTOLISP AND ADS FUNCTION
get_tile *and* ads_get_tile
            Gets the runtime value of a tile.

S

(setvar *var val*)
ads_setvar

External applications: Sets system variable *var* to value *var*.

Example	Result
(setvar "osmode" 2)	2

ADS FORMAT
```
int ads_setvar(const char *sym, const struct resbuf *val);
```

PARAMETERS
- *var*   The name of the system variable.
- *val*   The value of the system variable.

TIP
- The AutoCAD command **SetVar** accepts degrees for system variable **AngBase** but the AutoLISP function **setvar** only accepts radians for **AngBase**.

RELATED AUTOLISP AND ADS FUNCTIONS
getvar   Gets the value of an AutoCAD system variable.

setcfg   Sets the value of a variable in the Acad.Cfg file.

setenv   Sets the value in the environment.

(setview *viewd [vport]*)
ads_rsetview

Display control: Specifies the 3D view for viewport *vport.*

Example	Result
(setview ven 0)	((0 . "VIEW") (2 . "PLR") (70 . 0) (40 . 5.70802) (10 111.27 4.45461) (41 . 12.2996) (11 0.0 0.0 1.0) (12 0.0 0.0 0.0) (42 . 50.0) (43 . 0.0) (44 . 0.0) (50 . 0.0) (71 . 0))

ADS FORMAT
int ads_setview(const struct resbuf *view, const int vport);

PARAMETERS
- *viewd*   View descriptor table (as returned by **tblsearch**).

- *vport*   (*Optional*) The viewport ID number (as returned by system variable **CvPort**; default value = 0).

TIPS
- You can use the results of the **tblsearch** function for the *viewd* argument.

- You can get the value for *vport* from the **CvPort** system variable.

RELATED AUTOLISP AND ADS FUNCTIONS
vport *and* ads_vport
        Gets the viewport parameters.
tblsearch *and* ads_tblsearch
        Searches a table entry (such as "VIEW") for associated data.

RELATED SYSTEM VARIABLES
CvPort   Number of the current viewport.

ViewCtr   Center 3D coordinates of the current viewport.

(sin *ang*)

■■■

Geometric function: Returns the sine of angle *ang* in radians.

Example	Result
(sin 1)	1.22461e-016
(sin (/ pi 2)	1.0

*The sine of an angle is height **y** divided by distance **r**:*

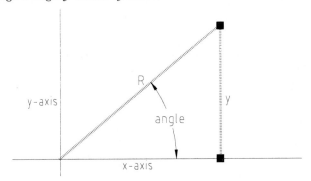

PARAMETER
■ *ang*   Angle in radians.

TIP
■ The *ang* argument must always be in radians, no matter the setting of **Units**.

RELATED AUTOLISP FUNCTIONS
cos	Finds the cosine of the angle.
atan	Finds the arctangent.

(slide_image *x y wid hgt sld*)
ads_slide_image

Dialog box: Displays an AutoCAD *sld* file at screen coordinate *x,y* (the upper-left corner) with width *wid* and height *hgt* (the lower-right corner); *sld* is either an SLD slide file or SLB slide library file.

Examples	Result
(slide_image 10 10 120 140 "colorwh.sld")	
(slide_image 20 30 110 150 "ddim.slb(dimmata8)")	

*The **AutoCAD Help** window showing topic **Line:***

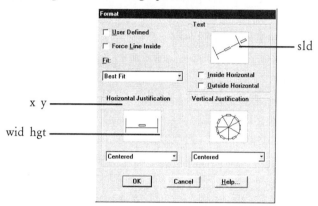

ADS FORMAT
int ads_slide_image(short x1, short y1, short wid, short hgt, char *sldname);

PARAMETERS
- *x*　　　　X-coordinate of the upper left corner.
- *y*　　　　Y-coordinate of the upper left corner.
- *wid*　　　Width in the x-direction.
- *hgt*　　　Height in the negative y-direction.
- *sld*　　　Name of the slide to display.

TIP
- When the slide is in an SLB slide library file, use the format of "slbfile(sldname)".

RELATED AUTOLISP AND ADS FUNCTIONS
ads_dimension The dimensions of a tile.

dim_x　　　The x-dimension of a tile.

dim_y　　　The y-dimension of a tile.

(snvalid *sym [flag]*)
ads_snvalid

Object handler: Checks symbol table *sym* for valid characters (*short for Symbol Name VALID*).

Example	Result
(snvalid "VIEW")	T
(snvalid "VIEW" 1)	T

ADS FORMAT
int ads_snvalid(const char *tbstr, int pipetest);

PARAMETERS
- *sym*   Name of a symbol in the table section of the DWG file.

- *flag*   (*Optional*) Determines if the pipe (| , vertical bar) is valid in symbol name:

AutoLISP	ADS	Meaning
0	FALSE	Pipe (	) is not allowed.
1	TRUE	Pipe (	)is allowed.

TIP
- A symbol table name contains alphanumeric characters, as well as the $, _, and - characters.

RELATED AUTOLISP AND ADS FUNCTION
tblsearch *and* ads_tblsearch
         Searched the tables.

(sqrt *num*)

■ ■ ■

Math function: Returns the square root of number *num*; *num* cannot be negative.

Examples	Result
(sqrt 2)	1.41421
(sqrt pi)	1.77245

PARAMETER

■ *num*   Any positive real or integer number.

RELATED AUTOLISP FUNCTIONS

expt   Raises a number to a power, including x^2.

log   Returns the natural log of a number.

(ssadd [ename [ss]])
ads_ssadd

Object handler: Adds object *ename* to selection set *ss*; creates a new selection set if *ss* does not exist (*short for Selection Set ADD*).

Example	Results
(ssadd)	<Selection set: 1>
(ssadd en)	<Selection set: 2>
(ssadd en ss1)	<Selection set: 2>

ADS FORMAT
int ads_ssadd(const ads_name ename, const ads_name sname, ads_name result);

PARAMETERS
- *ename*   (*Optional*) The entity name of an object.

- *ss*   (*Optional*) The name of a selection set.

TIPS
- AutoCAD can have up to 128 selection sets open at a time.

- This function performs three actions, depending on the arguments:

Argument	Action
none	Creates a new selection set with no object.
ename	Creates a new selection set with *ename*.
ename and *ss*	Adds *ename* to selection set *ss*.

RELATED AUTOLISP AND ADS FUNCTIONS
ssdel *and* ads_ssdel
> Removes an item from a selection set.

ssget *and* ads_ssget
> Gets a selection set.

(ssdel *ename ss*)
ads_ssdel

Object handler: Deletes object *ename* from selection set *ss* (*short for Selection Set DELete*).

Example	Result
(ssdel en ss1)	<Selection set: 1>

ADS FORMAT
```
int ads_ssdel(const ads_name ename, const ads_name ss);
```

PARAMETERS
- *ename*   The entity name of an object.
- *ss*   The name of a selection set.

RELATED AUTOLISP AND ADS FUNCTIONS
ssadd *and* ads_ssadd
        Adds an item from a selection set.
ads_ssfree   Frees up a selection set.
ssget *and* ads_ssget
        Get a selection set.

S

...

ads_ssfree

Object handler: Frees up a selection set.

Example	Result
ads_ssfree(ss1)	RTNORM

ADS FORMAT
int ads_ssfree(const ads_name sname);

PARAMETER
■ *ssname*   The name of a selection set.

TIP
■   AutoCAD can have up to 128 selection sets open at a time.

RELATED AUTOLISP AND ADS FUNCTIONS
ssdel *and* ads_ssdel
                Removes an item from a selection set.
ssget *and* ads_ssget
                Get a selection set.

(ssget [[mode] [pt1] pt2] [list]] [filter])
ads_ssget

Object handler: Prompts the user to select objects, which are turned into a selection set (*short for Select Set GET*).

Example	Results
(ssget)	Select objects:
	Select objects:
	<Selection set: 4>
(ssget "L")	<Selection set: 4>

ADS FORMAT
```
int ads_ssget(const char *str, const void *pt1, const ads_point
pt2, const struct resbuf *entmask, ads_name ss);
```

PARAMETERS
- *mode*   (*Optional*) String specifying the type of object selection:

mode	Meaning
none	Single point.
"C"	Crossing window.
"CP"	Crossing polygon window.
"F"	Fence (open polygon).
"I"	Implied.
"L"	Last object created in drawing.
"P"	The Previous selection set.
"W"	Windowed (default).
"WP"	Windowed Polygon (fenced window).
"X"	The entire database.

- *pt1, pt2*   (*Optional*) Two points, as required by *mode* "C" and "W".
- *list*   (*Optional*) List of points, as required by *mode* "F", "CP', and "WP".

- *filter*   (*Optional*) A filter list in dotted pair format, such as:

    ((0 . "LINE") (-3 . ("APPNAME")))

to select all lines with extended entity data attached; or:

Relation test:

filter	Meaning
"*"	Everything.
"="	Equals.
"!="	Not equal to.
"/="	Not equal to.
"<>"	Not equal to.
"<"	Less than.
"<="	Less than or equal to.
">"	Greater than.
">="	Greater than or equal to.
"&"	Bitwise AND (integers only).
"&="	Bitwise masked equal (integers only).

Logical groupings:

filter	Meaning
"<AND" ... "AND>"	One or more operands.
"<OR" ... "OR>"	One or more operands.
"<XOR" ... "XOR>"	Two operands.
"<NOT" ... "NOT>"	One operand .

TIPS

- AutoCAD can have up to 128 selection sets open at a time.
- The "X" option selects all objects in the drawing database.
- This function ignores any abject snap modes currently set.
- Objects are only highlighted when this function is used without arguments.

RELATED AUTOLISP AND ADS FUNCTIONS

entget *and* **ads_entget**

       Get the entity name of an object.

all SSxxx functions

(ssgetfirst)
ads_ssgetfirst

Object handler: Returns two selection sets: (1) objects gripped but not selected; and (2) objects gripped *and* selected.

Example	Result
(ssgetfirst)	(nil <Selection set: 7>)

An AutoCAD drawing showing gripped (shown by small blue squares) and selected objects (shown by the dashed lines):

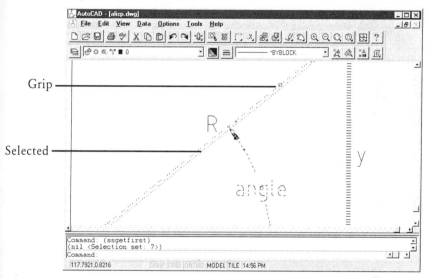

ADS FORMAT
```
int ads_ssgetfirst(struct resbuf** grip_set, pResbuf* pickfirst_set);
```

PARAMETERS
none

RELATED AUTOLISP AND ADS FUNCTION
sssetfirst *and* **ads_sssetfirst**
> Sets objects that have handles and those that are selected.

(sslength *ss*)
ads_sslength

Object handler: Returns the number of objects in selection set *ss*.

Example	Result
(sslength ss1)	7

ADS FORMAT
```
int ads_sslength(const ads_name sname, long *len);
```

PARAMETER
- *ss*   The name of a selection set.

RELATED AUTOLISP AND ADS FUNCTIONS
ssname *and* ads_ssname
> Returns the name of a specific entity in the selection set.

ssget *and* ads_ssget
> Gets a selection set.

ssadd *and* ads_ssadd
> Adds an item from a selection set.

(ssmemb *ename ss*)
ads_ssmemb

Object handler: Checks if object *ename* is a member of selection set *ss*.

Example	Results
(ssmemb en ss1)	en

ADS FORMAT
int ads_ssmemb(const ads_name ename, const ads_name ss);

PARAMETERS
- *ename*   The entity name of an object.
- *ss*   The name of a selection set.

TIP
- This function returns **nil** when object *ename* is not in selection set *ss*.

RELATED AUTOLISP AND ADS FUNCTIONS
ssnamex and ads_ssnamex
> Describes how an object was selected.

ssname and ads_ssname
> Returns the name of an object in the selection set.

(ssname *ss idx*)
ads_ssname

Object handler: Returns the *idx*'th member of selection set *ss*; the first member has the index number of 0.

Example	Results
(ssname ss1 3)	<Entity name: 1fe25a8>

ADS FORMAT
```
int ads_ssname(const ads_name ss, long i, ads_name entres);
```

PARAMETERS
- *ss*   The name of a selection set.

- *idx*   An integer or real number.

TIPS
- The first value of *idx* is 0, not 1.

- Use a real number for *idx* = 32768.0 or higher.

- This function returns **nil** when *idx* is negative or larger than the number of objects in selection set *ss*.

RELATED AUTOLISP AND ADS FUNCTIONS
sslength *and* ads_sslength

     Returns the number of items in a selection set.

ssnamex *and* ads_ssnamex

     Describes how the object was selected.

(ssnamex *ss* [*idx*])
ads_ssnamex

Object handler: Returns information on how the *idx*'ed object in selection set *ss* was created.

Example	Results
(ssnamex ss1)	((0 <Entity name: 1fe2600> 0)
	(0 <Entity name: 1fe25f8> 0)
	(0 <Entity name: 1fe25f0> 0)
	. . .
	(0 <Entity name: 1fe0500> 0))
(ssnamex ss1 3)	((0 <Entity name: 1fe25e0> 0))

ADS FORMAT
int ads_ssnamex(struct resbuf** rbpp, const ads_name ss, const long i);

PARAMETERS
- *ss*　　　　The name of a selection set.

- *idx*　　　　(*Optional*) An integer number.

TIPS
- Selection method ID number returned by **ssnamex**:

ID	Meaning
0	Any other selection method.
1	Pick.
2	Window or WPolygon.
3	Crossing or CPolygon.
4	Fence.

- Point descriptor ID number returned by **ssnamex**:

ID	Meaning
0	Xline (infinite construction line).
1	Ray (semi-infinite construction line).
2	Line segment.

RELATED AUTOLISP AND ADS FUNCTIONS
sslength *and* ads_sslength

　　　　Returns the number of items in a selection set.

ssname *and* ads_ssname

　　　　Describes the *index*th object in the selection set.

(sssetfirst *ss1* *[ss2]*)
ads_sssetfirst

Object handler: Sets the grip and pick modes of objects: those in selection set *ss1* are gripped; those in selection set *ss2* are gripped *and* picked.

Example	Result
(sssetfirst ss1)	SS1

ADS FORMAT
```
int ads_ssetfirst(const ads_name grip_set, const ads_name
pickfirst_set);
```

PARAMETERS
- *ss1*   The name of a selection set.

- *ss2*   (*Optional*) The name of another selection set.

RELATED AUTOLISP AND ADS FUNCTIONS
ssgetfirst *and* ads_ssgetfirst

>   Gets which objects are gripped and which are selected.

ssget *and* ads_ssget

>   Gets a selection set.

(startapp *app file*)

■ ■ ■

External applications: Starts Windows application *app* along with filename *file* (*short for START APPlication; an external function defined in AcadApp.Exe*).

Example	Result
(startapp "notepad" "3d.lsp")	1

The Notepad text editor launched with 3d.Lsp file:

```
3d.lsp - Notepad
File  Edit  Search  Help
;;;------------------------------------------------------------------
;;; Draw a cone

(defun cone (/ elev cen1 rad top h numseg cen2 oldelev e1 e2)
  (setq numseg 0)
  (initget 17)                    ;3D point can't be null
  (setq elev (caddr (setq cen1 (getpoint "\nBase center point: "))))
  (initget 7 "Diameter")          ;Base radius can't be 0, neg, or null
  (setq rad (getdist cen1 "\nDiameter/<radius> of base: "))
  (if (= rad "Diameter")
    (progn
      (initget 7)                 ;Base diameter can't be 0, neg, or null
```

PARAMETERS

■ *app*   Filename of the application.

■ *file*   Filename to have the application open.

TIP

■   This function returns **nil** when unsuccessful (not 0, as indicated by the Autodesk documentation.)

RELATED AUTOLISP AND ADS FUNCTIONS

load   Loads an AutoLISP application.

xload *and* **ads_xload**

   Loads an ADS application.

arxload *and* **ads_arxload**

   Loads an ARx application.

help *and* **ads_help**

   Launches the help engine.

(start_dialog)
ads_start_dialog

Dialog box: Displays dialog box.

Example	Results
(start_dialog)	0

ADS FORMAT
`int ads_start_dialog(ads_hdlg hdlg, int *status);`

PARAMETERS
none

TIPS
- Returns the following status code:

Status	Meaning
1	User pressed [OK].
0	User pressed [Cancel].
-1	term_dialog was used.

RELATED AUTOLISP AND ADS FUNCTIONS
done_dialog *and* ads_done_dialog

    Dismisses dialog box.

new_dialog *and* ads_new_dialog

    Initializes the dialog box before starting it.

term_dialog *and* ads_term_dialog

    Terminates all dialog boxes.

(start_image *key*)
ads_start_image

Dialog box: Signals the start of image *key* in dialog box.

Example	Result
(start_image kn)	

ADS FORMAT
```
int ads_start_image(ads_hdlg hdlg, char *key);
```

PARAMETER
- *key*   A string that specifies the dialog box tile.

TIP
- Follow this function with the **fill_image, slide_image,** and **vector_image** functions.
- Complete the **start_image** function with the **end_image** function.

RELATED AUTOLISP AND ADS FUNCTIONS
fill_image *and* ads_fill_image

      Fills the tile with a solid color.

slide_image *and* ads_slide_image

      Displays an SLD slide file in the tile.

vector_image *and* ads_vector_image

      Draws a vector in the image tile.

end_image *and* ads_end_image

      Ends the creation of the image.

(start_list *key [opr [idx]]*)
ads_start_list

Dialog box: Signals the start of processing a list in a dialog box tile.

Example	Results
(start_list kn)	

ADS FORMAT
```
int ads_start_list(ads_hdlg hdlg, char *key, short opr, short idx);
```

PARAMETERS

- *key*   A string that specifies the dialog box tile.

- *opr*   (*Optional*) Operation to be performed:

opr	Meaning
1	Change contents of selected list.
2	Append new entry to list.
3	Delete list and create new list (default).

- *idx*   (*Optional*) Index value (used only when *opr* = 1).

TIP
- The first element in *idx* is #0, not #1.

RELATED AUTOLISP AND ADS FUNCTIONS
add_list *and* ads_add_list

Adds a string to the current list.

end_list *and* ads_end_list

Ends processing of the list.

(strcase *str [flag]*)
ads_tolower *and* ads_toupper

Conversion: Converts string *str* to uppercase; if *flag* is **T** (or not **nil**), string *str* is converted to lowercase (*short for STRing CASE*).

Example	Results
(strcase "Quick Ref")	"QUICK REF"
(strcase "Quick Ref" T)	"quick ref"

ADS FORMAT
```
int ads_tolower(int c);
int ads_toupper(int c);
```

PARAMETERS
- *str*   A string of text.

- *flag*   (*Optional*) If **T**, then text is converted to lowercase; otherwise uppercase.

RELATED ADS FUNCTIONS
ads_toupper   Converts all text in string to uppercase.

ads_tolower   Converts all text in string to lowercase.

(strcat *str1 [str2 ...]*)

∎∎∎

String manipulation: Concatenates string *str1* with string *str2* (*short for STRing ConcATenation*).

Example	Result
(strcat "Quick" " Ref")	"Quick Ref"

PARAMETERS

- *str1*   A string of text.

- *str2*   (*Optional*) Another string of text.

TIP

- This function is extremely useful to combining fixed text and variables into a single string, such as:

    (strcat "The answer is " ans)

RELATED AUTOLISP FUNCTIONS

strlen   Returns the length of a string.

strsub   Returns a substring.

(strlen *[str]* ...)

■■■

String manipulation: Returns the number of characters in string *str* (*short for STRing LENgth*).

Examples	Result
(strlen)	0
(strlen "Quick")	5
(strlen "Quick" "Ref")	8

PARAMETER
■ *str*   (*Optional*) One or more strings of text; when missing or "", returns 0.

TIP
■ This function adds up the number of characters in all strings provided as the argument.

RELATED AUTOLISP FUNCTION
strsub   Returns a substring.

S

(subst *new old list*)

■ ■ ■

List manipulation: Replaces every occurance of *old* with *new* in *list* (*short for SUBSTitute*).

Example	Result
(subst 'x 'y '(y y z t))	(X X Z T)

PARAMETERS
- *new*   New item to use as replacement.
- *old*   Old item to be replaced.
- *list*   List of items to perform replacement on.

TIP
- Use this function with the **assoc** function to manipulate the contents of entity data.

RELATED AUTOLISP FUNCTIONS
assoc   Searches for an association in a list.

length   Returns the length of the list.

member   Searches for an item in a list and returns it and all following items.

(substr *str start [length]*)

■ ■ ■

String manipulation: Returns a portion of string *str*, beginning at character *start* for *length* characters long (*short for SUB STRing*).

Example	Result
(substr "Quick Ref" 7)	"Ref"

PARAMETERS

■ *str* A string of text.

■ *start* Start at character #.

■ *length* (*Optional*) Length of substring to extract, in number of characters; when missing, this function returns all characters to the end of the *str*.

TIP

■ The first character is #1, unlike **nth** and **ssname**.

RELATED AUTOLISP FUNCTIONS

strlen Returns the length of a string.

strcat Joins two or more strings together into a single string.

(tablet *flag [row1 row2 row3 dir]*)
ads_tablet

User input: When *code* is 0, returns tablet calibration parameters; when *code* is 1, sets the tablet calibration specified by 3D points *row1*, *row2*, and *row3*, in direction *dir*.

Example	Result	
(tablet 0)	nil	*(if mouse is attached)*
(tablet 1 '(1 0 0) '(0 1 0) '(0 0 1) '(0 0 1))		

ADS FORMAT
```
int ads_tablet(const struct resbuf *args, struct resbuf **result)
```

PARAMETERS

■ *flag*   Determines how tablet is used:

flag	Meaning
0	Return tablet calibration parameters.
1	Sets tablet calibration.

■ *row1, row2,* and *row3*

    (*Optional*) Three 3D (x,y,z) points that specify the transformation matrix; used only when *flag* = 1.

■ *dir*   A 3D point specifying a vector in the WCS (world coordinate system).

TIPS

■ Argument *row3* must always equal 1.

■ When *dir* is expressed incorrectly, the **tablet** function corrects it and returns it corrected.

■ The ErrNo system variable holds the error message number when **tablet** encounters an error.

RELATED AUTOLISP AND ADS FUNCTION
grread *and* ads_grread
    Reads input from any AutoCAD input device.

RELATED SYSTEM VARIABLES
TabMode   Toggles whether AutoCAD sees the tablet:

Tabmode	Meaning
0	No tablet attached.
1	Tablet attached.

ErrNo   Holds the error number returned by AutoLISP, ADS, and ARx apps.

(tblnext *tbl [flag]*)
ads_tblnext

Object handler: Returns the next item in the symbol table *tbl*; when *flag* is **T**, returns the first entry in the symbol table (*short for TaBLe NEXT*).

Example	Result
(tblnext "VIEW")	((0 . "VIEW") (2 . "PLR") (70 . 0) (40 . 5.70802) (10 111.27 4.45461) (41 . 12.2996) (11 0.0 0.0 1.0) (12 0.0 0.0 0.0) (42 . 50.0) (43 . 0.0) (44 . 0.0) (50 . 0.0) (71 . 0))
(tblnext "VIEW" T)	((0 . "VIEW") (2 . "PLR") (70 . 0) (40 . 5.70802) (10 111.27 4.45461) (41 . 12.2996) (11 0.0 0.0 1.0) (12 0.0 0.0 0.0) (42 . 50.0) (43 . 0.0) (44 . 0.0) (50 . 0.0) (71 . 0))

ADS FORMAT
```
struct resbuf *ads_tblnext(const char *tblname, int rewind);
```

PARAMETER
■ *tbl*   A string identifying one of the table sections in the DWG file:

tbl	Meaning
"APPID"	Application ID names.
"BLOCK"	Block (symbol) names.
"DIMSTYLE"	Dimension style names.
"LAYER"	Layer names.
"LTYPE"	Linetype names.
"STYLE"	Text style names.
"UCS"	User coordinate systems.
"VIEW"	View names.
"VPORT"	Viewport names.

RELATED AUTOLISP AND ADS FUNCTIONS
tblobjname *and* ads_tblobjname
> Returns the entity name of a specified symbol in a table.

tblsearch *and* ads_tblsearch
> Searches a table for a symbol name.

entget *and* ads_entget
> Returns entity data.

vports *and* ads_vports
> Returns viewport data.

(tblobjname *tbl sym*)
ads_tblobjname

Object handler: Returns the entity name of symbol *sym* in table *tbl* (*short for TaBLe OBJect NAME*).

Example	Result
(tblobjname "VIEW" "PLR")	<Entity name: 1fe2568>

ADS FORMAT
int ads_tblobjname(char* tblname, char* sym, ads_name objid);

PARAMETERS

■ *tbl*   A string identifying one of the table sections in the DWG file.

■ *sym*   The name of Autodesk- and user-defined symbol in the table; Autodesk defined symbol names include:

sym	Meaning
"CONTINUOUS"	The default linetype.
"0"	The default layer name.
"ASHADE"	Layer used by Render.
"DEFPOINTS"	Layer used by associative dimensions.
"AME-FRZ"	Layer used by AME and ACIS solids.
"STANDARD"	The default dimension style.
"STANDARD"	The default text style.

RELATED AUTOLISP AND ADS FUNCTIONS
tblnext *and* ads_tblnext
          Finds the next item in the table section.
tblsearch *and* ads_tblsearch
          Searches a table for a symbol name.
entget *and* ads_entget
          Returns entity data.
vports *and* ads_vports
          Returns viewport data.

RELATED SYSTEM VARIABLES
CeLayer   The current layer name.

CeLtype   The current linetype name.

DimStyle   The current dimension style.

InsName   The name of the current block.

TextStyle   The name of the current text style.

UcsName   The name of the current UCS view.

(tblsearch *tbl sym [flag]*)
ads_tblsearch

Object handler: Returns data associated with symbol *sym* in table *tbl.*

Example	Result
(tblsearch "VIEW" "PLR")	((0 . "VIEW") (2 . "PLR") (70 . 0) (40 . 5.70802) (10 111.27 4.45461) (41 . 12.2996) (11 0.0 0.0 1.0) (12 0.0 0.0 0.0) (42 . 50.0) (43 . 0.0) (44 . 0.0) (50 . 0.0) (71 . 0))
(tblsearch "VIEW" "PLR" T)	((0 . "VIEW") (2 . "PLR") (70 . 0) (40 . 5.70802) (10 111.27 4.45461) (41 . 12.2996) (11 0.0 0.0 1.0) (12 0.0 0.0 0.0) (42 . 50.0) (43 . 0.0) (44 . 0.0) (50 . 0.0) (71 . 0))

ADS FORMAT
struct resbuf *ads_tblsearch(const char *tblname, const char *sym, int setnext);

PARAMETERS
- *tbl*   A string identifying one of the table sections in the DWG file.
- *sym*   The name of Autodesk- and user-defined symbol in the table.
- *flag*   (*Optional*) If **T**, the **tblnext** counter returns the next entry after the one returned by **tblsearch.**

RELATED AUTOLISP FUNCTIONS
tblnext *and* ads_tblnext
> Finds the next item in the table section.

tblobjname *and* ads_tblobjname
> Returns the entity name of a specified symbol in a table.

entget *and* ads_entget
> Returns entity data.

vports *and* ads_vports
> Returns viewport data.

(term_dialog)
ads_term_dialog

Dialog box: Terminates all dialog boxes.

Example	Results
(term_dialog)	nil

ADS FORMAT
```
int  ads_term_dialog(void);
```

PARAMETERS
none

TIP
■ Use this function for terminating nested dialog boxes.

RELATED AUTOLISP AND ADS FUNCTION
unload_dialog *and* ads_unload_dialog

Unloads a DCL file.

(terpri)

...

Output function: Prints the \n (newline) character to the AutoCAD 'Command:' prompt area (*short for TERminal PRInt*).

Example	Result
(terpri)	nil

PARAMETERS
none

TIP
■ Does not write to a file, only to the screen.

RELATED AUTOLISP AND ADS FUNCTIONS

ads_printf   An AutoCAD-specific version of the C **printf** function.

princ   Prints as prin1 but control characters are retained.

print   Prints a newline before *expr* and a space following.

prompt *and* ads_prompt

　　　　Displays a string at the 'Command:' prompt area.

(textbox *elist*)
ads_textbox

Object handler: Returns the 3D coordinates of a rectangle that bounds a text box; *elist* must refer to a text object — such as **Text, MText,** and **Attributes** — but not text in dimensions or blocks.

Example	Result
(textbox '((1 . "Quick Ref")))	((0.06 0.00550253 0.0) (2.22 0.396569 0.0))

The bounding box is a rectangle that tightly encloses a text object:

Bounding box   (2.22 0.396569 0.0)

Quick Ref

(0.0 0.0 0.0)

ADS FORMAT
```
int ads_textbox(const struct resbuf *ent, ads_point p1, ads_point p2);
```

PARAMETER
- *elist*   The entity name of a text object.

TIP
- The x-coordinate of the first coordinate pair refers to the distance from the text insertion point to the lower-left corner of the rectanglular boundary of the text. This value is not 0.0 when the text contains letters with decenders (g, j, p, q, and y), oblique text, and vertical text.

RELATED AUTOLISP AND ADS FUNCTIONS
none

(textpage)
ads_textpage

Display control: Forces the display of the AutoCAD Text window, then clears all text; does not clear the Text window on Windows systems.

Example	Result
(textpage)	nil

ADS FORMAT
int ads_textpage();

PARAMETERS
none

RELATED AUTOLISP AND ADS FUNCTION
textscr *and* ads_textscr

Forces the display of the AutoCAD Text window.

(textscr)
ads_textscr

Display control: Forces the display of the AutoCAD Text window, without clearing text.

Example	Results
(textscr)	nil

The AutoCAD Text window, as displayed under Windows 95:

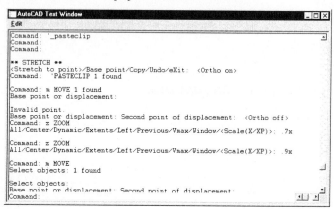

ADS FORMAT
int ads_textscr();

PARAMETERS
none

RELATED AUTOLISP AND ADS FUNCTION
textpage *and* ads_textpage

Forces the display of the AutoCAD Text window, then clear text.

...

ads_tolower

Conversion: Converts the character to lowercase.

Example	Results
ads_tolower(c1)	

ADS FORMAT
```
int ads_tolower(int c);
```

PARAMETER
■ *c*   A character.

RELATED AUTOLISP AND ADS FUNCTIONS

strcase   Changes the case of a string of text to all upper or all lowercase.

ads_toupper   Changes the case of a character to uppercase.

...

ads_toupper

Conversion: Converts the character to uppercase.

Example	Result
ads_toupper(c1)	

ADS FORMAT
`int ads_toupper(int c);`

PARAMETERS
- *c*   A character.

RELATED AUTOLISP AND ADS FUNCTIONS

strcase   Changes the case of a string of text to all upper or all lowercase.

ads_tolower   Changes the case of a character to lowercase.

(trace *func* ...)

■■■

Error handler: Displays the name of function *func* each time it is executed, as a primitive form of debugging.

Example	Results
(trace func)	FUNC

PARAMETER
■ *func*   The name(s) of AutoLISP function(s).

RELATED AUTOLISP FUNCTION
untrace   Turn off function tracing.

(trans *pt from to [flag]*)
ads_trans

Geometric function: Translates point *pt* from one to another coordinate system; if *flag* is non-nil, *pt* is a 3D vector displacement (*short for TRANSlate*).

Examples	Result
(trans pt1 0 1)	(2.39204 9.54109 0.0)
(trans pt1 0 1 T)	(4.39204 11.5411 0.0)

ADS FORMAT
```
int ads_trans(const ads_point pt, const struct resbuf *from, const
struct resbuf *to, int flag, ads_point result);
```

PARAMETERS

- *pt*　　A list of three real numbers that is either (1) a 3D point; or (2) a 3D displacement vector, depending on the setting of *flag*.

- *from*　The current coordinate system:

from/to	Meaning
0	WCS (world coordinate system).
1	UCS (user coordinate system).
2	Current DCS (display coordinate system) when used with code 0 and 1.
2	Current model space DCS when used with code 3.
3	Paper space DCS (use only with 2).

- *to*　　The coordinate system to change to.

- *flag*　(*Optional*) Determines how *pt* should be treated:

flag	Meaning
T	3D displacement.
nil	3D point.

RELATED AUTOLISP AND ADS FUNCTION
ads_xform　　Transforms an ojbect via a transformation matrix.

(type *item*)

■■■

List manipulation: Returns the type of *item*.

Example	Result
(type pt1)	LIST

PARAMETER
- *item* An AutoLISP item.

TIP
- Types returned by this function:

Type	Description
REAL	Floating-point number.
SUBR	Internal function.
FILE	File descriptor.
EXSUBR	External ADS function.
STR	String.
PICKSET	Selection set.
INT	Integer.
ENAME	Entity name.
SYM	Symbol.
PAGETB	Function paging table.
LIST	Lists (and user function).

RELATED AUTOLISP AND ADS FUNCTIONS

numberp	Determines whether an item is a number (real or integer).
zerop	Determines whether a number is zero.
listp	Determines whether an item is a list.
boundp	Determines whether an item is bound to a symbol.
atom	Determines whether an item is an atom.
not	Determines whether an item evaluates to nil.
null	Determines whether an item is bound to nil.

...

ads_undef

External fnctions: Undefine the external function.

Example	Result
ads_undef(*sn1,fn)	RTNORM

ADS FORMAT
```
int ads_undef(const char *sname, short funcno);
```

PARAMETERS
- *sname*   Name of the function.
- *funcno*   Non-negative integer code of the function.

RELATED ADS FUNCTION
ads_defun   Defines an external function.

(unload_dialog *dcl*)
ads_unload_dialog

Dialog box: Uncloads DCL file.

Example	Result
(unload_dialog id)	nil

ADS FORMAT
```
int ads_unload_dialog(int dcl_id);
```

PARAMETER
■ *dcl*   The DCL identification number obtained from **new_dialog**.

RELATED AUTOLISP AND ADS FUNCTIONS
new_dialog *and* **ads_new_dialog**

        Specifies a new dialog box.

load_dialog *and* **ads_new_dialog**

        Loads a dialog box.

U-V

...
ads_usrbreak

User input: Checks if the user has pressed **[Ctrl]+C** or **[Esc]** (*short for USeR-initiated BREAK*).

Example	Result
ads_usrbreak()	1

ADS FORMAT

int ads_usrbrk();

PARAMETERS

none

RELATED ADS FUNCTION

ads_isctrl   Checks if the character is a control character.

(untrace *func* ...)

...

Error handler: Turn off the trace function for *func*.

Example	Result
(untrace func)	FUNC

PARAMETER
- *func*   Name of the function.

RELATED AUTOLISP FUNCTION
trace   Turns on tracing for the function.

(vector_image *x1 y1 x2 y2 clr*)
ads_vector_image

Dialog box: Draws a vector from *x1,y1* to *x2,y2* in color *clr* within the current
dialog box image.

Example	Result
(vector_image 1.2 3.4 5.6 10.0 1)	nil

ADS FORMAT
int ads_vector_image(short x1, short y1, short x2, short y2, short clr);

PARAMETERS
- *x1* and *y1*   The starting coordinates of the vector.
- *x2* and *y2*   The ending coordinates of the vector.
- *clr*   The color of the vector:

Clr	ADI Mnemonic	Meaning
0 *thru* 255	...	Standard AutoCAD colors.
-2	BGLCOLOR	Current background of the AutoCAD graphics screen.
-15	DBGLCOLOR	Dialog box background color.
-16	DFGLCOLOR	Dialog box foreground color for text.
-18	LINELCOLOR	Current dialog box line color.

TIP
- The origin (0,0) is the upper-left corner of the tile.

RELATED AUTOLISP AND ADS FUNCTIONS
ads_dimensions_tile

        Coordinates of the current tile.

dim_x *and* dim_y

        Coordinates of the current tile.

(ver)

■■■

Miscellaneous: Returns the current AutoLISP version number and language as a string.

Example	Result
(ver)	"AutoLISP Release 13.0 (en)"

PARAMETERS
none

TIP
■ AutoLISP returns the following language codes:

Code	Meaning
de	German.
en	English (US and UK).
es	Spanish.
fr	French.
it	Italian.

RELATED AUTOLISP FUNCTIONS

getenv   Gets data from the environment.

getvar   Gets the value of AutoCAD system variables, including the version number, serial number, and platform type.

U-V

(vmon)

■ ■ ■

Memory management (obsolete): Turns on the virtual memory manager (*short for Virtual Memory ON*).

Example	Result
(vmon)	nil

PARAMETERS
none

TIP
■   This function is only provided for compatibility for AutoLISP code written with older versions of AutoCAD.

RELATED AUTOLISP FUNCTION
mem   Reports on the memory used by AutoLISP.

(vports)
ads_vports

Display control: Returns a list describing the current viewport configuration.

Example	Result
(vports)	((2 (0.0 0.0) (1.0 1.0)))

ADS FORMAT
int ads_vports(struct resbuf **result);

PARAMETERS
none

TIPS
■ The result depends on the setting of the **TileMode** system variable, as follows:

TileMode	Meaning
1 (On)	Viewport was created with VPORTS command. Range of coordinate values is 0.0 to 1.0 Lower-left corner is (0,0). Upper-right corner is (1,1). First viewport is 2.
0 (Off)	Viewport was created with MVIEW command. Coordinates are in paper space units. First viewport is 1.

■ The first viewport listed is the current viewport.

RELATED AUTOLISP AND ADS FUNCTIONS
none

RELATED SYSTEM VARIABLES
TileMode   1 (on) is the default.

CvPorts   The current viewport number.

U-V

(wcmatch *str pat*)
ads_wcmatch

String manipulation: Matches a wild-card *pattern* to string *str* (*short for Wild Card MATCHing*).

Example	Result
(wcmatch "Quick" "Ref")	nil
(wcmatch "Quick" "*")	T

ADS FORMAT
```
int ads_wcmatch(const char *str, const char *pat);
```

PARAMETERS
- *str* The string being compared.

- *pat* The pattern being compared with:

pat	Matches
*	Any pattern.
?	Single character.
#	Single digit.
@	Single alphabetic character.
.	Singe non-alphanumeric character.
~	Anything except *pat*.
[ ]	Any enclosed character.
[~]	Any character not enclosed.
[—]	A range of single character.
,	Separates two patterns.
\\	\ (backslash)
`	Read next character literally.

TIPS
- The *str* and *pat* can be either a string or a variable.
- This function is case-sensitive: upper- and lower-case characters are matched.
- Any text beyond the first 500 characters in *str* and *pat* is ignored.

RELATED AUTOLISP AND ADS FUNCTIONS
none

(while *test expr*)

■■■

Conditional: Repeats the evaluation of expression *expr* while *test* remains true (not nil).

Example	Result
(while (< x 10) (setq x (1+ x)))	10

PARAMETERS
- *test*   The text expression.
- *expr*   The expression to execute while *test* is **T**.

RELATED AUTOLISP FUNCTIONS
cond   Conditional evaluation.

if   If conditional.

repeat   Repeat conditional.

W-Z

(write-char *num [filed]*)

■■■

File function: Writes ASCII charcacter *num* as a character to the screen or to *filed*.

Example	Result
(write-char 65)	A65
(write-char 65 fn)	A

PARAMETERS

- **num**   A single ASCII character.

- **filed**   (*Optional*) The file descriptor attached to an open file; when missing, this function writes to the screen.

RELATED AUTOLISP AND ADS FUNCTIONS

open	Opens a file for writing.
write-line	Writes a line of text to file.
ascii	Converts first character into its ASCII value.
chr	Converts an ASCII number into its equivalent character.

(write-line *str [file]*)

■■■

File function: Writes string *str* to the screen or to *file.*

Example	Result
(write-line "Quick Ref")	Quick Ref"Quick Ref"
(write-line "Quick Ref" fn)	Quick Ref

PARAMETERS

- *str*   A string of text.

- *filed*   (*Optional*) The file descriptor attached to an open file; when missing, this function writes to the screen.

TIP

■   Note that the quotation marks are left out when writing to the file.

RELATED AUTOLISP FUNCTIONS

write-char   Writes a single ASCII character to file.

read-line   Reads a line of text from file.

open   Opens a file for writing.

(xdroom *ename*)
ads_xdroom

Object hndler: Returns the amount of xdata space available in object *ename*; 16,383
bytes when no xdata has been used (*short for eXtended entity Data ROOM*).

Example	Result
(xdroom en1)	16383

ADS FORMAT
int ads_xdroom(const ads_name ent, long *result);

PARAMETER
■ *ename*   Name of an object.

TIP
■   The maximum amount of extended data attached to an object is 16KB.

RELATED AUTOLISP AND ADS FUNCTIONS
xdsize *and* ads xdsize

> Size of the list of extended data attached to an object

entgetx *and* ads_entgetx

> Gets entity data and extended entity data from an object.

(xdsize *list*)
ads_xdsize

Object handler: Returns the number of bytes that a *list* of xdata will occupy (*short for eXternal Data SIZE*).

Example	Result
(xdsize el)	

ADS FORMAT
`int ads_xdsize(const struct resbuf *xd, long *result);`

PARAMETER
■ *list*   The list of data.

TIPS
■ The maximum amount of extended data attached to an object is 16KB.

■ The *list* must contain valid data, otherwise this function reports an error message via system variable **ErrNo**.

RELATED AUTOLISP AND ADS FUNCTIONS
xdroom *and* ads xdroom

        Amount of room remaining for extended data attached to an object

entgetx *and* ads_entgetx

        Gets entity data and extended entity data from an object.

...

ads_xformss

Selection set: Applies transformation matrix to the selection set.

Example	Result
ads_xformss(ss1,mat1)	RTNORM

ADS FORMAT
int ads_xformss(const ads_name ssname, ads_matrix genmat);

PARAMETERS
- *ssname*   Name of the selection set.
- *genmat*   A 4x4 transformation matrix.

TIPS
-

RELATED ADS FUNCTION
ads_ssget   Gets a selection set.

(xload *app [flag]*)
ads_xload

External applications: Loads an ADS application.

Example	Result
(xload "render")	"render"
(xload "whois" "failed")	"failed"

ADS FORMAT
int ads_xload(const char *app);

PARAMETERS
- *app*   Name of ADS application to load.
- *flag*   (*Optional*) Message to display when ADS application does not load.

TIP
- Performs these functions:

  1. Checks that the filename relates to an ADS application

  2. Checks that the versions of ADS, the ADS application, and AutoLISP are compatibile.

  3. Displays the application's name when the load is successful.

  4. Displays an error message (or *flag*) when the load is unsuccessful.

  5. Displays a message is the application is already loaded.

RELATED AUTOLISP AND ADS FUNCTIONS
ads *and* ads_loaded
      Names of ADS applications loaded.
xunload *and* ads_xunload
      Unloads an ADS application.
load   Loads an AutoLISP file.
arxload *and* ads_arxload
      Loads an ARx program.

(xunload *app [fail]*)
ads_xunload

External applications: Unloads the ADS application *app* from AutoCAD memory.

Example	Result
(xunload "render")	"render"
(xunload "whois" "failed")	"failed"

ADS FORMAT
```
int ads_xunload(const char *app);
```

PARAMETERS
- *app*   Name of ADS application to load.

- *flag*   (*Optional*) Message to display when ADS application does not load.

RELATED AUTOLISP AND ADS FUNCTIONS
ads *and* ads_loaded
          Names of ADS applications loaded.
xload *and* ads_xload
          Loads an ADS application.
load   Loads an AutoLISP file.
arxload *and* ads_arxload
          Loads an ARx program.

(zerop *num*)

...

Symbol handler: Returns **T** if *num* is zero; otherwise, returns **nil**.

Example	Result
(zerop 0)	T
(zerop 1)	nil

PARAMETER
- *num*   Any number.

RELATED AUTOLISP AFUNCTIONS

numberp   Determines whether an item is a number (real or integer).

listp   Determines whether an item is a list.

boundp   Determines whether an item is bound to a symbol.

atom   Determines whether an item is an atom.

not   Determines whether an item evaluates to nil.

null   Determines whether an item is bound to nil.

W-Z

(+ [nbr1 nbr2 ...])

...

Math function: Adds two or more numbers.

Example	Result
(+)	0
(+ 1.23)	1.23
(+ 1.2 3.4)	4.6
(+ 5 10 4 7)	26
(+ 5.0 10 4 7)	26.0

PARAMETER
■ *nbr1,nbr2*   Any real or integer numbers.

TIPS
■ A single plus sign adds all numbers inside the parentheses, unlike in other programming languages.

■ The + function returns an integer when all arguments are integers.

■ To return a real number, include a decimal-zero in at least one number, such as the 5.0 in (+ **5.0** 10 5 7).

■ When there are no arguments, or just one argument, the + function adds the number to zero.

■ Use the **setq** function to store the result of this function:

(setq a (+ 1.2 3.4))

RELATED AUTOLISP FUNCTIONS

1+	Adds one to a number or variable.
-	Subtracts one or more number from the first number.
setq	Stores the result of this function in a variable.

(- [nbr1 nbr2 ...])

■■■

Math function: Subtracts two or more numbers.

Example	Result
(-)	0
(- 1.23)	-1.23
(- 1.2 3.4)	2.2
(- 5 10 4 7)	-16
(- 5.0 10 4 7)	-16.0

PARAMETER
■ *nbr1,nbr2*   Any real or integer numbers.

TIPS
■ A single minus sign subtracts all numbers inside the parentheses, unlike in other programming languages.

■ The - function returns an integer when all arguments are integers.

■ To return a real number, include a decimal-zero in at least one number, such as the 5.0 in (- **5.0** 10 5 7).

■ When there are no arguments, or just one argument, the - function subtracts the number from zero.

■ Use the **setq** function to store the result of this function:

```
(setq a (- 1.2 3.4))
```

RELATED AUTOLISP FUNCTIONS

1-	Subtracts one from a number or variable.
+	Adds one or more number to the first number.
setq	Stores the result of this function in a variable.

(* [nbr1 nbr2 ...])

...

Math function: Multiplies two or more numbers.

Example	Result
(*)	0
(* 1.23)	1.23
(* 1.2 3.4)	4.08
(* 5 10 4 7)	1400
(* 5.0 10 4 7)	1400.0

PARAMETER
■ *nbr1,nbr2*   Any real or integer numbers.

TIPS
■ A single asterisk multiplies all numbers inside the parentheses, unlike in other programming languages.

■ The * function returns an integer when all arguments are integers.

■ To return a real number, include a decimal-zero in at least one number, such as the 5.0 in (* 5.0 10 5 7).

■ *Caution:* The integer returned loops around when the result becomes too large, such as:

```
(* 500 1000 400 500)        ; returns 1215752192
(* 5000 10000 4000 5000)    ; returns -1530494976
```

■ When there is just one argument, the * function multiplies the number by one.

■ When there are no aguments, the * function returns zero.

■ Use the **setq** function to store the result of this function:

(setq a (* 1.2 3.4))

RELATED AUTOLISP FUNCTIONS
/   Divides one into a number or variable.

setq   Stores the result of this function in a variable.

(/ [nbr1 nbr2 ...])

...

Math function: Divides the second and following numbers into the first number.

Example	Result
(/)	0
(/ 1.23)	1.23
(/ 1.2 3.4)	2.83333
(/ 5 10 4 7)	0
(/ 5.0 10 4 7)	0.0178571

PARAMETER
- *nbr1,nbr2*   Any real or integer numbers.

TIPS
- A single slash divides all numbers inside the parentheses, unlike in other programming languages.

- The / function returns an integer when all arguments are integers.

- To return a real number, include a decimal-zero in at least one number, such as the 5.0 in (/ **5.0** 10 5 7).

- *Caution:* Integer division may return unexpected results; use at least one real number to ensure accurate results, such as:

```
(/ 1 2)   ; returns 0
(/ 1 2.0) ; returns 0.5
```

- When there are no arguments, the / function returns zero.

- When there is just one arguement, the / function divides the number by 1.

- Use the **setq** function to store the result of this function:

```
(setq a (/ 1.2 3.4))
```

RELATED AUTOLISP FUNCTIONS
rem	Returns the remainder after dividing two numbers.
fix	Converts a real number into an integer by rounding down.
float	Converts an integer number into a real.
*	Multiplies one or more numbers.
setq	Stores the result of this function in a variable.

(= var1 [var2 ...])

...

Symbol handler: Returns T when all items (variables, numbers, or strings) are equal; returns **nil** otherwise.

Example	Result
(= 1)	T
(= 1.2 1.2)	T
(= 1 1.0)	T
(= 1 1.2)	nil
(= "hgt" "hgt")	T
(= "hgt" "wth")	nil

PARAMETER
- *var1,var2*   Any variable, string, real or integer number.

TIPS
- This function is *not* for setting one expression equal to another; use the **setq** function for that purpose.

- Contrary to Autodesk documentation, the = function *does* handle variables, such as:

```
(setq a "hgt")
(setq b "hgt")
(setq c "wth")
(= a b)        ; returns T
(= a c)        ; returns nil
```

RELATED AUTOLISP FUNCTIONS

eq   Determines whether two expressions are equal.

equal   Determines whether two expression are equal wtihin a fuzz factor.

setq   Stores the result of a function in a variable.

(/= var1 [var2 ...])

■■■

Logical function: Returns **T** when the first item is not equal to all items (variables, numbers, or strings) following the first item; returns **nil** otherwise (*short for not equal to*).

Example	Result
(/= 1.2)	T
(/= 1 1.0)	nil
(/= 1 1.2)	T
(/= "hgt" "hgt")	nil
(/= "hgt" "wth")	T

PARAMETER
■ *var1,var2*   Any variable, string, real or integer numbers.

TIPS
■ This function is often used with conditional functions, such as **if**, **cond**, and **while**.

■ Contrary to Autodesk documentation, the /= function *does* handle variables, such as:

```
(setq a "hgt")
(setq b "hgt")
(setq c "wth")
(/= a b)        ; returns nil
(/= a c)        ; returns T
```

RELATED AUTOLISP FUNCTIONS

=	Determines whether two expressions are equal.
<	Determines whether one expression is less than other expressions.
<=	Determines whether one expression is less than or equal to other expressions.
>	Determines whether one expression is greater than other expressions.
>=	Determines whether one expression is greater than or equal to other expressions.
if	Executes an expression if it is true.
cond	Executes the first expression found to be true.
while	Executes an expression while it remains true.

(< var1 [var2 ...])

■■■

Logical function: Returns **T** when the first item is less than all items (variables, numbers, or strings) following the first item; returns **nil** otherwise (*short for less than*).

Example	Result
(< 1.2)	T
(< 1 1.0)	nil
(< 1 1.2)	T
(< "hgt" "hgt")	nil
(< "hgt" "wth")	T

PARAMETER
■ *var1,var2*   Any variable, string, real or integer numbers.

TIPS
■ This function is often used with conditional functions, such as **if, cond,** and **while**.

■ Contrary to Autodesk documentation, the < function *does* handle variables, such as:

```
(setq a "hgt")
(setq b "hgt")
(setq c "wth")
(< a b)        ; returns nil
(< a c)        ; returns T
```

RELATED AUTOLISP FUNCTIONS

=	Determines whether two expressions are equal.
/=	Determines whether one expression is not equal to other expressions.
<=	Determines whether one expression is less than or equal to other expressions.
>	Determines whether one expression is greater than other expressions.
>=	Determines whether one expression is greater than or equal to other expressions.
if	Executes an expression if it is true.
cond	Executes the first expression found to be true.
while	Executes an expression while it remains true.

(<= var1 [var2 ...])

...

Logical function: Returns **T** when the first item is less than or equal to all items (variables, numbers, or strings) following the first item; returns **nil** otherwise (*short for less than or equal to*).

Example	Result
(<= 1.2)	T
(<= 1 1.0)	T
(<= 1 1.2)	T
(<= "hgt" "hgt")	T
(<= "hgt" "wth")	T

PARAMETER
■ *var1,var2*   Any variable, string, real or integer numbers.

TIPS
■ This function is often used with conditional functions, such as **if, cond**, and **while**.

■ Contrary to Autodesk documentation, the <= function *does* handle variables, such as:

```
(setq a "hgt")
(setq b "hgt")
(setq c "wth")
(<= a b)        ; returns T
(<= a c)        ; returns T
```

RELATED AUTOLISP FUNCTIONS

=	Determines whether two expressions are equal.
<	Determines whether one expression is less than other expressions.
/=	Determines whether one expression is not equal to other expressions.
>	Determines whether one expression is greater than other expressions.
>=	Determines whether one expression is greater than or equal to other expressions.
if	Executes an expression if it is true.
cond	Executes the first expression found to be true.
while	Executes an expression while it remains true.

(>= var1 [var2 ...])

...

Logical function: Returns **T** when the first item is greater than or equal to all items (variables, numbers, or strings) following the first item; returns **nil** otherwise (*short for greater than or equal to*).

Example	Result
(>= 1.2)	T
(>= 1 1.0)	T
(>= 1 1.2)	nil
(>= "hgt" "hgt")	T
(>= "hgt" "wth")	nil

PARAMETER

- *var1,var2*   Any variable, string, real or integer numbers.

TIPS

- This function is often used with conditional functions, such as **if**, **cond**, and **while**.
- Contrary to Autodesk documentation, the >= function *does* handle variables, such as:

```
(setq a "hgt")
(setq b "hgt")
(setq c "wth")
(>= a b)      ; returns T
(>= a c)      ; returns T
```

RELATED AUTOLISP FUNCTIONS

=	Determines whether two expressions are equal.
<	Determines whether one expression is less than other expressions.
<=	Determines whether one expression is less than or equal to other expressions.
>	Determines whether one expression is greater than other expressions.
/=	Determines whether one expression is not equal to other expressions.
if	Executes an expression if it is true.
cond	Executes the first expression found to be true.
while	Executes an expression while it remains true.

(> var1 [var2 ...])

...

Logical function: Returns **T** when the first item is greater than all items (variables, numbers, or strings) following the first item; returns **nil** otherwise (*short for greater than*).

Example	Result
(> 1.2)	T
(> 1 1.0)	nil
(> 1 1.2)	nil
(> "hgt" "hgt")	nil
(> "hgt" "wth")	nil

PARAMETER
- *var1,var2*   Any variable, string, real or integer numbers.

TIPS
- This function is often used with conditional functions, such as **if**, **cond**, and **while**.
- Contrary to Autodesk documentation, the > function *does* handle variables, such as:

```
(setq a "hgt")
(setq b "hgt")
(setq c "wth")
(> a b)       ; returns nil
(> a c)       ; returns nil
```

RELATED AUTOLISP FUNCTIONS
=	Determines whether two expressions are equal.
<	Determines whether one expression is less than other expressions.
<=	Determines whether one expression is less than or equal to other expressions.
/=	Determines whether one expression is gnot equal to other expressions.
>=	Determines whether one expression is greater than or equal to other expressions.
if	Executes an expression if it is true.
cond	Executes the first expression found to be true.
while	Executes an expression while it remains true.

(~ *int*)

...

Logical function: Returns the bitwise NOT of *int*.

Example	Result
(~ -2)	1
(~ -1)	0
(~ 0)	-1
(~ 1)	-2
(~ 2)	-3

PARAMETER
- *int*   Any integer number.

RELATED AUTOLISP FUNCTIONS
and   Returns the logical AND of two or more expressions.

or   Returns the logical OR of two or more expressions.

(1+ *nbr*)

■■■

Math function: Adds one to number *nbr*.

Example	Result
(1+ 2)	3
(1+ 1.2)	2.2

PARAMETER
- *nbr*   Any real or integer number.

TIPS
- This function is useful for incrementing a counter.
- This function is the equivalent to (+ *nbr* 1).
- This function is often used with conditional functions, such as **if, repeat,** and **while.**
- Use the **setq** function to store the result of this function:

      (setq a (1+ 1.2))

RELATED AUTOLISP FUNCTIONS
1-   Subtracts one from a number or variable.

+   Adds one or more number to the first number.

setq   Stores the result of this function in a variable.

(1- *nbr*)

...

Math function: Subtracts one from number *nbr*.

Example	Result
(1- 2)	1
(1- 1.2)	0.2

PARAMETER
- *nbr*   Any real or integer number.

TIPS
- This function is useful for decrementing a counter.
- This function is the equivalent to (- *nbr* 1).
- This function is often used with conditional functions, such as **if**, **repeat**, and **while**.
- Use the **setq** function to store the result of this function:

    (setq a (1- 1.2))

RELATED AUTOLISP FUNCTIONS
1-   Adds one to a number or variable.

-         Subtracts one or more numbers from the first number.

setq   Stores the result of this function in a variable.

Introduction to Diesel Programming

Autodesk first introduced Diesel programming in AutoCAD Release 12 for DOS. Its purpose is to customize the status line. The status line window display messages to the CAD operator, which — by default — is the display of the O, S, and P indicators, the x,y-coordinates, the current color, and the layer name.

The default status line in AutoCAD LT and Release 12 for Windows:

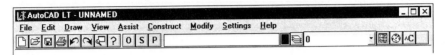

The default status line in AutoCAD Release 13 for Windows:

Diesel allows users to change the status line to display other information, such as the time, the DWG filename, and the z-coordinate. The text is truncated after 32 characters, no matter how long the window (39 chraracters in Release 13 for Windows).

Diesel is the acronym for "direct interactively evaluated string expression language." Despite the word "string" and the $ prefix, Diesel mostly operates on numbers, not strings.

It uses an unusual format for its macro language: $(*function*, *variable*), where *function* is one of 28 function names (15 in AutoCAD LT). All Diesel functions take at least one variable; some take as many as nine variables.

The function acts on the variables, each separated by a comma. The function and variables are prefixed by '$(' and suffixed by ')'. Notice that $ is the traditional way of indicating strings in programming and that the parentheses are reminisent of AutoLISP.

TIPS

■ Each argument is separated by a comma.

■ The maximum length of a Diesel statement is approximately 460 characters.

■ Use the ModeMacro system variable to output Diesel expressions to the status line.

■ Use quoted strings to prevent evaluation of a Diesel expression: "$(+,1)"

■ To display quotation marks on the status line, use double quotations: ""Test""

■ ModeMacro outputs directly to the status line, until it reaches a $(, then it begins evaluating.

■ Use AutoLISP's **strcat** function to string together a Diesel expression within AutoLISP.

■ Use the $M= construct to use Diesel expressions in a menu macro.

Diesel Error Messages

Cryptic error messages are printed by Diesel on the status line, as shown below:

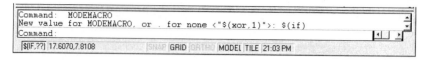

Error Message	Meaning	Example
$?	Right parenthesis is missing.	$(+,1,2
	Left quotation mark is missing.	$(eq,"To
$(*function*)??	**Wrong name of *function*.**	$(hoots)
$(*func*,??)	Wrong number of arguments for function *func*.	$(if)
$(++)	Output string too long.	

The MacroTrace System Variable

To help debug Diesel expressions, turn the **MacroTrace** system variable on, as follows:

```
Command: macrotrace
New value for MACROTRACE <0>: 1
```

Once turned on, MacroTrace displays the step-by-step evaluation of the Diesel expression in the Text window. Here is an example for the following Diesel macro: $(+,25, $(getvar,elevation))

```
Eval: $(+, 1, 2)
===> 3
Eval: $(+, 25, $(getvar,elevation))
Eval: $(GETVAR, elevation)
===> 0
===> 25
Eval: $(+, 25, $(getvar,elevation))
Eval: $(GETVAR, elevation)
===> 0
===> 25
Eval: $(+, 25, $(getvar,elevation))
Eval: $(GETVAR, elevation)
===> 0
===> 25
Eval: $(+, 25, $(getvar,elevation))
Eval: $(GETVAR, elevation)
===> 0
===> 25
```

Diesel Quick Starts

Using Diesel at the Command Prompt

1. The easiest way to put Diesel to work modifying the status line is at the 'Command:' prompt. You must use the **ModeMacro** system variable:

```
Command: modemacro
New value for MODEMACRO, or . for none <"">: The Illustrated
    AutoCAD Quick Reference.
```

2. In Release 12 and LT, the area of the left of the coordinate readout is replaced by a text box containing part of the sentence; in Release 13 for Windows, a new area is added to the left of the coordinate display.

The Diesel display in AutoCAD LT and Release 12 for Windows:

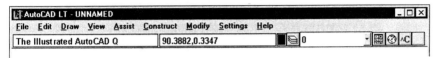

The Diesel display in Release 13 for Windows:

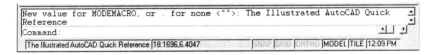

3. Typing the ModeMacro system variable with the "" null string restores the status line, as follows:

```
Command: modemacro
New value for MODEMACRO, or . for none <>: ""
```

Using Diesel in AutoLISP

There are two ways to use Diesel expressions inside an AutoLISP function:

1. The **setvar** function in conjunction with the **ModeMacro** system variable. The following AutoLISP routine displays the two chamfer distances on the status line:

```
Eval: $(GETVAR, chamferb)
===>  0
Command:
Chamfer A: 0 Chamfer B: 0  17.6070,7.8108          SNAP  GRID  ORTHO  MODEL  TILE  21:31 PM
```

Note the use of the **strcar** function to submit all of the Diesel data to the **ModeMacro** variable in one chunk:

```
(defun c:chab ()
  (setvar "modemacro"
    (strcat "Chamfer A: $(getvar,chamfera)"
            "Chamfer B: $(getvar,chamferb)"
    )
  )
)
```

2. The second method is for using Diesel macros within AutoLISP instead of displaying data on the status line. Use **menucmd** function in conjunction with the **M=** menu macro construct:

```
(defun c:chab ()
  (menucmd "M=Chamfer A: $(getvar,chamfera)
            Chamfer B: $(getvar,chamferb)"
  )
)
```

When this routine is run, the following happens:

```
Command: chab
"Chamfer A: 0 Chamfer B: 0"
```

$(and, [int1, int2, ..., int9])

Logical function: Returns the bitwise logical AND of *int1* through *int9*.

Example	Result
$(and)	1
$(and,2)	2
$(and,2,3)	2
$(and,4.5,5.6,6.7)	4

PARAMETER

■ *int1,int2*   Any integer or real number.

TIPS

■ A maximum of nine integer numbers can be ANDed together; using this function with no arguments results in 1.

■ This function accepts real numbers but converts them to integers via a fix-like function, such as 6.7 becomes 6.

RELATED DIESEL FUNCTIONS

all logic functions

RELATED SYSTEM VARIABLES

all that contain a real or integer number

$(angtos, *val [, fmt, prec]*)

Conversion function: Converts *val* into an angle using the optional *fmt* and *prec*; if *fmt* or *prec* are left out, **angtos** uses the values stored in system variables **AUnits** and **AuPrec**.

Example	Result
$(angtos,45,1,4)	58d18'36"

PARAMETERS

■ *val*   Any real or integer number.

■ *fmt*   (*Optional*) The format to convert to; when *fmt* is missing, this function uses the value stored in system variable **AUnits**; otherwise, *fmt* is permitted to be one of the following:

fmt	Meaning
0	Decimal degrees (0.0000)
1	Degrees-minutes-seconds (00d00'00".0000)
2	Grad (0.0000g)
3	Radian (0.0000r)
4	Surveyor units (N0'0.0000"E)

■ *prec*   (*Optional*) The precision in decimal places; when *prec* is missing, this function uses the value stored in system variable **AuPrec**; otherwise, *prec* has a range of 0 to 8 decimal places (default = 4).

TIPS

■ This function assumes that *val* is valid format for an angle.

■ The following Diesel code converts radians to degrees using the value stored in system variable **LastAngle**:

```
$(fix,$(*,$(getvar,lastangle),$(/,180,3.14159)))
```

RELATED DIESEL FUNCTIONS
all conversion functions

RELATED SYSTEM VARIABLES
AUnits   Holds the type of units set by the **Units** and **DdUnits** commands.

AuPrec   Holds the number of decimal places set by the **Units** and **DdUnits** commands.

$(edtime,*time,fmt*)

Get fucntion: Returns the system date and time from *time* as specified by *fmt*.

Example	Result
$(edtime,$(getvar,time),DD MON"," YYYY)	"15 Sep, 1996"

PARAMETERS

- *time*   A source for the time and time, such as system variable **date**.
- *fmt*   The format of the date and time.

TIPS

- For example, to display current date and time in 24-hour format:

  $(edtime,$(getvar,time),DD MON"," YYYY"," HH:MM)

returns "18 Sep, 1995, 17:25"

- The date and day format specifiers are:

fmt	Meaning	Example
D	Date	9
DD	Date padded with zero	09
DDD	Abbreviated day	Mon
DDDD	Full day	Monday

- The month and year format specifiers are:

fmt	Meaning	Example
M	Month	9
MO	Month padded with zero	09
MON	Abbreviated month	Sep
MONTH	Full month	September
YY	Abbreviated year	95
YYYY	Full year	1995

- The time format specifiers are:

fmt	Meaning	Example
H	Hour	4
HH	Hour padded with zero	04
MM	Minutes	25
SS	Seconds	38
MSEC	Millisec(1/1000th second)	500
AM, PM	Display AM or PM	AM
am, pm	Display am or pm	am
A, P	Display A or P	A
a, p	Display a or p	a

RELATED DIESEL FUNCTIONS

all get functions

RELATED SYSTEM VARIABLES

CDate   System date and time in YYYYMMDD.HHMMSSDD format, such as 19960306.17371122, which translates into 6 March, 1996, at 5:37:11.22 in the afternoon.

Date   System date expressed in Julian format, such as 2448860.54043252

TdCreate   Time and date drawing originally created, in Julian format.

TdInDwg   Duration drawing has been loaded into AutoCAD, in Julian format.

TdUpDate   Duration since drawing was laste updated, in Julian format.

TdUsrTimer   Duration since user timer began (via the **Time** command), in Julian format.

$(eq, *str1, str2*)

Logical function: Returns 1 if *str1* is identical to *str2*; otherwise returns 0.

Example	Result
$(eq,"Quick","Ref")	0
$(eq,"Quick","Quick")	1
$(eq,1.0,1)	1
$(eq,"","")	1

The result of comparing "quick" with "Quick" is 0:

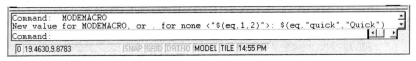

PARAMETER
■ *str1,str2*   Any number or string, including the empty string, "".

TIPS
■ This function requires the use of two arguments; unlike the = function, **eq** works equally well with numbers and strings.

■ Use this function to check if a system variable holds a string:

   $(eq,$(getvar,platform),"Microsoft Windows")

results in 1 if system variable **Platform** = "Microsoft Windows".

■ Use this function together with the **getvar** function to compare the value of user system variables, such as **UserI3**, with other system variables, such as **Elevation**:

   $(=,$(getvar,elevation),$(getvar,useri3))

results in 1 if the current value of system variables **UserI3** and **Elevation** both are 96.

RELATED DIESEL FUNCTIONS
all logic functions

RELATED SYSTEM VARIABLES
all that contain a real or integer number

$(eval,*str*)

String function: Passes *str* to Diesel for evaluation.

Example	Result
$(eval,234.56)	234.56
$(eval,"Time to save your drawing.")	Time to save your drawing.

*Using **eval** to display a prompt on the status line:*

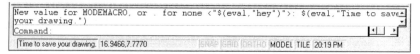

PARAMETER
■ *str* Any string or numbers.

TIPS
■ This function is useful for displaying a prompt on the status line.

■ Using the **ModeMacro** system variable without any Diesel expression is the equivalent to the **eval** function, as follows:

```
Command: modemacro
New value for MODEMACRO, or . for none <>: This is a test.
```

results in 'This is a test.' appearing on the status line.

RELATED DIESEL FUNCTIONS
all string functions

RELATED SYSTEM VARIABLES
none

$(fix, *val*)

Conversion function: Truncates the decimal portion of *val*, a real number.

Example	Result
$(fix,45.14)	45

PARAMETER
- *val*   Any real or integer numbers.

TIP
- Too large a real number, such as 10000000000000000000000000.1, returns 0.

RELATED DIESEL FUNCTIONS
all conversion functions

RELATED SYSTEM VARIABLES
all that contain a real or integer number

$(getenv,*var*)

Get stuff function: Return the value of a *var* in the initialization file, Acad.Ini.

Example	Result
$ (getenv,prototypedwg)	acad.dwg
$ (getenv,acad)	d:\acad13\com\SUPPORT;d:\acad13\win\SUPPORT; d:\acad13\win\TUTORIAL;d:\acad13\com\FONTS;

PARAMETER
■ *var*　　　　Name of any of AutoCAD's system variables..

TIPS
■ A maximum of nine numbers can be added together in LISP-like fashion.

■ Even though the name of the system variable is a string, you do not place quote marks around the name.

■ **Getenv** only works with AutoCAD INI variables located in the **[General]** section of Acad.Ini .

■ For example, if variable **PrototypeDwg** is "Acad.Dwg", then:

　　$ (getenv,prototypedwg)

returns acad.dwg.

RELATED DIESEL FUNCTIONS
all get functions

RELATED SYSTEM VARIABLES
none

$(getvar, *var*)

Get stuff function: Returns the value of a system *var*.

Example	Result
$(getvar,filletrad)	0.5
$(getvar,errno)	0

PARAMETER
- *var*   Name of any of AutoCAD system variable.

TIPS
- **Getvar** works with all of AutoCAD's system variables.

- Even though the name of the system variable is a string, you do not place quote marks around the name.

- For example, if system variable **FilletRad** holds the fillet radius of 0.5000, then:

  $(getvar,filletrad)

returns the value 0.5.

- To display the current grid spacing on the status line:

```
Command: modemacro
New value for MODEMACRO, or . for none <"""">: Grid spacing:
   $(getvar,gridunit)
```

As you change the grid spacing with the Grid or DdRModes commands, the display on the status line automatically upates:

```
and: modemacro
value for MODEMACRO, or . for none <"""">: Grid spacing: $(getvar,gridunit)
Command:
Grid spacing: 0.5,0.5  11.4520,7.7041        SNAP GRID ORTHO MODEL TILE 20:37 PM
```

RELATED DIESEL FUNCTIONS
all get functions

RELATED SYSTEM VARIABLES
all

$(if, *expr, true* [, *false]*)

Logical function: If *expr* is 1 (true), performs *true*; if *expr* is 0 (false), performs *false*.

Example	Result
$(if,$(<,useri1,0),($getvar,useri2)	1

PARAMETERS

- *expr*   Any Diesel expression.
- *true*   Any Diesel expression to evaluate when *expr* equals 1.
- *false*   Any Diesel expression to evaluate when *expr* equals 0.

TIPS

- The value of 1 can be taken as 'true' and 0 as 'false'.

- This function an be used to change the value of toggle system variables, such as **TileMode**. For example, to toggle the display of a check mark in a pull-down menu:

[$(if,$(getvar,tilemode),!.)/TTileMode]^C^Ctilemode $M=$(-,1,$(getvar,tilemode))

This complex-looking menu macro *toggles* (switches the value between 0 and 1) the state of the **TileMode** system variable, as well as toggle the display of the checkmark in front of the TileMode label in the menu. When TileMode = 1, the checkmark appears.

To better understand this combination Diesel and menu macro, let's break it down bit by bit:

[	Start of the menu label.
$(if,	Start of the Diesel **If** function.
$(getvar,tilemode),	The *expr* that obtains the value of variable **TileMode**.
!.	The *true*, which displays the checkmark, ✓, in front of the TileMode menu item when **TileMode** = 1.
)	The end of the Diesel expression; there is no *false* part..
/TTileMode]	The remainder of the menu label, **TileMode**.
^C^Ctilemode	The start of the menu macro, which cancels any other command and executes the **TileMode** system variable.

This is the remainder of the menu macro:

$M=$(-,1,$(getvar,tilemode))

. It changes the value of system variable **TileMode** to either 1 or 0:

$M=	Start of a Diesel macro within a menu macro.
$(-,	Subtraction function.
1,	Subtract 1 from the value of ...
$(getvar,tilemode))	... system variable **TileMode**.

$(index,*val,str*)

String function: Finds and returns the *val* found in *str*, a comma-delimited string;

Example	Result
$(index,1,$(getvar,lastpoint))	2.17741935
$(index,1,"1,2")	2
$(index,99,"1,2")	""

PARAMETERS

- *val* Any real or integer numbers.
- *str* Any comma-delimited string.

TIPS

- Use this function to extract one element of a comma-separated series, such as coordinates from a system variable:

val	Meaning
0	x-coordinate.
1	y-coordinate.
2	z-coordinate.

- The index *val* begins with 0; the second item is #1; when *str* contains fewer items than the value of *val*, this function returns "" the null string.

- The index *str* must consist of a single argument holding a series of comma-separated values, such as system variables **EntMax, GridUnit, InsBase, LastPoint, LimMax, ScreenSize, SnapBase,Target, UscOrg, ViewCtr,** and **VsMax.**

- For example, if system variable **LastPoint** holds the x,y,z-coordinates of (44.3906,2.1774,0.0000), then the following **index** expression returns the value of the x-coordinate (index = 0):

 $(index,0,$(getvar,lastpoint))

returns the x-coordinate, 44.3906,

 $(index,1,$(getvar,lastpoint))

returns the y-coordinate, 2.1774, and

 $(index,2,$(getvar,lastpoint))

returns the z-coordinate, 0.

RELATED DIESEL FUNCTIONS
all string functions

RELATED SYSTEM VARIABLES
all that contain coordinates

$(linelen)

Function handler: Determines the longest status line (in characters) allowed by the host system.

Example	Result
$(linelen)	240

PARAMETERS
none

TIPS
■ This function tells you how long a message Diesel can print to the status line.

■ *Caution*: this number is only valid when the AutoCAD window is maximized; a smaller AutoCAD window allows fewer characters and is not reported by the **linelen** function.

RELATED DIESEL FUNCTIONS
all string functions

RELATED SYSTEM VARIABLES
none

$(nth,*val,expr0* [,*expr1,...,expr7]*)

String function: Finds and returns the n*th* *val* found in elements *expr0* through *expr7*.

Example	Result
$(nth,2,45,1,4)	4

PARAMETERS
- *val*   Any real or integer number.
- *expr0*   Any expression.

TIPS
- The index *value* begins with 0; the second item is #1.
- When *val* = 0, then **nth** returns the first element *expr0*.
- Use this function to return the n*th* expression from a list, which differs from the **index** function that returns the n*th* item of a string.

RELATED DIESEL FUNCTIONS
all string functions

RELATED SYSTEM VARIABLES
all that contain a string

$(or, [int1, int2, ..., int9])

Logical function: Returns the bitwise logical OR of *n1* through *n2*.

Example	Result
$(and)	0
$(and,2)	2
$(and,2,3)	3
$(and,4.5,5.6,6.7)	7

PARAMETER
- *int1,int2*   Any integer or real numbers.

TIPS
- A maximum of nine integer numbers can be ORed together; using this function with no arguments results in 0.

- This function accepts real numbers but rounds them to the nearest integer, such as 6.7 becomes 7.

RELATED DIESEL FUNCTIONS
all logic functions

RELATED SYSTEM VARIABLES
all that contain a real or integer number

$(rtos, *val* [, *fmt, prec]*)

Conversion function: Converts the *val* into a real number using the optional *fmt* and *prec*; if *fmt* and *prec* are left out, **rtos** uses the values stored in system variables **LUnits** and **LuPrec** (*short for Real TO String*).

Example	Result
$(rtos,45,1,4)	4.5000E+01

PARAMETERS

■ *val*   Any real or integer number.

■ *fmt*   (*Optional*) The format to convert to.

When *fmt* is missing, this function uses the value stored in system variable **LUnits**.

Otherwise, *fmt* is permitted to be one of the following:

fmt	Meaning	Example
0	Scientific	exponent notation (0.0000E+00)
1	Decimal	the default (0.0000)
2	Engineering	feet and decimal inches (0'-0.0000")
3	Architectural	feet-fractional inches (0'-0/64")
4	Fractional	unitless (0 0/64)

■ *prec*   (*Optional*) The precision in decimal places.

When *prec* is missing, this function uses the value stored in system variable **LuPrec**.

Otherwise, *prec* has a range of 0 to 8 decimal places (default = 4) or 0 to 1/256 for fractional (default = 1/64).

TIPS

■ This function assumes that *val* is valid format for an angle.

■ The following Diesel code converts radians to degrees using the value stored in system variable **LastAngle**:

```
$(fix,$(*,$(getvar,lastangle),$(/,180,3.14159)))
```

RELATED DIESEL FUNCTIONS
all conversion functions

RELATED SYSTEM VARIABLES

LUnits   Holds the type of units set by the **Units** and **DdUnits** commands.

LuPrec   Holds the number of decimal places set by the **Units** and **DdUnits** commands.

$(strlen,*str*)

String function: Returns the length (in number of characters) of the *str*.

Example	Result
$(strlen,"This is toast")	13
$(strlen,123.56)	6
$(strlen,123)	3

PARAMETER
- *str*   Any string or number.

TIPS
- The *string* can also be a real or integer number; when a real number, **strlen** counts the decimal place:

    $(strlen,245.15)

results in 6.

- **Strlen** works with system variables in conjunction with **GetVar**. For example, system variable **AcltVer** contains "2.0":

    $(strlen,$(getvar,acltver)

results in 3.

RELATED DIESEL FUNCTIONS
all string functions

RELATED SYSTEM VARIABLES
all that contain a string or number

$(substr,*str,start* [,*length*])

String function: Returns the substring (portion of the *str*), starting at character position *start* and continuing on for *length* characters; if *length* is not specified, all characters following the *start* position are returned:

Example	Result
$(substr,"This is toast",9)	toast
$(substr,123.45,3,3)	3.4

Diesel

PARAMETERS

- *str*   Any string or number.
- *start*   The position of the first chracter to return.
- *length*   (*Optional*) Number of characters to extract.

  When missing, returns all characters starting with *start* and following to end of *str*.

TIPS

- A maximum of nine numbers can be added together in LISP-like fashion.
- The *string* can also be a real or integer number:

      $(substr,245.15,4)

results in .15, which is a great way to simulate the **rem** function.

- **Substr** works with system variables in conjunction with **GetVar**. For example, system variable **CDate** contains today's date and time as 1995**0825**.20205319 (using the format YYYYmmdd.HHmmssddd):

      $(substr,$(getvar,cdate),5,4)

results in 0825, the current month and date (August 25).

RELATED DIESEL FUNCTIONS
all string functions

RELATED SYSTEM VARIABLES
all that contain a string or number

$(upper, *val*)

Conversion function: Returns the string *val* changed to all uppercase letters.

Example	Result
$(upper,"Quick")	QUICK
$(upper,"")	*nothing*

The text string "Quick" coverted to all uppercase, "QUICK":

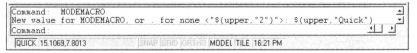

PARAMETER
■ *val*   Any string.

TIPS
■ Numbers and punctuation included as the string, such as "2" and ">", are not converted to uppercase.

■ When the null string "" is used as the argument, the Diesel display area disappears.

RELATED DIESEL FUNCTIONS
all conversion functions

RELATED SYSTEM VARIABLES
all that contain a string

$(xor,*int1* [,*int2*,...,*int9*])

Logic function: Returns the bitwise logical XOR (negative OR) of integers *int1* through *int9*.

Example	Result
$(xor,1)	1

PARAMETER
■ *int1,int2*   Any integer.

TIPS
■ A maximum of nine integer numbers can be XORed together; using this function with no arguments results in 0.

■ This function accepts real numbers but converts them to integers via a fix-like function, such as 6.7 becomes 6.

RELATED DIESEL FUNCTIONS
all logic functions

RELATED SYSTEM VARIABLES
none

$(+, *nbr1* [, *nbr2*, ..., *nbr9]*)

Math function: Add two or more numbers together.

Example	Result
$(+,1,3,5,7,11)	27
$(+,1)	1
$(+,1,2.0)	3
$(+,1,2.5)	3.5
$(+,96,$(getvar,elevation))	*adds 96 to variable* **Elevation**

The result of adding 1, 3, 5, 7, and 11 is shown as 27 on the status line:

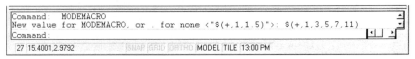

PARAMETER

■ *nbr1,nbr2*   Any real or integer numbers.

TIPS

■ A maximum of nine numbers can be added together with this function.

■ When a single argument is used, this function returns the number as if it were added to 0.

■ This function returns an integer (even when a real "integer," such as 2.0 is used) unless a "non-integer" real is used, such as 2.5.

■ Use this function together with the **getvar** function to change the values of system variables, such as **Elevation:**

    $(+,96,$(getvar,elevation))

adds 96 inches (8 feet) to the current value of system variable **Elevation.**

■ Create an increment counter by using this function together with one of the **UserI***n* system variables, such as **UserI1:**

    $(+,1,$(getvar,useri1))

There are five **UserI***n* system variables — **UserI1** through **UserI5** — which are designed to hold an integer number.

■ *Caution:* The value stored in the **UserI***n* variables is not saved after you exit AutoCAD.

RELATED DIESEL FUNCTIONS

all math functions

RELATED SYSTEM VARIABLES

all that contain a real or integer number

$(-, *nbr1* [, *nbr2*, ..., *nbr9]*)

Math function: Subtract one or more numbers from the first.

Example	Result
$(-,11,3,5,7)	-4
$(-,1)	1
$(-,1,2.0)	-1
$(-,1,2.5)	-1.5
$(-,96,$(getvar,elevation))	*subtracts 96 from Elevation*

PARAMETER
■ *nbr1,nbr2*   Any real or integer numbers.

TIPS
■ A maximum of nine numbers can be added together in LISP-like fashion: *nbr2* through *nbr9* are subtracted from *nbr1*, such as 11 - (3 + 5 + 7).

■ When a single argument is used, this function returns the number without subtracting it from 0.

■ This function returns an integer (even when a real "integer," such as 2.0 is used) unless a "non-integer" real is used, such as 2.5.

■ Use this function together with the **getvar** function to change the values of system variables, such as **Elevation**:

```
$(-,96,$(getvar,elevation))
```

subtracts 96 inches (8 feet) from the current value of system variable **Elevation**.

■ Create an decrement counter by using this function together with one of the **UserI***n* system variables, such as **UserI1**:

```
$(-,1,$(getvar,useri1))
```

There are five **UserI***n* system variables — **UserI1** through **UserI5** — which are designed to hold an integer number.

■ *Caution:* The value stored in the **UserI***n* variables is not saved after AutoCAD exits.

RELATED DIESEL FUNCTIONS
all math functions

RELATED SYSTEM VARIABLES
all that contain a real or integer number

$(*, nbr1 [, nbr2, ..., nbr9])

Math function: Multiply two or more numbers.

Example	Result
$(*,3,5,7)	105
$(*,10)	10
$(*,10,2.5)	25
$(*,3,2.5)	7.5

PARAMETER
- *nbr1,nbr2* Any real or integer numbers.

TIPS
- A maximum of nine numbers can be multipled together.
- Multiply two or more numbers in scientific notation:

  $(*,3e+5,7e+11)

results in 2.10000000e+17.

- The largest displayable number is 1.0e+308.
- When a single argument is used, this function returns the number, as if multiplying the number by 1.
- This function returns an integer (even when a real "integer," such as 2.0 is used) unless a "non-integer" real is used, such as 2.5.

RELATED DIESEL FUNCTIONS
all math functions

RELATED SYSTEM VARIABLES
all that contain a real or integer number

$(/, nbr1 [, nbr2, ..., nbr9])

Math function: Divide one or more numbers into the first number:

Example	Result
$(/,13,5,7)	0.37242857
$(/,10)	10
$(/,2.0,1)	2
$(/,1,2.5)	0.4

Diesel

PARAMETER

■ *nbr1,nbr2*   Any real or integer numbers.

TIPS

■ A maximum of nine numbers can be divided in LISP-like fashion: *nbr2* through *nbr9* are divided into the first number, *nbr1*, such as 13 / (5 * 7).

■ Results are displayed to eight decimal places.

■ When a single argument is used, this function returns the number, as if dividing the number by 1.

■ This function returns an integer (even when a real "integer," such as 2.0 is used) unless a "non-integer" real is used, such as 2.5.

RELATED DIESEL FUNCTIONS

all math functions

RELATED SYSTEM VARIABLES

all that contain a real or integer number

$(=, *nbr1*, *nbr2*)

Logical function: Returns 1 if two variables are equal; returns 0 if unequal.

Example	Result
$(=,2.0,2)	1
$(=,2,3)	0
$(=,$(getvar,elevation),96)	1

PARAMETER
- *nbr1,nbr2*   Any real or integer numbers.

TIPS
- This function requires the use of two arguments; it does not work with non-numbers.
- Use this function to check if a system variable is toggled on or off:

    $(=,$(getvar,gridmode),1)

results in 1 if system variable **GridMode** = 1 (grid is turned on).

- Use this function together with the **getvar** function to check the value of system variables, such as **Elevation**:

    $(=,$(getvar,elevation),96)

results in 1 if the current value of system variable **Elevation** = 96.

RELATED DIESEL FUNCTIONS
all logic functions

RELATED SYSTEM VARIABLES
all that contain a real or integer number

$(!=, *nbr1, nbr2*)

Logical functions: Returns 1 if *nbr1* is not equal to *nbr2*; otherwise returns 0.

Example	Result
$(!=,3.4,3.4)	0
$(eq,1.2,5,6)	1
$(eq,1.0,1)	0

PARAMETER
■ *nbr1,nbr2*   Any real or integer numbers.

TIP
■ This function requires the use of two arguments; != works only with numbers.

RELATED DIESEL FUNCTIONS
all logic functions

RELATED SYSTEM VARIABLES
all that contain a real or integer number

$(<, *nbr1, nbr2*)

Logical function: Returns 1 if *nbr1* is less than *nbr2*; otherwise returns 0:

Example	Result
$(<,$(getvar,elevation),97)	1

PARAMETER
- *nbr1,nbr2*   Any real or integer numbers.

TIP
- This function requires the use of two arguments; < works only with numbers.

RELATED DIESEL FUNCTIONS
all logic functions

RELATED SYSTEM VARIABLES
all that contain a real or integer number

$(<=, *nbr1*, *nbr2*)

Logical function: Returns 1 if *nbr1* is less than or equal to *nbr2*; otherwise returns 0.

Example	Result
$(<=,12,12)	1

PARAMETER
■ *nbr1,nbr2*   Any real or integer numbers.

TIP
■ This function requires the use of two arguments; <= works only with numbers.

RELATED DIESEL FUNCTIONS
all logic functions

RELATED SYSTEM VARIABLES
all that contain a real or integer number

$(>, *nbr1, nbr2*)

Logical function: Returns 1 if *nbr1* is greater than *nbr2*; otherwise returns 0.

Example	Result
$ (>,12,12)	0

PARAMETER
- *nbr1,nbr2*   Any real or integer numbers.

TIP
- This function requires the use of two arguments; > works only with numbers.

RELATED DIESEL FUNCTIONS
all logic functions

RELATED SYSTEM VARIABLES
all that contain a real or integer number

$(>=, *nbr1*, *nbr2*)

Logical function: Returns 1 if *nbr1* is greater than or equal to *nbr2*; otherwise returns 0.

Example	Result
$ (>=,12,12.1)	0

PARAMETER
■ *nbr1,nbr2*   Any real or integer numbers.

TIP
■ This function requires the use of two arguments; >= works only with numbers.

RELATED DIESEL FUNCTIONS
all logic functions

RELATED SYSTEM VARIABLES
all that contain a real or integer number

Introduction to Linetype Programming

Autodesk first introduced linetype programming in AutoCAD version 2. The first implementation was strictly 1D: linetypes are made up of lines, gaps, and dots. In Release 13, Autodesk extended linetypes to allow 2D shapes and text, such as zigzags and — GAS — for a gas line.

Some of the 1D (left) and 2D (right) linetypes provided with AutoCAD Release 13:

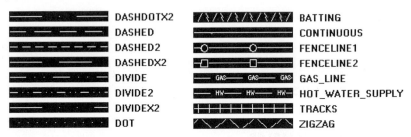

Linetypes are defined in a file external to AutoCAD. The file has an extension of LIN. The file must be loaded into AutoCAD before the linetype definition can be applied to objects and layers; only the 'Continuous' linetype is predefined in every new AutoCAD drawing.

Autodesk calls the 1D linetypes "simple" and the 2D linetypes "complex." AutoCAD defines 38 simple linetypes in \acadr13\com\support\Acad.Lin; eight complex linetypes are defined in \acadr13\com\support\Ltypeshp.Lin.

TIPS

■ The only linetype defined in a new AutoCAD drawing is CONTINUOUS.

■ Linetypes must be loaded from a LIN file into the drawing before they can be used.

■ Complex linetypes are simple linetypes with one or more shape characters added.

■ Change in Release 13: Every object can have its own linetype scale; previously, a single linetype scale applied to all objects in the drawing.

RELATED SYSTEM VARIABLES

CeLtype   The name of the current linetype (defualt = .

LtScale   The current linetype scale factor (default = 1.0).

PlineGen   Controls how linetypes are generated for polylines:

PlineGen	Meaning
0	Generate from vertex to vertex (default).
1	Generate linetype from end to end.

PsLtScale   Lintype scale relative to paper space (default = 1.0).

Linetype Quick Starts

Programming a 1D Linetype at the 'Command:' Prompt

To create a custom linetype on-the-fly:

1. Type the **Linetype Create** command:

```
Command: linetype
?/Create/Load/Set:  C
```

2. Name the linetype in three steps:

- The linetype name:

```
Name of linetype to create: [enter up to 31 characters]
```

- The LIN filename: append linetype description to Acad.Lin or create new LIN file.

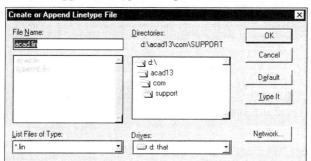

- Describe the linetype:

```
Descriptive text: [enter up to 47 characters]
```

3. Define the linetype pattern by using five codes:

- Positive number for dashes; 0.5 is a dash 0.5 units long.

- Negative number for gaps; -0.25 is a gap 0.25 units long.

- Zero is for dots; 0 is a single dot.

- "**A**" forces the linetype to align between two endpoints (linetypes start and stop with a dash).

- Commas (,) separate values.

Example:

```
*DASHDOT,__ . __ . __ . __ . __ . __ . __ . __ .
A,.5,-.25,0,-.25 [Enter]
```

4. Press **[Enter]** to end linetype definition.

5. Use the **Linetype Load** command to load pattern into drawing.

```
Linetype to load: [type name]
```

6. Use the **Linetype Set** command to set the linetype.

```
New object linetype (or ?) <>: [type name]
```

Alternatively, use the **Change** command to change objects to the linetype.

Programming a Simple (1D) Linetype with a Text Editor

To create a custom linetype by editing the Acad.Lin file:

1. Start a text editor (not a word processor), such as NotePad.

2. Load the Acad.Lin file from subdirectory \Acadr13\com\support\.

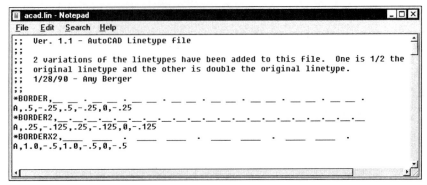

3. You can modify an existing linetype or add a new linetype.

4. The linetype definition consists of two lines of text:

;   (*Semi-colon*) A comment line; ignored by AutoCAD.

Line 1 is the header, such as `*BORDER,__ __ . __ __ . __ __ .`

*   (*Asterisk*) Indicates the start of a new linetype definition.

BORDER Name of the lintype. This name should be unqiue in the file; if not, AutoCAD will use the first linetype it finds with the name.

,   (*Optional*) Separator between name and description.

__ __ .   (*Optional*) Description of the linetype displayed by the **Linetype ?** command. Maximum 47 characters; if you need more room, use a comment line, such as:

```
; long dashed triplicate dotted line
*ACAD_ISO06W100,____  ...  ____  ...  ____
```

Line 2 is the data, such as `A,.5,-.25,.5,-.25,0,-.25`

A   (*Optional*) Alignment flag; when present forces AutoCAD to start and end the linetype with a line (rather than a gap or dot).

,   Separator.

.5   Length of a dash when **LtScale** = 1.0; a positive number indicates a dash. Every linetype data line must begin with a dash.

-.25   Length of a gap when **LtScale** = 1.0; a negative number indicates a gap. Every linetype data line must follow the initial dash with a gap.

0   A dot; gaps usually surround a dot since it makes little sense to have a dash on either side of a dot.

---

5. Save the LIN file with the same name or a new name.

TIPS

■ The data line is limited to: 1 line, 80 characters, and 12 dash lengths.

■ When the A-flag is used, the data line must start with a dash or a dot, such as .5 or 0.

■ When the A-flag is used, the initial dash must be followed with a gap, such as -.25.

■ When the A-flag is used, the minimum length of a data line is a single dash-gap or dot-gap combination, such as .5,-.25 or 0,-.25.

■ Then the line segment is too short to draw the linetype pattern, AutoCAD draws a continuous line.

Programming a Complex (2D) Linetype with a Text Editor

To create a custom linetype by editing the Ltypeshp.Lin file:

1. Start a text editor (not a word processor), such as NotePad.

2. Load the Ltypeshp.Lin file from subdirectory \Acadr13\com\support\.

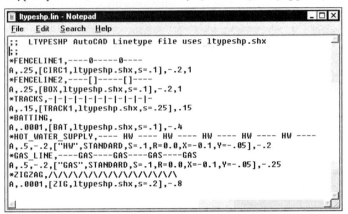

```
Itypeshp.lin - Notepad
File   Edit   Search   Help
;;   LTYPESHP AutoCAD Linetype file uses ltypeshp.shx
;;
*FENCELINE1,----0-----0----
A,.25,[CIRC1,ltypeshp.shx,s=.1],-.2,1
*FENCELINE2,----[]-----[]----
A,.25,[BOX,ltypeshp.shx,s=.1],-.2,1
*TRACKS,-|-|-|-|-|-|-|-|-|-|-
A,.15,[TRACK1,ltypeshp.shx,s=.25],.15
*BATTING,
A,.0001,[BAT,ltypeshp.shx,s=.1],-.4
*HOT_WATER_SUPPLY,---- HW ---- HW ---- HW ---- HW ----
A,.5,-.2,["HW",STANDARD,S=.1,R=0.0,X=-0.1,Y=-.05],-.2
*GAS_LINE,----GAS----GAS----GAS----GAS
A,.5,-.2,["GAS",STANDARD,S=.1,R=0.0,X=-0.1,Y=-.05],-.25
*ZIGZAG,/\/\/\/\/\/\/\/\/\/\/\/\
A,.0001,[ZIG,ltypeshp.shx,s=.2],-.8
```

3. You can modify an existing linetype or add a new linetype.

4. The linetype definition consists of two lines of text:

;   (*Semi-colon*) A comment line; ignored by AutoCAD.

Line 1 is the header, such as *GAS_LINE, - - - - GAS - - - - GAS - - - - GAS

*   (*Asterisk*) Indicates the start of a new linetype definition.

GAS_LINE Name of the linetype. This name should be unique in the file; if not, AutoCAD uses the first linetype it finds with the name.

,   (*Optional*) Separator between name and description.

- - GAS   (*Optional*) Description of the linetype displayed by the **Linetype ?** command. Maximum 47 characters; if you need more room, use a comment line, such as:

```
; complex linetype for an underground gas line
*GAS_LINE, - - - - GAS - - - - GAS - - - - GAS - - - - GAS
```

Line 2 is the data, such as A, .5, - .2, ["GAS",STANDARD,S=.1,R=0.0,X=-0.1,Y=-.05],-.25

A   (*Optional*) Alignment flag; when present forces AutoCAD to start and end the linetype with a line (rather than a gap or dot).

,   Separator.

.5   Length of a dash when **LtScale** = 1.0; a positive number indicates a dash.

-.2   Length of a gap when **LtScale** = 1.0; a negative number indicates a gap.

0   A dot; gaps usually surround a dot since it makes little sense to have a dash on either side of a dot.

EMBEDDING TEXT

`A,.5,-.2,["GAS",STANDARD,S=.1,R=0.0,X=-0.1,Y=-.05],-.25`

[...]   Indicates the "complex" portion of the linetype, which consists of specifying the text (shape) and an optional transformation.

"GAS"   The text string to be printed in the linetype.

STANDARD   (*Optional*) The name of the text style to apply to the text string; when missing, AutoCAD uses the current text style (as indicated by the **TextStyle** system variable.)

S=.1   (*Optional*) Scale multiplier: multiplies the text size as defined by the text style; when the text style defines a height of 0, then S= defines the height.

R=0.0   (*Optional*) Relative rotation (degrees): the text is rotated relative to the linetype; this means text changes orientation with the line.

A=0.0   (*Optional*) Absolute rotation (degrees): the text is rotated relative to the x-axis; this means the text is always oriented in the same direction, no matter the direction of the line.

*Text in a complex linetype with **R=0.0** (left), **R=30.0** (center) and **A=30.0** (right):*

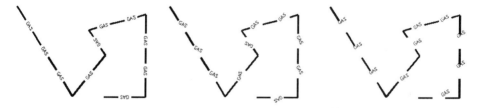

■ Use **d** for degrees; **r** for radians; **g** for grads, such as R=1.5r and A=200g.

■ The rotation is constrained between the text baseline and capital height.

X=-0.1   (*Optional*) X offset: shifts the text in the x-direction from the linetype definition vertex.

Y=-0.05   (*Optional*) Y offset: shifts the text in the y-direction from the linetype definition vertex.

■ Units are in linetype scale factor; LtScale = 1.0 by default.

EMBEDDING A SHAPE

`*ZIGZAG,/\/\/\/\/\/\/\/\/\/\/\/\/\`
`A,.0001,[ZIG,ltypeshp.shx,s=.2],-.8`

ZIG   Name of shape; when shape is missing, linetype is drawn without it.

ltypeshp.shx

    Name of compiled shape file; when missing, linetype is drawn without the shape.

Introduction to Hatch Patterns

Autodesk first introduced hatch pattern customization in AutoCAD version 1.4. Like linetypes, a hatch pattern consists of dashes, gaps, and dots; unlike the linetype, the hatch pattern can specify an offset and angle, resulting in a 2D, repeating pattern.

Some of the hatch patterns provided with AutoCAD Release 13:

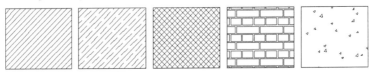

Hatch patterns are defined in a file external to AutoCAD. The file has an extension of PAT. The file must be loaded into AutoCAD before the hatch definitions can be applied to objects and layers; no hatch patterns are predefined in a new AutoCAD drawing. AutoCAD defines 67 hatch patterns in \acadr13\com\support\Acad.Pat.

It is considered that AutoCAD generates an infinite number of parallel lines from each definition. Hence, a hatch pattern can only consist of lines, line segments (dashes), dots, and gaps. AutoCAD cannot create hatch patterns made of circles or other non-linear objects; AutoCAD cannot solid fill an arbitrary area.

TIPS

■ Hatch patterns must be loaded into a drawing from a PAT file before they can be used.

■ New hatch patterns can be added to the Acad.Pat file or placed in their own PAT file.

■ *Change in Release 13*: Hatching can be associative and be edited via the **BHatch** and **HatchEdit** commands; previously, hatching was fixed and uneditable.

■ The hatch patterns displayed by the **BHatch** command are slide files stored in the Acad.Slb slide library file, when the slide name matches the hatch pattern name.

■ As Autodesk notes, "developing a hatch pattern definition for AutoCAD requires some knowledge, practice, and patience... ." After 12 years, Autodesk still has not made the process at all intuitive.

RELATED SYSTEM VARIABLES

HpAng	Angle of the hatch pattern lines in degrees (default = 0 degrees).
HpDouble	Toggle if hatch pattern is applied a second time at 90 degrees (default = 0).
HpName	Name of the current hatch pattern (default = ANSI31).
HpScale	Current scale factor (default = 1.0).
HpSpace	Spacing between hatch pattern lines (default = 1.0 units).
SnapAng	Rotation angle of the hatch pattern in degrees (default = 0 degrees).
SnapBase	x,y-coordinates of the origin for the hatch pattern (default = 0,0).

Hatch Pattern Quick Starts

Customizing a Hatch Pattern at the 'Command:' Prompt

To create a custom hatch pattern on-the-fly:

1. Type the **Hatch User-defined** command:

```
Command: hatch
Pattern (? or name/U,style): u
```

2. Specify the parameters of the hatch pattern:

```
Angle for crosshatch lines <0>: 90
Spacing between lines <1.0000>: 2
Double hatch area? <N> y
```

3. Select the object or boundary to hatch:

```
Select hatch boundaries or RETURN for direct hatch option,
Select objects: [Enter]
Retain polyline? <N> y
From point: [pick]
Arc/Close/Length/Undo/<Next point>: [pick]
Arc/Close/Length/Undo/<Next point>: a
Angle/CEnter/CLose/Direction/Line/Radius/Second pt/Undo/
   <Endpoint of arc>: end of [pick]
Angle/CEnter/ ... /Undo/<Endpoint of arc>: [Enter]
From point or RETURN to apply hatch: [Enter]
```

4. Unlike a custom linetype created on-the-fly, your custom hatch pattern cannot be saved to file.

Customizing a Hatch Pattern with a Text Editor

To create a custom hatch pattern by adding to the Acad.Pat file:

1. Start a text editor (not a word processor), such as NotePad.

2. Load the Acad.Pat file from subdirectory \Acadr13\com\support\.

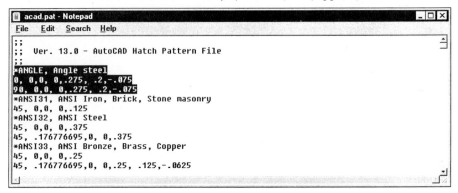

```
acad.pat - Notepad
File   Edit   Search   Help
;;
;;    Ver. 13.0 - AutoCAD Hatch Pattern File
;;
*ANGLE, Angle steel
0,  0,0,  0,.275, .2,-.075
90, 0,0,  0,.275, .2,-.075
*ANSI31, ANSI Iron, Brick, Stone masonry
45, 0,0, 0,.125
*ANSI32, ANSI Steel
45, 0,0, 0,.375
45, .176776695,0, 0,.375
*ANSI33, ANSI Bronze, Brass, Copper
45, 0,0, 0,.25
45, .176776695,0, 0,.25, .125,-.0625
```

3. You can modify an existing linetype or add a new linetype.

4. The linetype definition consists of two or more lines of text:

;   (*Semi-colon*) A comment line; ignored by AutoCAD.

Line 1 is the header, such as `*ANGLE, Angle steel`

*   (*Asterisk*) Indicates the start of a new hatch pattern definition.

ANGLE   Name of the hatch pattern. This name should be unique in the file; if not, AutoCAD will use the first pattern it finds with the name.

,   (*Optional*) Separator between name and description.

Angle Steel   (*Optional*) Description of the linetype displayed by the **Hatch ?** command.

      ■ Maximum 80 characters for the name, comma, and description; if you need more room, use comment lines, such as:

```
; The following hatch patterns AR-xxxxx
; come from AEC/Architectural
*AR-B816, 8x16 Block elevation stretcher bond
```

Lines 2 and following are the data, such as:

```
0,  0,0,  0,.275,  .2,-.075
90, 0,0,  0,.275,  .2,-.075
```

,   Separator.

A hatch pattern data line uses the following format:

```
angle, x-origin, y-origin, x-offset, y-offset [, dash1, ...]
```

- There is no limit to the number of data lines for a hatch pattern definition.
- Each line of data applies to a single pattern segment; for example, the two lines of data (*above*) represent a hatch pattern with two lines.
- Write one line of data for every line (or dash) in the pattern definition.

angle   Angle for this line hatch pattern data.

Hatch pattern angles at (left to right) 0, 30, 45, 90, and 135 degrees:

- To change the angle of a hatch pattern upon placing it in the drawing, set the angle in system variable **SnapAng**.
- The setting in **SnapAng** is additive; for example, if the hatch pattern defines the lines drawn at 30 degrees and **SnapAng** is 90 degrees, then AutoCAD drawns the hatch lines at 120 degrees.

x-origin   The first line of the hatch pattern passes through this x-coordinate.

y-origin   The first line of the hatch pattern passes through this y-coordinate.

- Hatch pattern lines are considered infinite in length.
- To change the x,y-origin of a hatch pattern upon placing it in the drawing, use system variable **SnapBase**.
- The setting in **SnapBase** is additive; for example, if the hatch pattern defines the lines start at 1,1 and **SnapBase** is 10,10, then AutoCAD drawns the hatch line origin 11,11.

*The effect on a hatch pattern as **SnapBase** changes (left to right) from 0,0 to 1,1 to 2,2 to 5,5 to 10,10 and to 15,15:*

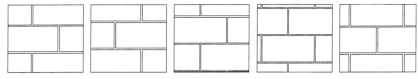

x-offset   Distance between line segments.

- This parameter only makes sense specifying the offset for vertical or diagonal lines. Thus, the *x-offset* has a value of 0.0 in most hatch patterns.
- Even though it is rarely used, this parameter is not optional.
- Use the *dash1* parameter to specify the distance between dashes.

---

y-offset   Distance between lines.

■ This parameter defines the vertical distance between repeating lines; thus, the *y-offset* is seen in every hatch pattern.

■ Both *x-offset* and *y-offset* are unaffected by the *angle* parameter; *x-offset* is in the direction of the line and *y-offset* is perpendicular to the line.

The Ar-816 hatch pattern, showning the x-offset and y-offset distances:

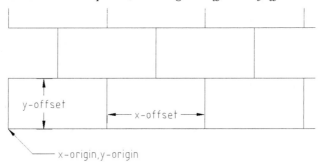

dash1   Defines dashes in the hatch pattern, like linetyes:

dash1	Meaning
positive number	Length of a dash, such as .25
0	A dot.
negative number	Length of a gap, such as -.25

*The **dash1** linecodes:*

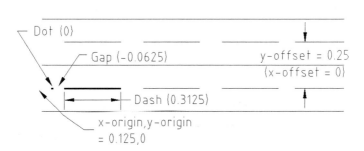

■ The "dot" drawn by the hatch pattern is actually a zero-length line.

■ The dot in a hatch pattern is not printed by some plotters, especially laser printers; therefor, you may want to use a very short line segment, such as 0.01, in place of a dot (0).

- You cannot specify a "weight" (or width) for a hatch pattern line. The workaround is to define two or more very closely spaced lines, such as:

```
*Thick_Line, Closely spaced lines
0, 0,0, 0,.25
0, 0,.01, 0,.25
0, 0,.02, 0,.25
```

*The **Thick_Line** hatch pattern at scale factor 5.0 (left) and 1.0 (right):*

5. Save the PAT file with the same name or a new name.

TIPS

- The data line is limited to 80 characters in length.
- Each data line must include the angle, x- and y-origin, and the x- and y-offset.
- Each data line defines a single line or a dash-gap-dot pattern.
- There is no limit to the number of data lines for each hatch patter definition, unlike linetype definitions. *Caution*: a complex hatch pattern takes a long time to draw.
- Simulate circlular elements with a series of very short dashes.
- To draw dash and gap segments at an angle, use the sine of the anglein degrees, such as:

Angle	Dash length (sine)
0	0
30	.433
45	.707
60	.866
90	1

- The angle specifier points the dash pattern in a particular direction; 90 degrees sends the dash pattern up, while 270 degrees (and -90 degrees) sends the dash pattern down. This does not affect continueous lines.
- To make it easier to read a hatch pattern definition, format the code as follows:

```
*AR-SAND, Random dot pattern
;angle    x,-yorigin    x,y-offset        dash codes
37.5,     0,0,          1.123,1.567,      0,-1.52, 0,-1.7, 0,-1.625
7.5,      0,0,          2.123,2.567,      0,-.82, 0,-1.37, 0,-.525
-32.5,    -1.23,0,      2.6234,1.678,     0,-.5, 0,-1.8, 0,-2.35
-42.5,    -1.23,0,      1.6234,2.678,     0,-.25, 0,-1.18, 0,-1.35
```

Introduction to Command Aliases

Autodesk first introduced command name customization (aliases) in AutoCAD Release 9. Commands can be redefined in two ways:

1. Eliminate a command via the **Undefine** command (restore the command with the **Redefine** command).

2. Give a command name a shortcut via an alias in the Acad.Pgp file.

Undefine/Redefine Quick Start

You undefine and redefine a command, as follows:

1. Start the **Undefine** command:

    Command: **undefine**

2. Type the name of the command to undefine, such as **Line**:

    Command name: **line**

3. AutoCAD now acts as if it never heard of the **Line** command:

    Command: **line**
    Unknown command "LINE". Type ? for list of commands.

4. Bring back command recognition with the **Redefine** command, as follows:

    Command: **undefine**
    Command name: **line**

5. AutoCAD once again recognizes the command name:

    Command: **line**
    From point:

TIPS

■ When a command is unavailable due to the **Undefine** command, the dot (.) prefix tempoarily brings it back, as follows:

    Command: **line**
    Unknown command "LINE". Type ? for list of commands.
    Command: **.line**
    From point:

■ AutoCAD does not provide a list of undefined command names.

■ While any and all command names can be undefined, command options and system variables cannot be undefined.

■ AutoLISP function names can be "undefined" by defining them as a null function:

    Command: **(defun c:entmod () ())**
    Command: **entmod**
    nil

RELATED SYSTEM VARIABLE

CmdName   The most-recently used command name.

Command Alias Quick Start

Customizing a Command Name with a Text Editor

To create a custom command name by adding to or editing the Acad.Pgp file:

1. Start a text editor (not a word processor), such as NotePad.

2. Load the Acad.Ppg file from subdirectory \Acadr13\com\support\.

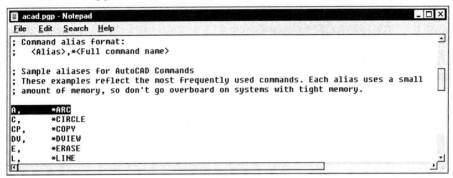

```
acad.pgp - Notepad
File   Edit   Search   Help
; Command alias format:
;    <Alias>,*<Full command name>

; Sample aliases for AutoCAD Commands
; These examples reflect the most frequently used commands. Each alias uses a small
; amount of memory, so don't go overboard on systems with tight memory.

A,         *ARC
C,         *CIRCLE
CP,        *COPY
DV,        *DVIEW
E,         *ERASE
L,         *LINE
```

3. You can modify an existing alias or add a new alias.

4. The alias definition consists of one line of text:

A,	*ARC
;	*(Semi-colon)* A comment line; ignored by AutoCAD.
A	Name of the alias. This name should be unique in the file; if not, AutoCAD will use the first alias it finds with the name.
,	Separator between alias and command name.
*	*(Asterisk)* Indicates the start of a new alias definition.
ARC	The full command name or system variable:

■ Use the - prefix for command names that take the - (command line version of a dialog box command) prefix, such as:

MT,   *-MTEXT

■ You can create an alias for command names and system variables.

■ You cannot create aliases for command options.

■ Use the **defun c:** to redefine an AutoLISP function.

TIPS

■ AutoCAD defines 34 aliases patterns in \acadr13\com\support\Acad.Ppg.

■ The alias of a transparent command can be used transparently.

■ Alises cannot be used in scripts.

Introduction to Script Programming

Autodesk first introduced script programming in AutoCAD version 1.4. Its purpose is to automate keystrokes. Anything you type at the 'Command:' prompt can be typed into a script file; the sole exception are comments (prefixed by ;). Until Release 12, the script file was the only way to automate the start up of AutoCAD.

TIPS

- AutoCAD includes no script files.

- Scripts are stored in files with SCR extension.

- Only one script can be loaded into AutoCAD at a time.

- The **Script** command loads, then automatically runs the script file.

- To re-run a script, use the **RScript** command.

- A script can branch off to an AutoLISP function, which, in turn, can call the same or another script file. For example, 'label' is the name of the Label.Lsp AutoLISP routine:

```
zoom e
qsave
label
```

and 'zeqsl' is the name of the Zeqsl.Scr script file:

```
(defun c:label ()
(getpoint "Pick a point: ")
(command "rscript" "zeqsl")
```

- AutoLISP code can be embedded in a script file in the same way that you type AutoLISP code at the 'Command:' prompt, such as:

```
(setq timer1 (getvar "date"))
regen
regen
regen
(setq time2 (getvar "date")
(setq times (- time2 time1))
(print times)
```

In fact, the **RScript** command was used in AutoCAD v2.17 and v2.18 to create loops in AutoLISP, which at that time was lacking conditional expressions.

- Since the **Script** command is a transparent command, it can be used during other command.

- The script file is limited because it cannot simulate mouse movements nor can it operate during a dialog box.

■ To allows script files to operate, AutoCAD includes non-dialog box versions of several commands:

Dialog Box Name	Command Line Name
Plot	Plot when variable CmdDia = 0
File-related commands, such as AcisIn,SaveAs,DxfOut, Files, and Export.	Set system variable FileDia = 0
Open	FileOpen
DdAttDef	AttDef
DdAttE	AttEdit
DdAttExt	AttExt
DdChProp	ChProp
DdColor	Color or Colour
DdEModes	Color,Layer,Linetype,Style,LtScale,Elev
DdInsert	Insert
DdLModes	Layer
DdLType	Linetype
DdOsnap	Osnap, Aperture
DdPtype	PdMode, PdSize
DdRename	Rename
DdRModes	Fill,QText,Blipmode,Orthomode,Highlight, Snap,Grid,Isomode
DdSelect	Select
DdUcs	Ucs
DdUnits	Units
DdView	View
DdVpoint	VPoint
BHatch	-BHatch
Boundary	-Boundary
HatchEdit	-HatchEdit
MText	-Mtext

Scripts

■ Some commands that display a dialog box have no command-line equivalent. These halt a script file: About, DdUcsP, DdEdit, DdGrips, DDim, DdModify, Filter, MlStyle, and others.

Script Quick Starts

WRITING A SCRIPT FILE

To create a custom script file by creating an SCR file:

1. Start a text editor (not a word processor), such as NotePad.

2. Begin typing.

- It is best to have one command per line.

- A script will stall when it comes across an invalid command name or command option.

- It is useful to have a command reference, such as *The Illustrated AutoCAD Quick Reference* (Delmar Publishers), that indicates the options for every command.

3. A script file may have the following special characters:

(Space) Equivalent to pressing the spacebar the 'Command:' prompt.

(End of line) Equivalent to pressing the **[Enter]** key at the 'Command:' prompt.

;   *(Semi-colon)* Allows you to place comments in the script file; ignored by AutoCAD.

*   *(Asterisk)* When used as a prefix to the **VSlide** command, preloads the slide file.

4. Here is an example of a script file. This script places a door symbol into the drawing:

```
; Inserts the DOOR2436 block at x,y = 76,100
insert door2436 76,100
; x-scale = 0.5, y-scale=1.0, rotation=90 degrees
0.5 1.0 90
```

5. Save the script file with the SCR extension.

RUNNING A SCRIPT FILE

To run a script file by loading an SCR file:

1. Type the **Script** command:

    Command: **script**

2. AutoCAD displays the **Select Script File** dialog box:

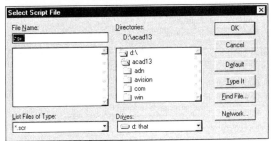

3. Select the name of a script file and click **OK**.

4. AutoCAD loads and runs the script file.

5. To run the script file again, type the **RScript** command:

    Command: **rscript**

6. To interrupt a script file, press **[Backspace]**.

7. To continue the interrupted script file, type the **Resume** comand:

    Command: **resume**

8. To stop a script file, press **[Esc]** (or **[Ctrl]+C** prior to Release 13).

STARTING AUTOCAD WITH A SCRIPT FILE

To start AutoCAD and automatically run a script file:

1. In DOS, type the following at the DOS prompt or in a batch file

```
C:\> acad dwgname scrname
```

2. In Windows 95, edit the **Properties** of AutoCAD.Exe:

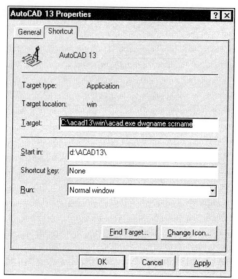

dwgname	The name of a drawing; this can be a dummy name, such as 'x'.
scrname	The name of the script file.

- AutoCAD begins running the script file as soon as it is loaded.

- This is useful for purging or plotting a drawing, or renaming layers.

'Delay *secs*

Script command: Delays the next script command, in milliseconds.

Example	Result
delay 1000	*pauses 1 second*

PARAMETER
■ *secs*   Delay time in millseconds:

RELATED SCRIPT COMMAND
■ Script   Initiates a script

TIPS
■ A transparent command; can be used in another command.

■ Use the **Delay** command to slow down the execution of a script file.

■ The maximum delay is 32767, just over 32 seconds.

'Resume

Script command: Resumes a script file after it has been paused by the user pressing the **[Backspace]** key.

Example	Result
resume	. . .

PARAMETERS
none

RELATED SCRIPT COMMANDS
- **RScript**   Reruns the current script file.
- **Script**   Loads and runs a script file.

TIPS
- A transparent command; can be used in another command.
- Use **[Backspace]** to pause the script file.
- Use **[Esc]** to stop the script file.

RELATED SYSTEM VARIABLES
none

'RScript

Script command: Repeats the script file (*short for Repeat SCRIPT*).

Example	Result
rscript	. . .

PARAMETERS
none

RELATED AUTOCAD COMMANDS
- **Resume**   Resumes a script file after being interrupted.
- **Script**   Loads and runs a script file.

TIPS
- A transparent command; can be used in another command.
- Use **[Backspace]** to pause the script file.
- Use **[Esc]** to stop the script file.

RELATED SYSTEM VARIABLES
none

'Script *fname*

Script command: Runs an ASCII file containing a sequence of AutoCAD instructions to automatically execute a series of commands.

Example	Result
script filename	*runs script*

PARAMETER
fname   Name of the script file; SCR extension not required.

RELATED SCRIPT COMMANDS
- **Delay**   Pauses, in milliseconds, before executing the next command.
- **Resume**   Resumes a script after a script has been interrupted.
- **RScript**   Repeats a script file.

TIPS
- Since the **Script** command is a transparent command, it can be used during another command.

- Prefix the **VSlide** command to preload it into memory for a faster slide show:

    *vslide

- AutoCAD can start with a script file on the command line:

    C:\ **acad13 dwgname scrname**

Since the script filename must follow the drawing filename, use a dummy drawing filename, such as 'X'.

- You can make a script file more flexible (pause for user input, branch with conditionals, and so on) by inserting AutoLISP functions.

RELATED SYSTEM VARIABLE
CmdNames   The name of the current command.

Introduction to Toolbar Programming

Autodesk first introduced the toolbar in Release 11 for Windows; the same toolbar system is used in R12, AutoCAD LT R1 and R2. (Toolbar is not available in the DOS versions.) In Release 13 and LT R3, the toolbar changed substantially.

AUTOCAD RELEASE 11 & 12, LT RELEASE 1 & 2

The toolbar and toolbox buttons are preconfigured by Autodesk with 60 commands. You can change the icon and the command assigned to any button; as well, you can add more buttons (to a maximum of 86). You cannot move the position of buttons, change the wording of tooltips, change the O, S, or P buttons, nor create new icons.

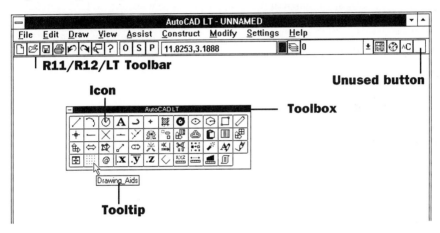

AUTOCAD RELEASE 13 AND LT RELEASE 3

In the newer version, you can edit the icons and have multiple floating toolbars. (The O, S, and P buttons are moved to the status line.)

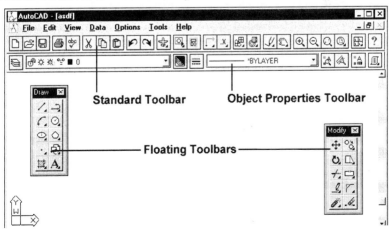

Special Characters

In addition to command and option names, you can use a limited number of special characters. For example, the space between each command is interpreted by LT as the same as pressing the **[Enter]** key. The complete list of special characters is as follows:

Character	Meaning
[Spacebar]	Equivalent to pressing [Enter] at the end of a command name.
;(semi-colon)	Suppresses the space that LT automatically adds to the end of a macro.
\2	Toggle **snap** mode, like pressing [Ctrl]+B on the keyboard.
\3	**Cancel** any command currently underway, like pressing [Ctrl]+C.
\4	Toggle **coordinate** display between on and off, like [Ctrl]+D.
\5	Switch between the three **isometric** planes, like [Ctrl]+E.
\7	Toggle display of the **grid** between on and off, like [Ctrl]+G.
\8	**Backspace**, like pressing the [Backspace] key.
\13	Like pressing the [Enter] key; required during **DText** command.
\15	Toggle **ortho** mode between on and off, like [Ctrl]+O.
\22	Switch to next **viewport**, like [Ctrl]+V.
\n	Start a **new line**; does not work with **DText** command.
\t	**Tab**; same effect as pressing [Spacebar].
\nnn	Any ASCII character nnn from 000 to 255.
\\	Allows \ (**backslash**) character in macros, such subdirectory.

TIPS

■ A toolbar and toolbox macro can be at most 255 characters long.

■ If you need to write a macro longer than 255 characters, use command aliases to save on space (see Alias). For example, using aliases for 'zoom e save plot' results in saving 50% of characters:

```
AutoCAD Command: z e sa pp
```

■ The maximum number of macros (buttons) that AutoCAD can display at one time:

Location	Buttons
Toolbar	26 (11 at 640x480 resolution).
Toolbox	60
Total	86

■ If you need more than 86 macros, consider storing the additional macros in a separate Acad.Ini file kept in another subdirectory.

■ Macros are stored in the Acad.Ini file:

Macro Type	Location
Toolbar	[General] section.
Toolbox	[ToolBox] section.

■ You can edit the macros directly by editing the Acad.Ini file with Notepad.

■ Always start the macro with \3\3\3. This ensures that any command currently underway is cancelled. While Autodesk recommends just \3\3, the extra \3 ensures cancellation of "deep" commands, such as **PEdit** and **Dim**. For example:

    AutoCAD Command: \3\3\3pedit

■ The exception to using the \3\3\3 prefix is when you want the macro to operate within another command. For example, to zoom to the previous view during another command:

    AutoCAD Command: 'zoom p

■ Toolbar-toolbox macros cannot pause for user input. To get around this, write two macros: one for before the user input, the other for after user input. For example, to supply the coordinates of a block being repeatedly inserted:

1. Click button 1:   \3\3\3insert

2. [Pick] insertion point.

3. Click button 2:   1 1 0

R11/R12/LT Toolbar Quick Starts

Changing a Toolbar/Toolbox Button

How to make any change to a toolbar or toolbox button:

1. Move the cursor over the button.

2. Press the rightmost button on the mouse. AutoCAD displays the **Toolbar Button Customization** dialog box:

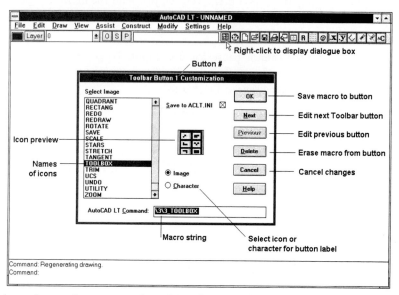

3. Click on the text box next to **AutoCAD Command**.

4. Erase the existing command and type the new command. Writing a macro is very similar to writing a script (see **Script**) but these special characters are allowed:

[Spacebar] Equivalent to the user pressing **[Enter]** at the end of a command name.

For example, **zoom e** results in:

    Command: zoom extents Regenerating drawing.

; (*Semi-colon*) Normally, LT automatically adds a space at the end of the macro; adding the semi-colon suppresses the space.

For example:

    .y;

\2 Toggles the snap mode, just like pressing **[Ctrl]+B** on the keyboard.

For example, **\2line** results in:

    Command: <Snap on> line From point:

■ *Toggle* means to turn on if off, and turn off if on.

■ Note the correlation between the letter 'B' (as in **[Ctrl]+B** being the second letter of the alphabet) and the '2' in the special character \2.

\3   Cancel any command currently underway, like pressing **[Ctrl]+C**.

Useful for ensuring that the macro starts at the 'Command:' prompt.

For example, **\3\3line** results in:

```
Command: *Cancel* line From point:
```

\4   Toggle coordinate display between on and off, like **[Ctrl]+D**.

Caution: Does not toggle relative display mode.

For example, **line\D** results in:

```
Command: line <Coords off> From point:
```

\5   Switch between the three isometric planes, like **[Ctrl]+E**.

Toggles from right to left to top isoplane.

For example, **\5ellipse** results in:

```
Command: <Isoplane top> ellipse
```

\7   Toggle display of the grid between on and off, like **[Ctrl]+G**. For example, **\7insert** results in:

```
Command: <Grid on> insert
```

\8   Backspace, like pressing the **[Backspace]** key.

Caution: Not documented by Autodesk.

\13   Enter, like pressing the **[Enter]** key. R

equired during **DText** command.

Caution: Not documented by Autodesk.

For example:

dtext 2,2 0.5 0 First line\13Second line\13\13;

results in:

```
Command: dext
Justify/Style/<Start point>: 2,2
Height: 0.5
Rotation angle: 0
Text: First line
Text: Second line
Text:
Command:
```

\15   Toggle ortho mode between on and off, like **[Ctrl]+O**.

Caution: Not documented by Autodesk.

\22	Switch to next viewport, like **[Ctrl]+V**.

\22   Switch to next viewport, like **[Ctrl]+V**.

Caution: Not documented by Autodesk.

For example:

     \22zoom w

results in:

     `Command: zoom w`

(The focus is switched to the next viewport).

\n   Start a new line.

     Does *not* work with **DText** command.

\t   Tab; same effect as pressing **[Spacebar]**.

     Caution: Undocumented by Autodesk.

nnn   Any ASCII character *nnn* from 000 to 255.

     Caution: Undocumented byAutodesk.

     For example, to toggle the grid, **\007** is the same as **\7**.

\\   Allows use of the \ (backslash) character in macros, such subdirectory.

     For example,

     fileopen c:\\acltwin\\office.dwg

results in

     `Command: fileopen`
     `Enter name of drawing: c:\acltwin\office.dwg`

5. The *icon* is the small picture that labels the button. To change the icon, select a different name from the list under **Select Image**. (The name of the icon becomes its *tooltip* label.)

     ■ Only toolbar icons can have a letter of the alphabet, rather than an icon.

6. Click on the **OK** button to dismiss the dialog box.

7. Click on the redefined button to check that it works correctly.

QUICK START: Writing a Macro

How to string together more than one command — this is called a *macro*.

1. The **Toolbar Customization** dialog box, below, shows a single button assigned three consecutive commands:

```
AutoCAD Command: zoom e save plot
```

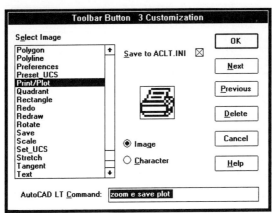

2. This macro replaces the **Plot** button with a useful three-step macro that zooms and saves the drawing before plotting:

- ■ **Zoom E**   Zooms the drawing to its extents.
- ■ **Save**   Saves the drawing.
- ■ **Plot**   Displays the **Plot Configuration** dialog box.

3. With a single click of the button, this macro saves 17 keystrokes or seven menu picks. To access this dialog box, click the rightmost mouse button over the toolbar or toolbox you want to change.

Toolbar

QUICK START: Understanding the INI File

AutoCAD stores the toolbar macros in the Acad.Ini (AcLt.Ini for AutoCAD LT) initialization file. Since INI files are in ASCII format, you can use the Notepad text editor to look at it.

The figure shows the first part of AcLt.Ini from AutoCAD LT:

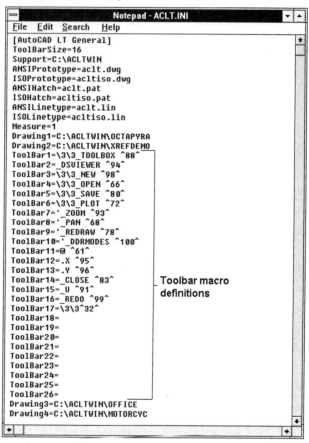

- You'll find the file in the same subdirectory as the AutoCAD executable (Acad.Exe or AcLt.Exe).

- The INI files are commonly used by Windows applications to store program settings between sessions; even Windows itself uses several INI files for its own purposes.

- Every INI file looks slightly different, depending on the settings in effect.

1. Start the NotePad text editor and load the Acad.Ini (or Aclt.Ini) file.

- INI files are often divided into sections.

- Section titles are in square brackets, such as **[AutoCAD LT General]**. It is here that we find the toolbar definitions, for example:

  ```
  ToolBar1=\3\3_TOOLBOX ^88^
  ```

- When AutoCAD loads, it reads the INI file; changes to the INI file do not come into effect until the next time AutoCAD loads.

2. Let's pick this mishmash apart, bit by bit, to see what it means:

Toolbar1= The "1" means this is the first toolbar button.

- Whatever is behind the equals sign in "Toolbar1=" is stuck onto the first toolbar button.

- The second toolbar button is defined by "Toolbar2=" and so on.

\3\3 Two Cancels in a row is like pressing **[Ctrl]+C** twice; this ensures any command in progress is cancelled before executing the macro.

_TOOLBOX The command that toggles the display of the toolbox.

- The underscore (_) internationalizes any English-language AutoCAD command.

- The command can be typed in UPPERCASE or lowercase — it doesn't matter.

(*Space*) There is a space after the command, which AutoCAD automatically appends to the macro: this acts like pressing the **[Enter]** key at the end of a command.

^88^ Specifies the icon displayed by the toolbar button. Number 88 happens to be the 88th bitmap stored by AutoCAD LT .

- The carets (^ ... ^) tell AutoCAD that the 88 refers to the icon and is not part of the macro.

- How do you know which icon number corresponds with which icon number? Not very easily, I'm afraid. Recall that the **Toolbar Button Customization** dialog box presented a list of 91 icon images. Those images are listed in alphabetical order and, by no coincidence, in numerical order. The icon of the Toolbox is the 88th icon in the list. Thus, if you want to a specific icon image, you'll need to count along to find out its number.

3. Let's look at another toolbar definition in the INI file:

```
ToolBar9='_DDLMODES ^56^
```
,
    (*Apostrophe*) Makes the **DdLModes** command transparent.

```
ToolBar13=
```
    This button is undefined since there is nothing behind the equal (=) sign. When you click on the 13th button, nothing happens. As well, the button itself is blank.

QUICK START: Environment Variables

How to edit the Aclt.Ini file with the **SetEnv** and **GetEnv** commands:

1. Type the **SetEnv** command; LT prompts you for the variable name:

```
Command: setenv
Variable name: toolbarsize
```

    ■ LT has one advantage over full-strength AutoCAD with its unique **SetEnv** command; even Release 13 lacks the command.

    ■ **SetEnv** lets you directly manipulate the values in the INI file.

    ■ **ToolBarSize** is the setting in AcLt.Ini (and Acad.Ini) that determines the size of the toolbar icons displayed by AutoCAD R11, R12, LT R1, and R2.

2. LT prompts you for the new value:

```
Value <16>: 24
```

    ■ If the variable exists, LT returns the value in angle brackets, such as <16>; by default, the value of **ToolBarSize** is 16, measured in pixels. You can change the number down to 6 to display more buttons but very tiny icons. Or you can increase the value to 32, which display very large but fewer buttons.

3. Type the new value and press [**Enter**]. AutoCAD records the new value in its INI file.

    ■ The new icon size does not come into effect until AutoCAD starts again.

4. To directly customize buttons on the toolbar:

```
Command: setenv
Variable name: toolbar13
Value: ^C^C_bmake^9^
```

5. Here we have assigned the **BMake** command (short for block make; displays the **Block Definition** dialog box in LT) to toolbar button #13 and uses icon #9, the **Block** icon. In the AcLt.Ini file, this appears as:

```
ToolBar13=^C^C_bmake^9^
```

6. To change the macro, **SetEnv** helpfully displays the current setting, as follows:

```
Command: setenv
Variable name: toolbar13
Value <^C^C_bmake^9^>: ^C^C_block^9^
```

7. The SetEnv command has numerous drawbacks:

■ **SetEnv** cannot cope with spaces. The first space you type ends the command and returns you to the 'Command:' prompt.

■ **SetEnv** only accesses INI items in the first section, **[AutoCAD LT General]**.

■ It cannot access INI items in later sections, such as **[AutoCAD LT ToolBox]**.

■ **SetEnv**does no syntax checking. When you type in an incorrect variable name, such as "ToolBat39=junk," **SetEnv** faithfully records it at the end of the **[AutoCAD LT General]** section.

Toolbar

R13 Toolbar Quick Starts

With Release 13 and LT Release 3, AutoCAD for Windows greatly expanded its toolbox ability. Instead of the one fixed toolbar and one floating toolbox found in previous releases, R13/LT R3 boasts many, many toolbars and icons. Clicking on an icon executes a command; pausing the cursor over the icon displays a tool tag explaining the icon's purpose.

While R13/LT R3 comes with most of its commands in icon form, you can create your own customized icons. To do this, AutoCAD has two commands: **Toolbar** and **TbConfig**.

The **Toolbar** command displays (and hides) one or more or all toolbars. Be careful, though: the **ALL Show** option completely fills your screen!

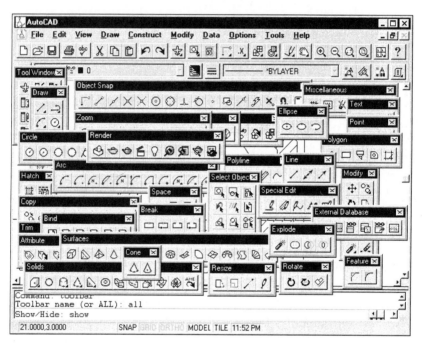

The **Toolbar ALL Hide** command gets rid of them again. To open just a couple of toolbars, select **Tools | Toolbars** from the menu bar.

The **TbConfig** command handles everything about customizing toolbars:

- macro behind the icon; the tooltip;
- location of the icon in the toolbar;
- the look of the icon.

Unfortunately, the customization process is not at all intuitive and involves several dialog boxes. Here's how to do it, step by step:

Creating an R13, LT R3 Toolbar Button

How to create a new toolbar with buuttons:

1. Type the **TbConfig** command. AutoCAD displays the **Toolbars** dialog box, which lists the names of all 50 currently-defined toolbars.

At the bottom of the dialog box, you can change whether AutoCAD displays small or large icons, and whether tooltips are displayed:

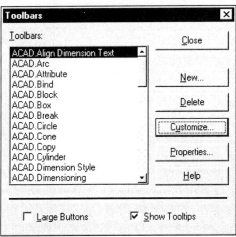

2. Click on the **New** button to create a new toolbar. The **New Toolbar** dialog box appears:

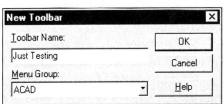

3. Type a name for the toolbar, such as "Just Testing" and click the **OK** button. A tiny, empty toolbar appears on the screen with the name **Just Testing** on the title bar; you'll probably see the first three letters, "Jus".

4. You've created a new toolbar but it is empty. Now you fill it with icons. Click on the

Toolbar dialog box's **Customize** button. AutoCAD displays the **Customize Toolbars** dialog box:

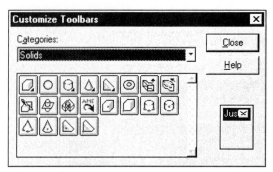

5. The **Categories** drop list box has the names of AutoCAD's groups of icons, such as Object Properties, Standard, and Solids.

■ You may have to hunt around for an icon by selecting one category after another. AutoCAD displays the group of icons associated with each category.

6. Drag an icon from the **Customize Toolbars** dialog box to the **Just Testing** toolbar. As you drag icons, your custom toolbar expands to accommodate the icons:

■ *Drag* means to hold down the left mouse button over the icon, then move the icon to its destination, and let go of the button.

■ If the icon has a small triangle, that means it is a flyout. A *flyout* displays one or more additional icons.

7. You now have a new toolbar with several icons in it.

Customizing an R13 Toolbar Button

How to customize the look and meaning of each icon.

1. Cick on the **Toolbar** dialog box's **Properties** button. AutoCAD displays the **Button Properties** dialog box:

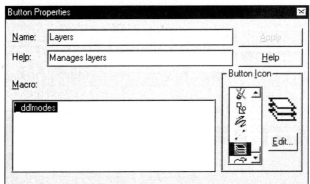

2. To change the action AutoCAD performs when you click on the icon, change the text of the **Macro** area.

3. To change the look of the icon, click on the **Edit** button. AutoCAD displays the **Button Editor**.

The tools along the top (from left to right) let you color individual pixels, draw a straight line, draw a circle, and change a pixel to grey (erase):

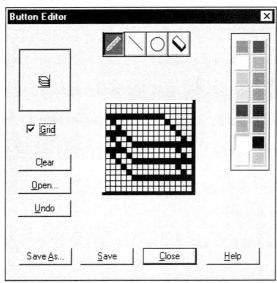

- The button editor lets you edit the icon or create a new one.

- You can insert any BMP (bitmap) file as the icon.

- When done, click on the **Save** and **Close** buttons.

4. Back in the **Button Properties** dialog box, click on the **Apply** button. AutoCAD saves the changes.

5. Test your customziation by clicking on the icon in the **Just Testing** dialog box to make sure it works as you expect.

6. When done, close all remaining dialog boxes related to the toolbox customization.

Introduction to Menu Programming

The menu bar, pop-up cursor menu, and mouse buttons are preconfigured by Autodesk. You can change the command assigned to almost any menu item; as well, you can add more menu items, move the position of menu items, and change the wording of menu items. You *cannot* change the **Edit** and **Help** menus.

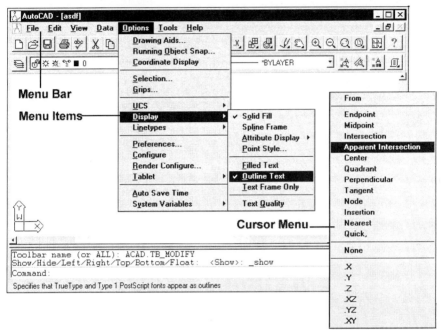

Menus display the following notations:

_   (*Underscore*) Keyboard shortcut; access **Dra<u>w</u>ing Aids** with **[Alt]+O D**

...   (*Ellipsis*) Displays a dialog box, such as **Drawing Aids...** displays the **Drawing Aids** dialog box.

✓   (*Check mark*) Item is toggled on, such as ✓**Outline Text**.

▶   (*Arrowhead*) Displays a child menu, such as **Display ▶**

To display the cursor menu, click the middle mouse button (or **[Shift]+[Right button]**) .

Menu Files

Extension	Meaning
.MNU	Source menu code.
.MNX	Compiled menu (DOS only).
.MNC	Compile menu (Windows only).
.MNR	Resource file (contains bitmaps).
.MNL	AutoLISP code used by menu.
.MND	Menu definitions (used by Mc.Exe).
.MNS	AutoCAD generated source code.

Mouse/Tablet Buttons

By default, the mouse and tablet buttons have the following meaning:

Button	Macro	Meaning	Notes
1	...	[Pick]	Cannot be redefined.
2	;	[Enter]	Rightmost button.
3	$p0=*	Screen menu.	Middle button.
4	^C^C	Cancel.	
5	^B	Snap toggle.	
6	^O	Ortho toggle.	
7	^G	Grid toggle.	
8	^D	Coordinate toggle.	
9	^E	Isoplane toggle.	
10	^T	Table toggle.	

TIPS

■ Button #1 (leftmost button) is always the **[pick]** button and cannot be redefined.

■ On a two-button mouse, press **[Shift]+[right button]** to display the screen menu.

■ The BUTTONS*n* (AUX*n* in LT) sections can be used to define additional functions for the mouse buttons in combination with the **[Ctrl]**, **[Shift]**, and **[Ctrl]+[Shift]** keys.

■ Each TABLET*n* section can have up to 32,766 items.

■ The TABLET1 section of Acad.Mnu has room for 255 boxes.

■ A menu macro can have up to 255 characters of AutoLISP code.

■ AutoCAD LT does not support the tablet toggle (button #10, **[Ctrl]+T**) because LT does not support tablets.

■ The pull-down menus and cursor menu are not available during the following commands: DText, DView, Sketch, VPoint, and Zoom Dynamic.

■ *Change in Release 13*: The ICON section becomes the IMAGE section; the ICON name will no longer be valid in Release 14.

RELATED AUTOCAD COMMANDS

Menu	Loads the menu file.
MenuLoad	(*Release 13 for Windows only*) Loads a portion of the menu.
MenuUnload	(*Release 13 for Windows only*) Unloads a portion of the menu.
Preferences	(*AutoCAD LT only*) Loads the menu file.
ReInit	Reinitializes the digitizer, plotter, Acad.Pgp file, and input-output ports.
Tablet	Configures the tablet.

RELATED SYSTEM VARIABLES

MenuCtrl	Displays side screen menu matching the command typed by user.
MenuEcho	Supresses the display of menu macros in the 'Command:' prompt area.
MenuName	Name of the current menu file.
PopUps	(*Read only*) Determines whether display device is capable of displaying pull-down menus.
Re-Init	Reinitialize input-output devices:

Value	Meaning
1	Digitizer port.
2	Plotter port.
4	Digitizer.
8	Plotter.
16	Reload PGP file.

ScreenBoxes	Number of menu lines displayed by the side screen menu.
TabMode	Tablet mode.
ToolTips	(*Windows only*) Toggles the display of tooltips.

Menu

Menu File Format

Understanding the Menu Structure

1. Load the Acad.Mnu file into the Wordpad text editor.

2. Look at the menu file.

The three different menus (menu bar, cursor menu, and mouse button menu) are defined by section names prefixed by *** (three asterisks)

MENUGROUP

***MenuGroup Name tag definition for use with the loading and unloading of partial menus.

BUTTONS

***Buttons*n* Mouse and digitizer buttons:

Section	Accessed By
***Buttons1	⌒🖰
***Buttons2	[Shift]+⌒🖰
***Buttons3	[Ctrl]+⌒🖰
***Buttons4	[Ctrl]+[Shift]+⌒🖰

***Aux*n* Auxilliary input device; under Windows, defines the system pointing device (mouse) buttons (⌒🖰) in combination with **[Shift]** and **[Ctrl]** keys. As such, the Aux*n* sections should be identical to the Buttons*n* sections:

Section	Accessed By
***Aux1	⌒🖰
***Aux2	[Shift]+⌒🖰
***Aux3	[Ctrl]+⌒🖰
***Aux4	[Ctrl]+[Shift]+⌒🖰

POP MENUS

***Pop0   The cursor menu.

From
Endpoint
Midpoint
Intersection
Apparent Intersection
Center
Quadrant
Perpendicular
Tangent
Node
Insertion
Nearest
Quick.
None
.X
.Y
.Z
.XZ
.YZ
.XY

***Pop*n*   The menu bar; maximum = 16 items.

The default Release 13 menu bar:

<u>F</u>ile   <u>E</u>dit   <u>V</u>iew   <u>D</u>ata   <u>O</u>ptions   <u>T</u>ools   <u>H</u>elp

Section	Accessed By
***Pop1	File
***Pop2	Edit
***Pop3	View
***Pop4	Data
***Pop5	Options
***Pop6	Tools
***Pop7	Help

Menu

TOOLBARS

***Toolbars   The definitions for toolbars.

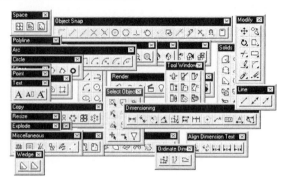

**STANDARD_TOOLBAR

**TB_TOOL_WINDOWS

**TB_SELECT_OBJECTS

**TB_OBJECT_SNAP

**TB_POINT_FILTERS

**TB_UCS

**TB_VIEW

**TB_REDRAW

**TB_PAN

**TB_ZOOM

**TB_SPACE

**TB_OBJECT_PROPERTIES

**TB_INQUIRY

**TB_DRAW

**TB_LINE

**TB_PLINE

**TB_ARC

**TB_CIRCLE

**TB_ELLIPSE

**TB_POLYGON

**TB_POINT

**TB_BLOCK

**TB_HATCH

```
**TB_TEXT
**TB_MODIFY
**TB_COPY
**TB_ROTATE
**TB_RESIZE
**TB_TRIM
**TB_BREAK
**TB_SPECIAL_EDIT
**TB_FEATURE
**TB_EXPLODE
**TB_DIMENSIONING
**TB_DIMRADIAL
**TB_DIMORDINATE
**TB_DIMTEXT
**TB_DIMSTYLE
**TB_SOLIDS
**TB_BOX
**TB_CYLINDER
**TB_CONE
**TB_WEDGE
**TB_SURFACES
**TB_EXTERNAL_REFERENCE
**TB_BIND
**TB_ATTRIBUTE
**TB_RENDER
**TB_EXTERNAL_DATABASE
**TB_MISCELLANEOUS
```

Menu

ICON MENUS

***Image   (*Release 13 only*) Image tiles; known as ***Icon in LT, Release 12 and earlier. *One of the rare icon menus used by Release 13:*

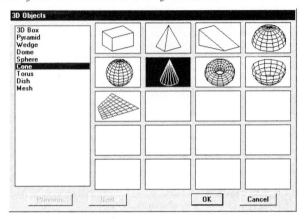

Uses the following format:

```
[3D Objects]
[acad(box3d,3D Box)]^C^Cai_box
```

where:

[3D Objects]   Title of the image (icon) box.

[acad   Name of the Acad.Slb slide library file.

(box3d,   Name of the slide file in SLB.

3D Box)]   Title of the image.

^C^Cai_box   The menu macro activated by selecting the image.

AutoCAD Release 13 Acad.Mnu file includes these image items:

**image_poly

**image_3DObjects (*see figure above*).

**image_vporti

SIDE SCREEN MENU

***Screen   Sidebar screen menu (not available in LT; turned off by default in the Windows versions of AutoCAD.)

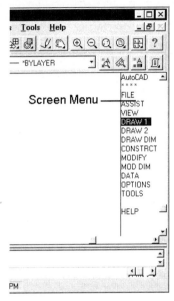

TABLET MENU

***Tablet*n*   Tablet menu; maximum = 4 items; not in LT.

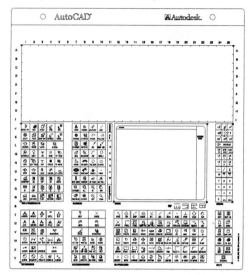

***TABLET1

    **TABLET1STD
    **ENDTAB1
    **TABLET1ALT
    **ENDTAB1A

***TABLET2

    **TABLET2STD
    **ENDTAB2
    **TABLET2ALT
    **ENDTAB2A

***TABLET3

    **TABLET3STD
    **ENDTAB3
    **TABLET3ALT
    **ENDTAB3A

***TABLET4

    **TABLET4STD
    **ENDTAB4
    ***TABLET4ALT
    **ENDTAB4A

HELP TOPICS

***Helpstrings Help text displayed on the status line, such as:

```
ID_New    [Creates a new drawing file]
```

where

ID_New   The menu item's name tag

[Creates a new drawing file]

The text displayed on the status line.

Moving the cursor over a menu item displays help on the status line:

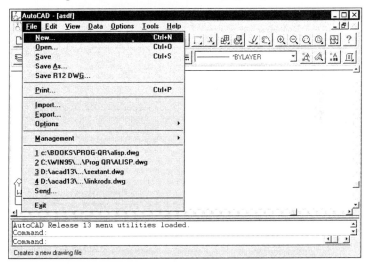

***Accelerators The definition of shortcut keys, including two redefinitions (^O and ^V), using the following format:

```
ID_Undo    [CONTROL+"Z"]
```

Shortcut	Meaning
CTRL+C	Copy (to Clipboard).
CTRL+L	^O (Ortho toggle).
CTRL+N	New.
CTRL+O	Open.
CTRL+P	Print (Plot).
CTRL+R	^V (Viewport toggle).
CTRL+S	Save.
CTRL+V	Paste.
CTRL+X	Cut.
CTRL+Z	Undo.

***Comment Comment section ignored by AutoCAD.

TIPS

■ Each pull-down menu (**POP***n*) can have a maximum of 999 items including all child menu items.

■ The cursor menu (**POP0**) can have a maximum of 499 items.

■ The button menu (**AUX***n*) can have a maximum of 15 items; the meaning of the first button is always **[pick]** and cannot be changed.

■ The resolution of the screen provides a more practical limit, such as 20 items.

■ Interface designers use the rule of "five items, plus or minus two": a minimum of 3, a maximum of 7.

■ The cursor menu (POP0) does not operate unless at least one pull-down menu (POP1) is defined.

■ The pulldown and cursor menus are made automatically wide enough to fit the widest text label.

■ The longest menu bar title is 14 characters.

■ The cursor menu does not display a title bar, unlike the pull-down and icon menus, but still must have a dummy section title.

■ AutoCAD LT forces the **File**, **Edit**, and **Help** items on the menu bar, along with these Windows-specific menu items:

■ If you create menu sections with titles **[File]** and **[Edit]**, LT automatically adds in the above Windows-specific menu items.

■ If you don't have any sections named **[File]** or **[Edit]**, AutoCAD adds the menus shown above. All your menus appear after these first two.

Menu Macro Syntax

Here are all the special characters that AutoCAD menu macros understand:

SECTION CHARACTERS

label   Start of section; for example: *****POP1**. Valid section names are:

Section Name	Meaning
***P0	Cursor menu.
***P1 *thru* *****P16**	Menu bar.
***S	Side screen menu.
***A1 *thru* *****A4**	Auxilliary menus.
***B1 *thru* *****B4**	Mouse/tablet button menus.
***T1 *thru* *****T4**	Tablet menus.
***I	Image (icon) menu.

R13 Windows only:

***ACCELERATORS	Shortcut keys.
***HELPSTRINGS	Status line text.
***MENUGROUP	Menu file group name.
***TOOLBARS	Toolbar definitions.

label   Start a subsection; for example: ****File.

- You can make a label using alphanumerics, $, -, and _.
- Maximum length of a label is 33 characters.

$n=label   Jump to a subsection; for example: **$I=icon_fonts1.**

- AutoCAD remembers a maximum of 8 jumps for the return paths.
- Valid jump-to section names are:

Section Name	Meaning
$P0	Cursor menu.
$P1 *thru* $P16	Menu bar.
$A1 *thru* $A4	Auxilliary menus.
$S	Side screen menu.
$B1 *thru* $B4	Button menus.
$T1 *thru* $T4	Tablet menus.
$I	Image (icon) menu.

$n=*   Display the current subsection; for example: **$P1=***

$n=   Return to previous subsection; for example: **$A1=**

$P*n*.*i*=~   Disable pull-down menu *n* and item *i*; for example: **$P4.3=~**

$P*n*.*i*=   Restore pull-down menu *n* and item *i*; for example: **$P4.3=**

$P@.@=   Restore current pull-down menu item; for example: **$P@.@=**

$P@.*i*=   Restore item *i* of the current pull-down menu for example: **$P@.3=**

MACRO CHARACTERS

\   (*Backslash*) Pause for user input.

Macro continues after you pick a point or press **[Enter]** or **[Spacebar]**.

For example:

```
[Insert Block]insert \\\
```

;   (*Semi-colon*) Equivalent of pressing **[Enter]**.

Easier to see than the space character in macros.

For example:

```
[Insert Block]insert;\\\
```

_   (*Underscore*) Internationalize the command.

For example:

```
[Insert Block]_insert;\\\
```

*   (*Asterisk*) Repeat the command until canceled with **[Ctrl]+C.**

Is equivalent to the **Multiple** command.

For example:

```
[Insert Block]*_insert;\\\
```

'   (*Apostrophe*) Transparent command.

Executes the command within another command.

For example:

```
[Zoom Windows]'_zoom w \\
```

+   (*Plus*) Continue a macro on the next line.

Required for very long macros; see the **+** signs in the example below.

=*   Display top menu (cursor, pull-down, image).

$M=($*code*) Include Diesel code in macro, as shown in **boldface** below (see **Diesel** section):

```
[$(if,$(getvar,dimaso),!.)/vAssociative +
Dimensions]'_dimaso $m=$(-, 1, $(getvar, +
dimaso))
```

CONTROL CHARACTERS

^B   Toggle (turn on and off) snap mode.

Same as pressing [Ctrl]+B or using \2 in a toolbar macro.

'^' is short for [Ctrl].

For example:

```
[Snap Toggle]'^B
```

^C   Cancel the current command.

For example:

```
[Insert Block]^C^C^C_insert;\\\\
```

^D   Toggle the real-time display of coordinates.

^E   Toggle isometric mode.

^G   Toggle grid display.

^H   Backspace to suppress the automatic [Enter].

For example, selecting angle from a menu, where the 'x' is the sacrificial character:

```
[90]90x^H
```

^I   Tab.

^M   Enter (carriage return or newline).

^O   Toggle ortho mode.

^P   Toggle menu echoing.

By default, the menu macro is displayed at the 'Command:' prompt. Adding the ^P to the macro turns off the echoing:

```
[Insert Block]^P^C^C^C_insert;\\\\
```

^Q   Echo output to the printer.

^T   Toggle tablet on or off.

^V   Switch focus to the next viewport.

^Z   Suppress the [Enter] at the end of the macro.

^@   Null character (same as ^Z).

^[Escape character, like ASCII code 27.

^\   File separator.

^]   Group separator.

^^   Record separator.

^_   Unit separator.

Menu

LABEL CHARACTERS

[*label*]   Start of the macro.

For example:

    [Insert Block]insert

[- -]   Draws a separator line in pull-down and cursor menus.

[-> *label*]   Starts a child menu.

[<- *label*]   End of the child menu.

[<-<- *label*] End of child and parent menu.

[~*label*]   Disable the menu item.

Text is displayed in grey and macro does not run; child menus are also disabled.

For example, the **boldface** portions of the following Diesel macro toggle the disabled/enabled state:

    [**$(if,$(getvar**,tilemode)**,~)**Paper + Space]^C^C^C_pspace;

[!c *label*]   Prefix label with a checkmark.

[/*nlabel*]   Underscore the following character (as in label) as shortcut key.

[<*nlabel*]   Format of the text displayed by the menu:

Format	Meaning
<B	Boldface.
<I	Italic.
<O	Outline.
<S	Shadow.
<U	Underlined.

[!*n* *label*]   Display a special character.

Normally, special characters like [, $, and ~ are not displayed because they perform macro functions.

Character	Meaning
!.	Check mark.
!<	Angle bracket.
!-	Dash.
!~	Tilde.
!+	Plus.
![	Open bracket.
!/	Forward slash.
!\	Backslash.
!*	Asterisk.
!$	Dollar.
!=	Equals.
!^	Caret.
!_	Underscore.

Prefixing the special character causes it to be displayed, rather than executed, as shown by the source code (*left*) and the resulting menu, right:

Toolbar Macro Programming

The ***Toolbar** section contains one subsection (such as **Standard_Toolbar**) for every toolbar. Within each subsection is code that displays the icon and executes the macro, such as:

```
**STANDARD_TOOLBAR
ID_Stdtbar  [_Toolbar("Standard Toolbar",_Top,_Show,0,38,1)]
ID_New      [_Button("New", ICON_16_NEW, ICON_32_NEW)]^C^C_new
```

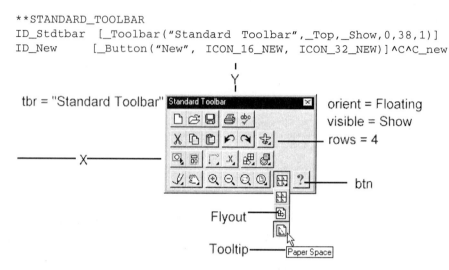

Each subsection can contain one or more of the following types of code:

TOOLBAR HEADER

The toolbar header describes the paramters of the toolbar:

```
tag [Toolbar ("tbr", orient, visible, x, y, rows)]
```

tag	Name tag that associates help information with the toolbar item, such as ID_Stdtbar (see ***Helpstrings**).
"tbr"	Wording for the toolbar's title bar, such as "Standard Toolbar".
orient	Initial orientation of the toolbar: floating, top, bottom, left, right.
visible	Initial visibility of the toolbar: show, hide.
x	Initial horizontal location of the toolbar, measured in pixels from left of screen to right of toolbar.
y	Initial vertical location of the toolbar, measured in pixels from top of screen to top of toolbar.
rows	Number of rows of icon buttons (the total number of icons automatically determines the number of columns).

For example:

```
ID_TbDraw  [_Toolbar("Draw",_Floating,_Show,1,101,5)]
```

BUTTON DEFINITION

> *tag* [**Button** (*"btn"*, *small*, *large*)] *macro*

"btn"   Wording for the tooltip.

small   Name of the 16x16-pixel bitmap.

large   Name of the 32x32-pixel bitmap.

macro   The menu macro to execute when user selects this button.

For example:

```
ID_Mlstyle [_Button("Multiline Style",ICON_16_MSTYLE,
    ICON_32_MSTYLE)]^C^C_mlstyle
```

FLYOUT DEFINITION

> *tag* [**Flyout** (*"fly"*, *small*, *large*, *flag*, *jump*)] *macro*

"fly"   Wording for the flyout's tooltip, such as "New".

small   Name of the 16x16-pixel bitmap.

large   Name of the 32x32-pixel bitmap.

flag   Display same icon or last icon selected by user: ownicon, othericon

jump   Name of the toolbar subsection (such as ****TB_VIEW**) to jump to and display as the flyout row of icons.

macro   The menu macro to execute when user selects this button.

For example:

```
ID_TbInq [_Flyout("Inquiry", ICON_16_LIST, ICON_32_LIST,
    _OtherIcon, ACAD.TB_INQUIRY)]
```

CONTROL DEFINITION

> *tag* [**Control** (*type*)]

type   One of three hardwired drop boxes: layer, linetype, color

For example:

```
ID_Layer [_Control(_Layer)]
```

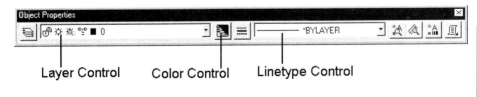

Layer Control   Color Control   Linetype Control

Menu Programming Quick Starts

QUICK START: Reloading a Menu File

How to load the menu file into AutoCAD after making a change:

1. Start a text editor, such as Wordpad (Notepad cannot handle such a large file).

2. Load the Acad.Mnu file, which contains the source code for the menus:

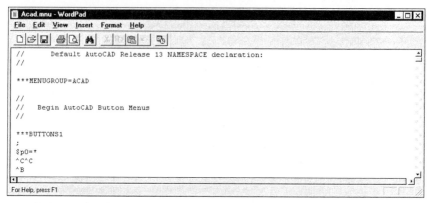

3. Make your editing changes.

4. Save the menu file by another name, such as MyMenu.Mnu.

5. Load the MyMenu.Mnu file with the **Menu** command.

```
Command: menu
Menu file name or . for none <acad>: mymenu
Menu loaded successfully. MENUGROUP: mymenu
Command:
AutoCAD Release 13 menu utilities loaded.
```

QUICK START: Creating a Simple Menu

How to create a custom menu:

1. Start the Notepad editor.

2. Decide what kind of menu you want to create – pulldown menu, cursor menu, button menu, or icon menu – then write the label, such as:

```
***POP1
```

3. Give the menu item a name using these characters:

[ ]	(*Square brackets*) Name the menu item.
/*n*	Underline a character for the **[Alt]**+*n* keyboard shortcut.

For example:

```
***POP1
[/FFile]
```

creates the <u>F</u>ile item on the menu bar:

4. To have a menu item execute an AutoCAD command, type the command at the appropriate spot in the Aclt.Mnu file. For example, here is the <u>N</u>ew command added under the **File** item on the menu bar:

```
***POP1
[/FFile]
[/NNew...] ^C^C_new
```

5. The menu macro has the following syntax:

[	Start of label.
/N	Underline the N.
New	Label name.
...	Alerts user that this will open a dialog box.
]	End of label.
^C^C	As with toolbar macros, it is prudent to start commands with a pair of cancels. Instead of \3\3, menu macros use ^C^C.
_	(*Underscore*) Internationalize the command.
New	The **New** command (finally!).

6. Save the menu file with the MNU extension and load into AutoCAD with the **Menu** command.

QUICK START: Advanced Menu Tricks

How to create child and sub menus, and toggle a check mark:

1. To create the child menu, use the -> and <- code, as follows:

```
[--]
[->/IImport/Export]
[/VView Slide...]^C^C_vslide
...
[<-/PBMP Out...]^C^C_savedib
```

> ■ ->   Adds the ▶ character and triggers the child menu.
> ■ <-   Indicates the last item of the child menu.
> ■ [--]   Draws a horizontal line between menu items.

2. Save the menu macro, then load menu file into AutoCAD.

3. Click on the **Import/Export ▶** menu item displays the child menu:

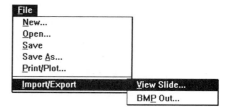

4. Related to the child menu is the submenu. This is where AutoCAD branches off to another part of the menu file:

```
...
[/TText Style...]$I=icon_fonts1 $I=*
...
***icon
**icon_fonts1
[Select Text Font]
[aclt(romans,Roman Simplex)]'_style romans romans
```

5. The boldface text, above, creates the jump to an icon submenu named "icon_fonts1" using these elements: **$I=*icon_fonts1*

> ■ $ Jump.
> ■ I   Type of submenu: Icon menu.
> ■ =   Name of the submenu, "icon_fonts1" in this case.

**icon_fonts1* Start of the submenu section.

- **$I=***   Displays the currently loaded menu; in this case, **icont_fonts1.
- **$I=**   Returns to the previous menu.

5. Clicking on ✓**Associative Dimensions** turns the check mark on and off:

!.   Prefix label with a check mark; for example:

```
!./vAssociative Dimensions
```

6. To display the checkmark is easy but turning the check mark on and off is tricky and requires the use of Diesel programming.

```
[$(if,$(getvar,dimaso),!.)/vAssociative Dimensions]'_dimaso
$m=$(-,1,$(getvar,dimaso))
```

The code shown above is a combination of menu macro code and Diesel programming code. The code checks whether system variable **DimAso** is 1 (on = show check mark) or 0 (off = don't display check mark). For more information, see the **Diesel** section.

- ■ The quick-start workaround is to copy the elements shown in **boldface**. Replace the parts in *italic* with the appropriate text and system variables. For example, here is the same code for toggling the grid:

```
[$(if,$(getvar,gridmode),!.)/GGrid Markings]'_gridmode
$m=$(-,1,$(getvar,gridmode))
```

- ■ The macro is one long line; don't split it into two lines in your menu file!

QUICK START: Designing an Icon Menu

The icon menu looks a bit like a dialog box, with a text list (at the left) and up to 16 "icon" image tiles on the right. The images are *not* icons (as on toolbar buttons); instead, they are small slides made with the **MSlide** command and **SlideLib.Exe** utility program.

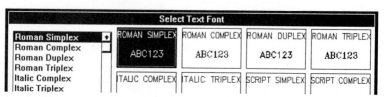

AutoCAD automatically generates the icon menu using just three macro programming elements:

How to create an icon menu:

1. AutoCAD automatically generates the icon menu using just three macro programming elements. Open the MNU file and start with an ***icon** section:

```
***icon
```

The icon section holds all icon menus.

2. Each separate icon menu starts with the ** (submenu section) tag. Start the icon menu with an ****icon_name*, such as:

```
**icon_fonts1
```

3. For the icon menu's title bar, place a label in square brackets, such as:

```
[Select Text Font]
```

4. Finally, a list of image tiles (shown in boldface) and related macro:

```
[aclt(romans,Roman Simplex)]'_style romans romans
```

This icon menu macro, taken from the Aclt.Mnu file, helps you select a text style. When you click on the picture of the RomanS font or select "Roman Simplex" from the list, AutoCAD runs the **Style** command. Here's what the elements mean:

[aclt   Name of the slide library file, Aclt.Slb.

(romans, Name of the slide image, the icon.

Roman Simplex)]

The label text.

'_style Start the macro with the **Style** command.

romans romans

Answer the first two **Style** command prompts with the name of the text style, RomanS.

QUICK START: Converting Slides into Icons

How to create slides for the icon menu:

1. To fit the area provided for the icon, the slide should have an aspect ratio of 2:3. Start AutoCAD with a new drawing and set up a viewport with the 2:3 aspect ratio. Use these commands:

```
Tilemode 0
MView 0,0 3,2
Zoom Extents
MSpace
Fillmode 0
```

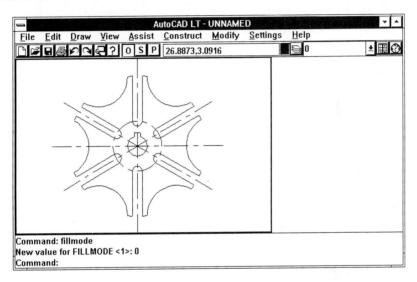

2. Draw the symbol or import a drawing with the **Insert** command.

3. After drawing the symbol in AutoCAD, save the image as an SLD slide file with the **MSlide** command.

4. Use the Notepad text editor to create the list of slide files to convert into a slide library file.

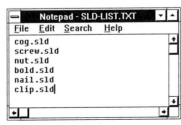

5. Save the file by any name with a TXT extension, such as Sld-List.Txt, in the \Acltwin subdirectory.

6. Double-click on the DOS icon in the Program Manager:

7. Change to the \acadr13\com\support (or \Acltwin subdirectory for AutoCAD LT) and run the **SlideLib** program ("parts" is the name of the slide library file, Parts.Slb):

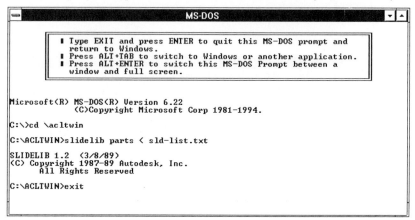

```
C:\> cd \acltwin
C:\acltwin\> slidelib parts < sld-list.txt
```

■ The SlideLib program creates the Parts.Slb slide library from the SLD slide files listed in the Sld-List.Txt file.

8. Exit from DOS back to Windows:

```
C:\acltwin\> exit
```

9. Write the menu macro to display the icons:

```
***icon
**icon_parts
[parts(cog,Six Segment Cog)]^C^Cinsert;cog;\\\
```

10. Save the MNU file and load with the **Menu** command. Test the command:

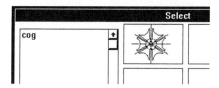

Introduction to Shape Programming

Autodesk first introduced shape (and custom text fonts) programming in AutoCAD version 1.0. The purpose is to create highly effecient symbols. However, blocks have taken over from shapes as the primary means of creating and placing symbols.

The source code for shapes and fonts is stored in SHP files. The first time you load a shape file (shapes with the **Load** command; fonts with the **Style** command), AutoCAD compiles the SHP file on-the-fly into a compiled SHX file. (AutoCAD also compiles PFB PostScript and TTF TrueType font files on-the-fly.)

Shapes (and fonts) are highly efficient; they take up very small amounts of memory. However, they are difficult to code.

TIPS

- The maximum length of an SHP file is 128 characters.

- More than one line of data can define a shape to a maximum of 2,000 characters.

- Use the ; (semi-colon) for comments; blank lines are ignored.

- A regular SHP file is limited to defining 258 shapes; to create more, start a second SHP file or use the BigFont specification, which allows 65,535 shapes.

- Three shape numbers are reserved for the following characters:

Number	Identifier
256	Degree_Sign
257	Plus_Or_Minus_Sign
258	Diameter_Symbol

- Shape names must be in UPPERCASE; lowercase characters are ignored.

- When the first character is a 0 (zero) the following two represent a hexadecimal value.

- All shapes are drawn to unit size. This allows easy scaling upon placement in a drawing.

Shape

Shape File Format

A shape definition consists of two or more lines: (1) one header line; and (2) one or more data lines, with the last line terminated by a 0 (zero). For example:

```
*150,8,FEEDTHRU
1,020,02C,028,024,2,04C,0
```

HEADER LINE
The header line has the following format:

> *nbr,bytes,NAME

*   (*Asterisk*) Signals the start of a new shape definition.

nbr   Each shape in the SHP file must have a unique number between 1 and 125.

■ Three shape numbers are reserved:

Number	Identifier
256	Degree_Sign
257	Plus_Or_Minus_Sign
258	Diameter_Symbol

■ Text font shapes should have a number corresponding to their ASCII code, such as 65 for letter A.

,   (*Comma*) Separator.

bytes   The number of bytes used to define the shape, including the terminating 0.

■ AutoCAD is limited to 2,000 bytes per shape definition (does not include the header line nor the commas.

■ The shape data below contains eight bytes of data:

> 1,020,02C,028,024,2,04C,0

NAME   The name of the shape.

■ This is the name displayed by the **Load ?** command.

■ Shape name must be in UPPERCASE characters.

■ Any part of the shape name in lowercase characters is ignored by AutoCAD and can be used for comments.

DATA LINES

The data lines have the following format:

```
byte1,byte2,...,0
```

byte1   The shape specification byte.

- The *byte* is a code number that specifies either: (1) a special code; or (2) the vector length and direction.

- A byte can be in decimal or hexadecimal (prefixed by a 0).

- Each line of data can be maximum of 128 characters.

- Total number of bytes cannot exceed 2,000.

,   (*Comma*) Separator.

0   (*Zero*) Required terminator.

VECTOR CODES

The shape data is either a vector code or a special code. The vector code is a three-digit code that specifies the length and the direction, such as 04A, in the format of:

```
0 length direction
```

0   (*Zero*) All vector codes are expressed only in hexadecimal; the 0 signals AutoCAD that the following code is a hexadecimal number.

length   The length of the vector in the range of 1 to 15 units long.

- A vector cannot be 0 units long.

- Expressed in hexadecimal:

Length	Hex Code
1 units	1
2 units	2
3 units	3
4 units	4
5 units	5
6 units	6
7 units	7
8 units	8
9 units	9
10 units	A
11 units	B
12 units	C
13 units	D
14 units	E
15 units	F

Shape

direction   One of 16 fixed directions, 22.5 degrees apart:

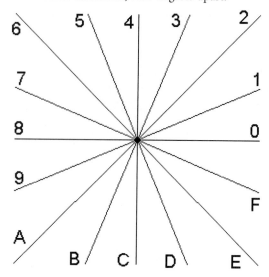

■ Vectors are "stretched" to the length shown in the figure, above. Thus, a vector in the A direction is longer than a vector in the C direction.

Code	Direction
0	0.0 degrees
1	22.5 degrees
2	45.0 degrees
3	67.5 degrees
4	90.0 degrees
5	112.5 degrees
6	135.0 degrees
7	157.5 degrees
8	180.0 degrees
9	202.5 degrees
A	225.0 degrees
B	247.5 degrees
C	270.0 degrees
D	292.5 degrees
E	315.0 degrees
F	337.5 degrees

SPECIAL CODES

The shape data is either a vector code or a special code. The special code is a three-digit code that specifies a variety of actions, such as defining arcs and subshapes, in the format of:

> [0 0] code

0   (*Zero; optional*) All vector codes are expressed in hexadecimal or decimal; the 0 signals AutoCAD that the following are hexadecimal numbers.

0   (*Zero; optional*) Padding. This zero is only used when the first zero is used.

code   A code number that specifies an action:

Meaning	Bytes	Decimal	Hex Code
End of shape definition.	1	0	000
Pen down.	1	1	001
Pen up.	1	2	002
Divide length.	2	3	003
Multiply length.	2	4	004
Push location on stack.	1	5	005
Pop location off stack.	1	6	006
Draw subshape.	2	7	007
X,y-offset.	3	8	008
Multiple x,y-offisets.	*n*	9	009
Octant arc.	3	10	00A
Fractional arc.	6	11	00B
Buldged arc.	4	12	00C
Multiple buldged arc.	*n*	13	00D
Vertical text.	2	14	00E

Shape

End of shape: 0 *or* 000

Shape code: Signals the end of the shape definition (*1 byte*).

Example

```
1,020,02C,028,024,2,04C,0
```

PARAMETERS

none

SAMPLE CODE

The code **0** ends the shape definition:

```
*128,8,CON1
3,20,032,0A0,06C,0A8,036,0
```

TIPS

■ The 0 (zero) is the last byte of a shape definition.

■ When a shape definition spans several lines, the 0 terminates only the last line.

■ When counting the total number of bytes in a shape definition, remember to include this termination byte.

RELATED SHAPE CODES

2 or **002**   Pen up. Stop drawing and move to another location without drawing vectors.

9 or **009**   Multiple x,y-offsets. This series of offsets must be terminated with a (0,0).

13 or **00D**   Multiple bulge arc. This polyarc must be terminated with a (0,0).

Pen down: [1,] 0*ld*, *[...]*

Shape code: Draws vectors; the default shape command (*1 or more bytes*).

Example	Result
1,020,02C,028,024,2,04C,0	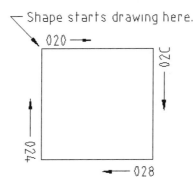

PARAMETERS
- **0*ld***   The vector code that indicates the direction and distance to draw.
- **,**   (*Comma*) Separator.

SAMPLE CODE
The code **1,020,02C,028,024** draws the four sides of the square:

```
*150,8,FEEDTHRU
1,020,02C,028,024,2,04C,0
```

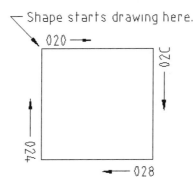

TIPS
- When a shape does not start with any code, AutoCAD assumes the Pen down code.
- All of the bytes following are vector length-direction codes.
- The shape keeps drawing vectors until it encounters another special code or a 0 (terminator) code.

RELATED SHAPE CODES
2 *or* **002**	Pen up. Move to another location without drawing vectors.
7 *or* **007**	Draw subshape.
10 *or* **00A**	Draw octant arc.
11 *or* **00B**	Draw fractional arc.
12 *or* **00C**	Draw bulge arc.
13 *or* **00D**	Draw polyarc.

Shape

Pen up: 2, 0*ld*, [...]

Shape code: Moves in the direction indicated by vector codes (*2 or more bytes*).

Example

```
3,20,040,2,054,1,0AC,2,054,070,1,058
```

PARAMETERS

■ **0*ld***   The vector code that indicates the direction and distance to move.

■ **,**   (*Comma*) Separator.

SAMPLE CODE

The code 2,080 (occurs twice) moves the pen up while drawing a PNP transistor:

```
*132,19,PNP
3,20,080,084,2,080,1,028,06A,0AC,2,080,1,028
066,03F,037,03D,0
```

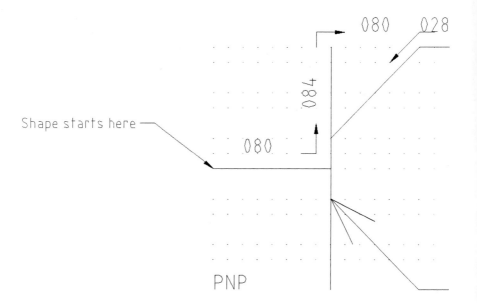

TIPS

■ All of the bytes following are vector length-direction codes.

■ The shape keeps moving according to the vectors until it encounters another special code or a 0 (terminator) code.

RELATED SHAPE CODE

0 *or* **000**   Terminator. End of shape definition.

Divide length: 3, *int*

Shape code: Divides all vectors by the following number (*2 bytes*).

Example

`3,20,080,084,2,080,1,028,06A,0AC,2,080,1,028`

PARAMETERS

- *int*   The divisor; an integer that ranges from 1 to 255.

- ,   (*Comma*) Separator.

SAMPLE CODE

The code 3,20 draws a PNP shape 20 times smaller than unit size:

```
*132,19,PNP
3,20,080,084,2,080,1,028,06A,0AC,2,080,1,028
066,03F,037,03D,0
```

TIPS

- When a divide or multiple scale factor is not provided, the shape is drawn at unit size.

- The dividing scale factor is cummulative: 3,20 followed later by 3,10 results in dividing by 200.

- Use the Multipling scale factor (4 or 004) code to reset the scale factor.

RELATED SHAPE CODE

4 *or* **004**   Multiple length. Scale factor.

Shape

Multiple length: 4,*int*

Shape code: Multiplies all vectors by the following number; acts like a scale factor (*2 bytes*).

Example

`4,20,080,084,2,080,1,028,06A,0AC,2,080,1,028`

PARAMETERS

- *int*   The multiplier; an integer that ranges from 1 to 255.
- ,   (*Comma*) Separator.

SAMPLE CODE

The code 4,20 draws a PNP transistor 20 times larger than unit size:

```
*132,19,PNP
4,20,080,084,2,080,1,028,06A,0AC,2,080,1,028
066,03F,037,03D,0
```

TIPS

- When a divide or multiple scale factor is not provided, the shape is drawn at unit size.
- The scale factor is cummulative: 4,5 followed later by 4,10 results in dividing by 50.
- Use the dividing scale factor (3 or 003) code to reset the scale factor.

RELATED SHAPE CODE

3 *or* 003   Divide length. Reducing scale factor.

Push onto stack: 5

Shape code: Stores the current location (*1 byte*).

Example

`5,7,150,7,150,0`

PARAMETERS

none

TIPS

- Use this function as a memory, to store the current coordinates for later use.
- This function is limited to four memories: you can store four locations.
- "Push onto the stack" means to store data in memory.
- "Pop off the stack" means to recall data from memory.
- The *stack* is a crude form of memory also used by some older PRN-style HP calculators.
- This function acts in FILO (first in, last out) manner: the last location pushed onto the stack becomes the first location popped off the stack.
- The number of pushes (stores) and pops (recalls) must balance in the shape definition.

ERROR MESSAGES

- When your code attempts to push more than four times (without an intervening pop) or attempts to pop (without any pushes) more than four times, the AutoCAD compiler complains, "Position stack overflow in shape *n*".
- When your code pops more times than there are pushes, the AutoCAD compiler complains, "Position stack underflow in shape *n*".

RELATED SHAPE CODE

6 *or* **006**   Pop off stack.

Shape

Pop off stack: 6

Shape code: Recalls a location (*1 byte*).

Example

6,7,150,7,150,0

PARAMETERS

none

TIPS

- Use this function as a memory, to recall the current coordinate.

- This function is limited to four memories: you can recall four locations.

- "Pop off the stack" means to recall data from memory.

- "Push onto the stack" means to store data in memory.

- The *stack* is a crude form of memory also used by some older PRN-style HP calculators.

- This function acts in FILO (first in, last out) manner: the last location pushed onto the stack becomes the first location popped off the stack.

- The number of pushes (stores) and pops (recalls) must balance in the shape definition.

ERROR MESSAGES

- When your code attempts to push more than four times (without an intervening pop) or attempts to pop (without any pushes) more than four times, the AutoCAD compiler complains, "Position stack overflow in shape *n*".

- When your code pops more times than there are pushes, the AutoCAD compiler complains, "Position stack underflow in shape *n*".

RELATED SHAPE CODE

5 *or* 005   Push onto stack.

Draw subshape: 7, *shp*

Shape code: Draws a shape referenced elsewhere in the SHP file (*2 bytes*).

Example
```
3,40,016,7,150,7,150,7,150,7,150,2,0C2,044,7,150,7,150,7,150,7,150,0
```

PARAMETERS
- *shp*   The number of another shape in the same SHP file; ranges from 1 to 255.
- ,   (*Comma*) Separator.

SAMPLE CODE
Shape #150 draws a square and moves down by an offset distance of 4 (2,04C):
```
*150,8,FEEDTHRU
1,020,02C,028,024,2,04C,0
```
Shape #151 now references shape #150 to draw eight squares in two rows.
```
*151,23,DIP8
3,40,                        ; Scale 40 times smaller.
016,                         ; Draw 1 unit at 135 degrees.
7,150,7,150,7,150,7,150,     ; Draw subshape 150 four times.
2,0C2,044,                   ; Move C (12) units at 45 degrees
                             ; and up 4 units.
7,150,7,150,7,150,7,150,     ; Draw subshape another 4 times.
0                            ; Terminate shape definition.
```
By drawing subshapes, shape #151 saves 40 bytes.

Shape #150 (FEEDTRHU)   Shape #151 (DIP8)

TIPS
- This function is a way of getting around the 2,000 byte limitation of shape definitions.
- The subshape must exist in the same SHP file.

RELATED SHAPE CODE
1 *or* 001   Draw vectors.

Shape

X,y-offset: 8, (x, y)

Shape code: Moves or draws using a 255-byte coordinate system (*3 bytes*).

Examples

8,-31,56
008,(-31,56)
8,(-31,+56)

PARAMETERS

- x The x-direction; an integer that ranges from -128 to 127.
- y The y-direction; an integer that ranges from -128 to 127.
- ,   (*Comma*) Separator.
- (...)   (*Optional*) Parentheses to enclose the x,y-offset; for easier reading of code.
- +   (*Optional*) Plus sign to indicate positive direction.

SAMPLE CODE

```
*49,27,nl
2,14,8,(-10,-21),14,5,8,(6,17),1,33,50,8,(0,-21),
  2,8,(9,0),14,6,14,8,(10,-9),0
```

TIPS

- Since draw (1 or 001) and move (2 or 002) codes are limited to 16 directions and 15 units, this function allows a greater range of movement.
- This function can be used to draw or to move.
- The 8 (or 008) code must be followed by the x and y displacement.
- To aid in easier reading of the code, use the optional parentheses (to enclose the x,y-offset) and plus sign (for positive directions).
- The x,y offsets are limited in range from -128 to +127.
- After executing the offset, the shape returns to draw mode (0 or 001) by default.

RELATED SHAPE CODES

9 *or* **009**   Multiple offsets.

1 *or* **001**   Pen down. Draw vectors.

2 *or* **002**   Pen up. Move to another location without drawing vectors.

Multiple offsets: 9, (*x, y*), (*x, y*), ... , (0,0)

Shape code: Move or draw using a list of vectors (*7 or more bytes*).

Examples

9,-31,56,15,-8,0,0
009,(-31,56),(15,-8),(0,0)
9,(-31,+56),(+15,-8),(0,0)

PARAMETERS

- *x*   The x-direction; an integer that ranges from -128 to 127.
- *y*   The y-direction; an integer that ranges from -128 to 127.
- ,   (*Comma*) Separator.
- (...)   (*Optional*) Parentheses to enclose the x,y-offset; for easier reading of code.
- +   (*Optional*) Plus sign to indicate positive direction.
- (0,0)   Terminator; indicates the end of the vector list.

SAMPLE CODE

```
1,014,8,(-10,-21),(14,5),(6,17),(1,33),(50,8),(0,-21),
    (2,8),(9,0),(14,6),(14,8),(10,-9),(0,0),0
```

TIPS

■ Since draw (1 or 001) and move (2 or 002) codes are limited to 16 directions and 15 units, this function allows a greater range of movement.

■ This function can be used to draw or move several times, based on the vector list following.

■ The 9 (or 009) code must be terminated by the x and y displacement of (0,0).

■ To aid in easier reading of the code, use the optional parentheses (to enclose the x,y-offset) and plus sign (for positive directions).

■ The x,y offsets are limited in range from -128 to +127.

RELATED SHAPE CODES

8 *or* 008	X,y-offset.
13 *or* 00D	Multiple-bulge arc.
1 *or* 001	Pen down. Draw vectors.
2 *or* 002	Pen up. Move to another location without drawing vectors.

Shape

Octant arc: 10,*rad,0se*

Shape code: Draws an arc with an angle in $^{PI}/_4$ increments (octants).

Examples

10,17,004
00A,245,-025

PARAMETERS

- **rad**   The radius of the arc; an integer that ranges from 1 to 255 units.
- **,**   (*Comma*) Separator.
- **0se**   The starting (variable *s*) and ending (variable *e*) octants of the arc;

  s and *e* are integers range from 0 (0 degrees) to 7 (315 degrees), in standard AutoCAD direction — starting at East, positive in the counterclockwise direction:

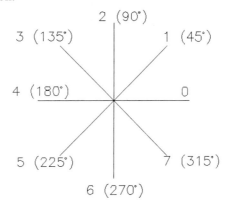

SAMPLE CODE

The following code draws a 16-unit radius, 225-degree arc shape that starts at 0 (0 degrees) and end at 5 (225 degrees):

```
10,(16,005)
```

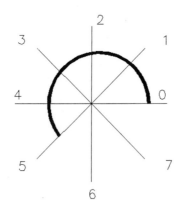

TIPS

- This function is limited to drawing an arc in 45-degree increments.
- For finer control, use the fractional arc (11 or 00B).
- Use a negative number to draw the arc shape clockwise, such as 10,(16,-005).
- To draw a full circle, use the 000 code, such as 10,(16,000).

RELATED SHAPE CODES

11 *or* 00B	Fractional arc.
12 *or* 00C	Bulge arc.
13 *or* 00D	Multiple bulge arc.

Shape

Fractional arc: 11, (*s, e, hrad, rad, 0se*)

Shape code: Draws an arc, with finer start and end points than octant arc (*6 bytes*).

Examples

11,0,0,0,10,004
11,(0,0,0,10,004)
00B,24,5,-025

PARAMETERS

■ *s* The arc's starting distance from an octant.

    Equals 0 when start point is on an octant.

■ , (*Comma*) Separator.

■ (...) (*Optional*) Parentheses to enclose the data for easier reading of code.

■ + (*Optional*) Plus sign to indicate positive direction.

■ *e* The arc's ending distance from an octant.

    Equals 0 when endpoint is on an octant.

■ *hrad* The most-significant 8 bits of the radius.

    Equals 0 when *rad* is 255 or less.

■ *rad* The radius of the arc.

    An integer that ranges from 1 to 255 units.

■ 0*se* The starting (s) and ending (e) octants of the arc.

    Integers that range from 0 (0 degrees) to 7 (315 degrees).

TIPS

■ Use this function to draw a finer arc than provided by the octant arc (10 or 00A).

■ To calculate the *s* or *e* parameter, use the following formula:

```
fix((start-or-end-of-arc)-(nearest-lower-octant)*(256/45))
```

where the start (or end) of arc is in degrees.

■ For example, for an arc to start at 30 degrees:

```
(30 - 0) * (256 / 45) = 170.67 = 170
```

■ For an arc to end at 72 degrees:

```
(72 - 45) * (256 / 45) = 153.60 = 153
```

■ When the frational arc starts (or ends) on an octant, *s* (and *e*) equal 0.

■ AutoCAD adds the value of the *s* (or *e*) parameter to the octant value specified by the 0*se* parameter.

Bulge arc: 12, (*x, y, b*)

Shape code: Draws an arc by applying a bulge factor to a vector (*4 bytes*).

Examples

12,0,5,127
00C,0,5,127
12,(0,5,-127)

PARAMETERS

- **x**   The x-distance from the start to the end of the arc.
- **y**   The y-distance from the start to the end of the arc.
- **b**   The bulge of the arc, an integer that ranges from -127 to 127.
- **,**   (*Comma*) Separator.
- **(...)**   (*Optional*) Parentheses to enclose the data; for easier reading of code.
- **+**   (*Optional*) Plus sign to indicate positive direction.

TIPS

- The largest arc this function can draw is limited to a half-circle, 180 degrees (*b* = 127).
- To draw an arc longer than 180 degrees, draw two bulge arcs in a row.
- When *b* = 0, this function draws a straight line (flat arc).
- The bulge is calculated from the x,y-offset (D) and the perpendicular height (H) using the following formula:

      bulge = fix ((2 * H/D) * 127)

When the x,y-offset is 2,3 and the height is 0.5, then the bulge works out to:

      bulge = ((2 * 0.5/3.6056) * 127) = 35.22 = 35

- The distance D is calculated from the square root of $x^2 + y^2$, or sqrt(2^2+3^2) = 3.6056.

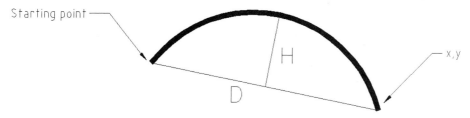

Starting point —   H   x,y   D

RELATED SHAPE CODES

10 *or* **00A**   Octant arc.

11 *or* **00B**   Fractional arc.

13 *or* **00D**   Multiple bulge arc.

Multiple bulge arc: 13, (*x, y, b*), (*x, y, b*), ... , (0,0)

Shape code: Draw two or more arcs by applying a bulge factor to a vector (*9 or more bytes*).

Examples

13,0,5,127,0,5,-127,0,0
00D,0,5,127,(0,5,-127),(0,0)
13,(0,5,-127),(0,5,127),(0,0)

PARAMETERS

- *x*   The x-distance from the start to the end of the arc.
- *y*   The y-distance from the start to the end of the arc.
- *b*   The bulge of the arc, an integer that ranges from -127 to 127.
- ,   (*Comma*) Separator.
- (...)   (*Optional*) Parentheses to enclose the data; for easier reading of code.
- +   (*Optional*) Plus sign to indicate positive direction.
- (0,0)   Terminator.

TIPS

- The largest arc this function can draw is limited to a half-circle, 180 degrees (*b* = 127); to draw an arc longer than 180 degrees, draw two bulge arcs in a row.
- When *b* = 0, this function draws a straight line (flat arc).
- This code must be terminated with (0,0).

RELATED SHAPE CODES

10 *or* 00A	Octant arc.
11 *or* 00B	Fractional arc.
12 *or* 00C	Bulge arc.

Vertical text: 14

Shape code: Vertical text processing flag (*1 flag*).

Example
14

PARAMETERS
none

SAMPLE CODE
The code for a text character ends with a move (code 8 or 008: x,y-displacement) to the next character's start point; this is how AutoCAD implements inter-character spacing. In vertical text, this is unnessary since the next character occurs below. The following code draws the uppercase letter A:

```
*65,39,uca
2,14,8,(-9,-21),      ; X,y-offset
14,5,                 ; Push to stack
8,(9,21),             ; X,y-offset
1,8,-8,-21,           ; Draw vector
2,8,8,21,             ; Move
1,8,8,-21,            ; Draw vector
2,8,-13,7,            ; Move
1,160,                ; Draw vector
2,8,4,-7,             ; Move
14,6,                 ; Pop off stack
14,8,(9,-9),0         ; X,y-offset and terminate.
```

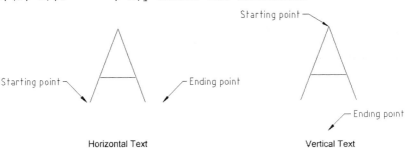

Horizontal Text   Vertical Text

TIPS
■ This function only works with a text font that is designed for horizontal and vertical orientations.

■ This function acts like a conditional:

Text orientation	Action
Horizontal	Skip next code.
Vertical	Process next code.

Shape

Introduction to DCL Programming

Autodesk first introduced DCL (short for dialog control language) programming in AutoCAD Release 11 for Windows as an undocumented feature. Part of a project code-named "Proteus," the purpose of DCL is to be syntax for creating platform-independent dialog boxes.

*The **Drawing Modes** dialog box from AutoCAD running under DOS:*

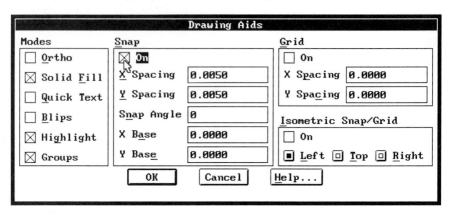

The same dialog box in AutoCAD Windows:

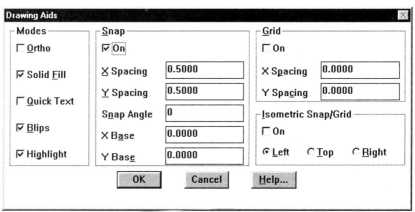

DCL allows programmers to create custom dialog boxes; most of AutoCAD's dialog boxes are DCL files and are not hard-coded. AutoLISP, ADS, and ARx applications load and display the dialog box.

   DCL is a structured language that describes all of the elements (called *tiles*) that make up a dialog box: edit box, list box, radio button, image tile, and so on. Each tile has one or more *attributes* that describe the tile, such as the action, positioning, background color, and tab stops. Autodesk provides no programming environment to help you create DCL files — it's hand coding all the way. However, third-party developers have DCL development tools available.

---

boxed_column

Tile cluster: Places an outline around a column with an optional title.

Example

```
: boxed_column {
    label = "Angle 0 Direction";
    fixed_width = true;
    width = 22;
}
```

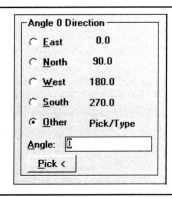

SYNTAX

```
: boxed_column {
    alignment
    children_alignment
    children_fixed_height
    children_fixed_width
    fixed_height
    fixed_width
    height
    label
    width }
```

ATTRIBUTES

- **alignment** = *position*;

  Vertical alignment.

  position: left (default), right, centered.

- **children_alignment** = *position*;

  Default alignment of the cluster's children.

  position: left (default), right, centered.

- **children_fixed_height** = *flag*;

  Default height for all tiles in a cluster.

  flag: true, false (default).

- **children_fixed_width** = *flag*;

  Default width for all tiles in a cluster.

  flag: true, false (default).

- **fixed_height** = *flag*;

    Determines whether height fills available space.

    flag: true, false (default).

- **fixed_width** = *flag*;

    Determines whether width fills available space.

    flag: true, false (default).

- **height** = *nbr*;

    Minimum height of tile.

    nbr: any real or integer number in units of character height.

- **label** = "*str*";

    Text of the box's title.

    str: a string.

- **width** = *nbr*;

    Minimum width of tile.

    nbr: any real or integer number in units of character width.

TIPS

- This tile is the same as the **column** except that it has a border around the column of tiles.
- If the **label** is missing or a null string ("") then the border appears with no title.

RELATED DCL TILES

dialog	The master tile that defines the entire dialog box.
column	A vertical column of tiles.
row	A horizontal row of tiles.
boxed_row	Places a border around a row of tiles.
boxed_radio_column	
	Places a border around a column of radio buttons.
boxed_radio_row	
	Places a border around a row of radio buttons.
radio_column	A radio button.
radio_row	A horizontal row of radio buttons.

boxed_radio_column

Tile cluster: Places an outline around a radio column with an optional title.

Example

```
: boxed_radio_column {
    label="File Format";
    width=40;
}
```

```
┌─ File Format ─────────────────────────┐
│                                       │
│  ⦿ Comma Delimited File (CDF)         │
│                                       │
│  ○ Space Delimited File (SDF)         │
│                                       │
│  ○ Drawing Interchange File (DXF)     │
│                                       │
└───────────────────────────────────────┘
```

SYNTAX

```
: boxed_radio_column {
    alignment
    children_alignment
    children_fixed_height
    children_fixed_width
    fixed_height
    fixed_width
    height
    label
    width }
```

ATTRIBUTES

- **alignment** = *position*;

    Horizontal alignment.

    Row **position**: top, centered (default), bottom.

- **children_alignment** = *position*;

    Default alignment of the cluster's children.

    Row **position**: top, centered (default), bottom.

- **children_fixed_height** = *flag*;

    Default height for all tiles in a cluster.

    flag: true, false (default).

- **children_fixed_width** = *flag*;

    Default width for all tiles in a cluster.

    flag: true, false (default).

- **fixed_height** = *flag*;

    Determines whether height fills available space.

    flag: true, false (default).

- **fixed_width** = *flag*;

     Determines whether width fills available spac.

     flag: true, false (default).

- **height** = *nbr*;

     Minimum height of tile.

     nbr: any real or integer number in units of character height.

- **label** = "*str*";

     Text of the box's title.

     str: a string.

- **width** = *nbr*;

     Minimum width of tile.

     nbr: any real or integer number in units of character width.

TIPS

- This tile is the same as the **radio_column** except that it has a border around the column of radio buttons.

- If the **label** is missing or a null string ("") then the border appears with no title.

RELATED DCL TILES

dialog   The master tile that defines the entire dialog box.

column   A vertical column of tiles.

row   A horizontal row of tiles.

boxed_column   Places a border around a column of tiles.

boxed_row   Places a border around a row of tiles.

boxed_radio_row

                Places a border around a row of radio buttons.

radio_column   A radio button.

radio_row   A horizontal row of radio buttons.

boxed_radio_row

Tile cluster: Places an outline around a radio row with an optional title.

Example

```
boxed_radio_row {
    label="Plot Rotation"
}
```

SYNTAX

```
: boxed_radio_row {
    alignment
    children_alignment
    children_fixed_height
    children_fixed_width
    fixed_height
    fixed_width
    height
    label
    width }
```

ATTRIBUTES

■ **alignment** = *position*;

> Horizontal alignment.

> Row **position**: top, centered (default), bottom.

■ **children_alignment** = *position*;

> Default horizontal alignment of the cluster's children.

> Row **position**: top, centered (default), bottom.

■ **children_fixed_height** = *flag*;

> Default height for all tiles in a cluster.

> **flag**: true, false (default).

■ **children_fixed_width** = *flag*;

> Default width for all tiles in a cluster.

> **flag**: true, false (default).

■ **fixed_height** = *flag*;

> Determines whether height fills available space.

> **flag**: true, false (default).

- **fixed_width** = *flag*;

  Determines whether width fills available space.

  flag: true, false (default).

- **height** = *nbr*;

  Minimum height of tile.

  nbr: any real or integer number in units of character height.

- **label** = "*str*";

  Text of the box's title.

  str: a string.

- **width** = *nbr*;

  Minimum width of tile.

  nbr: any real or integer number in units of character width.

TIPS

- This tile is the same as the **boxed_radio_column** except that it has a border around the row of radio buttons.

- If the **label** is missing or a null string ("") then the border appears with no title.

RELATED DCL TILES

dialog   The master tile that defines the entire dialog box.

column   A vertical column of tiles.

row   A horizontal row of tiles.

boxed_column   Places a border around a column of tiles.

boxed_row   Places a border around a row of tiles.

boxed_radio_column

  Places a border around a column of radio buttons.

radio_column   A radio button.

radio_row   A horizontal row of radio buttons.

boxed_row

Tile cluster: Places an outline around a row with an optional title.

Example

```
boxed_row : {
    label="Logical Colors";
}
```

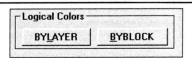

SYNTAX

```
: boxed_row {
    alignment
    children_alignment
    children_fixed_height
    children_fixed_width
    fixed_height
    fixed_width
    height
    label
    width }
```

ATTRIBUTES

- **alignment** = *position*;

    Vertical alignment.

    Row **position**: top, centered (default), bottom.

- **children_alignment** = *position*;

    Default horizontal alignment of the cluster's children.

    Row **position**: top, centered (default), bottom.

- **children_fixed_height** = *flag*;

    Default height for all tiles in a cluster.

    flag: true, false (default).

- **children_fixed_width** = *flag*;

    Default width for all tiles in a cluster.

    flag: true, false (default).

- **fixed_height** = *flag*;

    Determines whether height fills available space.

    flag: true, false (default).

- **fixed_width** = *flag*;

    Determines whether width fills available space.

    flag: true, false (default).

- **height** = *nbr*;

    Minimum height of tile.

    nbr: any real or integer number in units of character height.

- **label** = "*str*";

    Text of the box's title.

    str: a string.

- **width** = *nbr*;

    Minimum width of tile.

    nbr: any real or integer number in units of character width.

TIPS

- This tile is the same as the **boxed_radio_column** except that it has a border around the row of tiles.

- If the **label** is missing or a null string ("") then the border appears with no title.

RELATED DCL TILES

dialog   The master tile that defines the entire dialog box.

column   A vertical column of tiles.

row   A horizontal row of tiles.

boxed_column   Places a border around a column of tiles.

boxed_radio_column

     Places a border around a column of radio buttons.

boxed_radio_row

     Places a border around a row of radio buttons.

radio_column   A radio button.

radio_row   A horizontal row of radio buttons.

button

Active tile: Places a push button with a label.

Example

```
: button {
    label="Template File";
    mnemonic="T";
    key="tmpfil";
}
```

```
[ Template File... ]
```

SYNTAX

```
: button {
    action
    alignment
    fixed_height
    fixed_width
    height
    is_cancel
    is_default
    is_enabled
    is_tab_stop
    key
    label
    mnemonic
    width }
```

ATTRIBUTES

- action = "(*function*)"

  Callback: executes an AutoLISP function when user clicks on button.

  function: name of an AutoLISP function (cannot be ADS or ARx).

- alignment = *position*;

  Horizontal or vertical alignment.

  Column **position**: left (default), right, centered.

  Row **position**: top, centered (default), bottom.

- fixed_width = *flag*;

  Determines whether width fills available space.

  flag: true, false (default).

- fixed_width = *flag*;

  Determines whether width fills available space.

  flag: true, false (default).

- **height** = *nbr*;

    Minimum height of tile.

    nbr: any real or integer number in units of character height.

- **is_cancel** = *flag*;

    Selects button when user presses **[Ctrl]+C** or **[Esc]**.

    flag: true, false (default).

- **is_default** = *flag*;

    Selects button when user presses **[Enter]**.

    flag: true, false (default).

- **is_enabled** = *flag*;

    Determines if button is *not* initially grayed out.

    flag: true (default), false.

- **is_tab_stop** = *flag*;

    Button receives focus when user presses **[Tab]**.

    flag: true (default), false.

- **key** = "*str*";

    The name by which an AutoLISP, ADS, or ARx program refers to this tile.

    str: a string.

- **label** = "*str*";

    Text of the button's title.

    str: a string.

- **mnemonic** = "*char*";

    Button receives focus when user presses key.

    char: a character in the **label**.

- **width** = *nbr*;

    Minimum width of tile.

    nbr: any real or integer number in units of character width.

TIPS

- A button is generally used to exit a dialog box or display another box.
- Every diaogue box must have at least the OK button.

RELATED DCL TILES

edit_box	Enters a single line of text.
image_button	A non-vector image button.
list_box	A scrollable list.
popup_list	A dropbox with a list.
radio_button	A single-choice selector.
slider	A slider.
toggle	A multiple-choice selector.

column

Tile cluster: A column of tiles (including all other tiles except individual radio buttons) with an optional title.

Example
```
: column {
}
```

SYNTAX
```
: column {
    alignment
    children_alignment
    children_fixed_height
    children_fixed_width
    fixed_height
    fixed_width
    height
    label
    width }
```

ATTRIBUTES

■ **alignment** = *position*;

　　　　　　Horizontal alignment.

　　　　　　Row **position:** top, centered (default), bottom.

■ **children_alignment** = *position*;

　　　　　　Default alignment of the cluster's children.

　　　　　　Row **position:** top, centered (default), bottom.

■ **children_fixed_height** = *flag*;

　　　　　　Default height for all tiles in a cluster.

　　　　　　flag: true, false (default).

■ **children_fixed_width** = *flag*;

　　　　　　Default width for all tiles in a cluster.

　　　　　　flag: true, false (default).

■ **fixed_height** = *flag*;

　　　　　　Determines whether height fills available space.

　　　　　　flag: true, false (default).

- **fixed_width** = *flag*;

    Determines whether width fills available space.

    flag: true, false (default).

- **height** = *nbr*;

    Minimum height of tile.

    nbr: any real or integer number in units of character height.

- **label** = "*str*";

    Text of the box's title.

    str: a string.

- **width** = *nbr*;

    Minimum width of tile.

    nbr: any real or integer number in units of character width.

TIP

- A **column** can hold any tile except a solo **radio_button**.

RELATED DCL TILES

dialog   The master tile that defines the entire dialog box.

row   A horizontal row of tiles.

boxed_column Places a border around a column of tiles.

boxed_row   Places a border around a row of tiles.

boxed_radio_column

    Places a border around a column of radio buttons.

boxed_radio_row

    Places a border around a row of radio buttons.

radio_column A radio button.

radio_row   A horizontal row of radio buttons.

concantenation

Text tile: Concantenates one or more **text_part** tiles (an external function defined in Base.Dcl).

Example

```
: concantenate {



}
```

Number found: 0

SYNTAX

```
: concantenate {
    }
```

ATTRIBUTES

none

TIP

■ This function joins one of more text strings together.

RELATED DCL TILES

paragraph   Presents one of more lines of text.

text   A text tile.

text_part   A portion of text.

dialog

Tile cluster: The most important tile, since this defines the dialog box.

Example

```
: dialog {
    initial_focus = "OK"
    label = "Attribute Extraction"
}
```

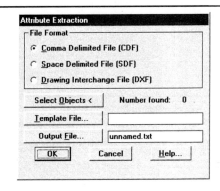

SYNTAX

```
: dialog {
    initial_focus
    label
    value }
```

ATTRIBUTES

■ **initial_focus** = "*str*";

        The key of the tile that receives the initial focus.

        str: a string.

■ **label** = "*str*";

        Text of the dialog box's title.

        str: a string.

■ **value** = "*str*";

        Optional text of the dialog box's title.

        str: a string.

TIP

■ Define either the **label** or the **value**; when both are defined, the **value** takes presidence over the **label**.

RELATED DCL TILES

column   A vertical column of tiles.

row   A horizontal row of tiles.

boxed_column   Places a border around a column of tiles.

boxed_row   Places a border around a row of tiles.

boxed_radio_column

                Places a border around a column of radio buttons.

boxed_radio_row

                Places a border around a row of radio buttons.

radio_column   A radio button.

radio_row   A horizontal row of radio buttons.

edit_box

Active tile: A field that allows the user to type one line of text; with an optional label.

Example

```
: edit_box {
    action = "(editext)";
    allow_accept = true;
    edit_limit = 31;
    edit_width = 31;
    label = "Name: ";
    mnemonic = "N";
    value = "STANDARD";
}
```

```
Name:     STANDARD
```

SYNTAX

```
: edit_box {
    action
    alignment
    allow_accecpt
    edit_limit
    edit_width
    fixed_height
    fixed_width
    height
    is_enabled
    is_tab_stop
    key
    label
    mnemonic
    value
    width }
```

ATTRIBUTES

- **action** = "(*function*)"

  Callback: executes an AutoLISP function when user clicks on button.

  function: name of an AutoLISP function (cannot be ADS or ARx).

- **alignment** = *position*;

  Horizontal alignment.

  Column **position**: left (default), right, centered.

- **allow_accept** = *flag*;

  Accepts the input when the users press [**Enter**] or double-clicks.

  flag: true, false (default).

- **edit_limit** = *int*;

  Maximum number of characters allows for input (maximum = 256).

  int: integer (default= 132).

- **edit_width** = *nbr*;

  Width of the edit box in characters.

  nbr: any real or integer number (default = 0, box stretches to fit available space.)

- **fixed_height** = *flag*;

  Determines whether height fills available space.

  flag: true, false (default).

- **fixed_width** = *flag*;

  Determines whether width fills available space.

  flag: true, false (default).

- **height** = *nbr*;

  Minimum height of tile.

  nbr: any real or integer number in units of character height.

- **is_enabled** = *flag*;

  Determines if button is *not* initially grayed out.

  flag: true (default), false.

- **is_tab_stop** = *flag*;

  Button receives focus when user presses [Tab].

  flag: true (default), false.

- **key** = "*str*";

  The name by which an AutoLISP, ADS, or ARx program refers to this tile.

  str: a string.

- **label** = "*str*";

  Text of the edit box's title.

  str: a string.

- **mnemonic** = "*char*";

  Button receives focus when user presses key.

  char: a character in the **label**.

■ **value** = "*str*";

> Optional, initial text placed in the edit box, which the user sees as the default value.

> **str**: a string.

■ **width** = *nbr*;

> Minimum width of tile.

> **nbr**: any real or integer number in units of character width.

TIPS

■ Text in the edit box is left justified.

■ AutoCAD automatically appends the null character (\0) to the end of the input string.

RELATED DCL TILES

button	A push button.
image_button	A non-vector image button.
list_box	A scrollable list.
popup_list	A dropbox with a list.
radio_button	A single-choice selector.
slider	A slider.
toggle	A multiple-choice selector.

errtile

Exit and error handler: Displays a message the the bottom of the dialog box (*an external function defined in Base.Dcl*).

Example	Result
: errtile;	

SYNTAX
```
: errtile;
```

ATTRIBUTES
none

TIPS
■ This tile is blank by default.

■ This tile is activated by setting another tile's **key** to "error".

■ The errtile code in Base.Dcl:
```
errtile : text {
    label = "";
    key = "error";
    width = 35;
    is_error_tile = true;
```

RELATED DCL TILES
ok_only   The **OK** button.

ok_cancel   The **OK** and **Cancel** buttons.

ok_cancel_help   The **OK**, **Cancel**, and **Help** buttons.

ok_cancel_help_errtile

         The **OK**, **Cancel**, and **Help** buttons and an optional message.

ok_cancel_help_info

         The **OK**, **Cancel**, **Help**, and **Info** buttons.

image

Decorator tile: A rectangle that outlines a vector image.

Example

```
image {
    action = "(dimvart)";
    height = 24;
    key = "dimvartile";
    width = 36;
}
```

SYNTAX

```
: image {
    action
    alignment
    aspect_ratio
    color
    fixed_height
    fixed_width
    height
    is_enabled
    is_tab_stop
    key
    label
    mnemonic
    value
    width }
```

ATTRIBUTES

■ action = "(*function*)"

Callback: executes an AutoLISP function when user clicks on button.

function: name of an AutoLISP function (cannot be ADS or ARx).

■ alignment = *position*;

Horizontal alignment.

Column **position**: left (default), right, centered.

■ aspect_ratio = *real*;

Specifies the ratio of width divided by height; tile is fitted to image size when when 0.0.

real: a real number (default = none).

- **color** = *clr*;

    Fill color for background of image tile.

    clr: name of the color (default = white):

clr	Meaning
black	
red	
yellow	
green	
cyan	Light blue.
blue	
magenta	Pink.
white	Default.
dialog_line	Current dialog box line color.
dialog_foreground	Current dialog box text color.
dialog_background	Current dialog box background color.
graphics_background	AutoCAD graphics screen color.
graphics_foreground	White.

- **fixed_height** = *flag*;

    Determines whether height fills available space.

    flag: true, false (default).

- **fixed_width** = *flag*;

    Determines whether width fills available space.

    flag: true, false (default).

- **height** = *nbr*;

    Minimum height of tile.

    nbr: any real or integer number in units of character height.

- **is_enabled** = *flag*;

    Determines if button is *not* initially grayed out.

    flag: true (default), false.

- **is_tab_stop** = *flag*;

    Button receives focus when user presses [Tab].

    flag: true (default), false.

- **key** = "*str*";

    The name by which an AutoLISP, ADS, or ARx program refers to this tile.

    str: a string.

- **label** = "*str*";

    Text of the button's title.

    str: a string.

- **mnemonic** = "*char*";

    Button receives focus when user presses key.

    char: a character in the **label**.

- **value** = "*str*";

    Optional, initial iamge placed in the image box, which the user sees as the default value.

    str: a string.

- **width** = *nbr*;

    Minimum width of tile.

    nbr: any real or integer number in units of character width.

TIPS

- The image is created using AutoLISP and ADS functions for drawing vector images in dialog box tiles.

- The image could include colors, text styles, linetypes, icons, and other images.

- Either specify both the **height** and **width**, or else one of those two along with the **aspect_ratio**.

RELATED DCL TILES

space   Inserts a space.

spacer_0   Inserts a zero-width space.

spacer_1   Inserts a unit-size space.

image_button

Active tile: A tile that displays an image instead of a label.

Example

```
: image_button{
    action = "(fontn)";
    key = "fontn";
}
```

SYNTAX

```
: image_button {
    action
    alignment
    allow_accept
    aspect_ratio
    color
    fixed_height
    fixed_width
    height
    is_enabled
    is_tab_stop
    key
    label
    mnemonic
    width }
```

ATTRIBUTES

■ **action** = "(*function*)"

Callback: executes an AutoLISP function when user clicks on button.

function: name of an AutoLISP function (cannot be ADS or ARx).

■ **alignment** = *position*;

Horizontal alignment.

Column **position:** left (default), right, centered.

■ *allow_accept* = *flag*;

Accepts the input when the user presses **[Enter]** or double-clicks.

flag: true, false (default).

■ **aspect_ratio** = *real*;

Specifies the ratio of width divided by height; tile is fitted to image size when 0.0.

real: a real number (default = none).

■ **color** = *clr*; Fill color for background of image tile.

clr: name of the color (default = white):

clr	Meaning
black	
red	
yellow	
green	
cyan	Light blue.
blue	
magenta	Pink.
white	Default.
dialog_line	Current dialog box line color.
dialog_foreground	Current dialog box text color.
dialog_background	Current dialog box background color.
graphics_background	AutoCAD graphics screen color.
graphics_foreground	White.

■ **fixed_height** = *flag*;

Determines whether height fills available space.

flag: true, false (default).

■ **fixed_width** = *flag*;

Determines whether width fills available space.

flag: true, false (default).

■ **height** = *nbr*;

Minimum height of tile.

nbr: any real or integer number in units of character height.

■ **is_enabled** = *flag*;

Determines if button is *not* initially grayed out.

flag: true (default), false.

■ **is_tab_stop** = *flag*;

Button receives focus when user presses **[Tab]**.

flag: true (default), false.

■ **key** = "*str*";

The name by which an AutoLISP, ADS, or ARx program refers to this tile.

str: a string.

■ **label** = "*str*";

Text of the button's title.

str: a string.

- **mnemonic** = "*char*";

    Button receives focus when user presses key.

    char: a character in the **label.**

- **width** = *nbr*;

    Minimum width of tile.

    nbr: any real or integer number in units of character width.

TIPS
- This function returns the coordinates of the user's pick point.
- This function displays a raster image instead of a vector image.
- Either specify both the **height** and **width,** or else one of those two along with the aspect_ratio.

RELATED DCL TILES

button	A push button.
edit_box	Enters a single line of text.
list_box	A scrollable list.
popup_list	A dropbox with a list.
radio_button	A single-choice selector.
slider	A slider.
toggle	A multiple-choice selector.

list_box

Active tile: A vertical list of strings with an optional scrollbar and title.

Example

```
: list_box {
    action = "(subdir)";
}
```

SYNTAX

```
: list_box {
    action
    alignment
    fixed_height
    fixed_width
    height
    is_enabled
    is_tab_stop
    key
    label
    list
    mnemonic
    multiple_select
    tabs
    value
    width }
```

ATTRIBUTES

■ action = "(*function*)"

> Callback: executes an AutoLISP function when user clicks on button.
>
> **function**: name of an AutoLISP function (cannot be ADS or ARx).

■ alignment = *position*;

> Horizontal alignment.
>
> Column **position**: left (default), right, centered.

■ fixed_height = *flag*;

> Determines whether height fills available space.
>
> **flag**: true, false (default).

■ fixed_width = *flag*;

> Determines whether width fills available space.
>
> **flag**: true, false (default).

- **height** = *nbr*;

    Minimum height of tile.

    nbr: any real or integer number in units of character height.

- **is_enabled** = *flag*;

    Determines if button is *not* initially grayed out.

    flag: true (default), false.

- **is_tab_stop** = *flag*;

    Button receives focus when user presses **[Tab]**.

    flag: true (default), false.

- **key** = "*str*";

    The name by which an AutoLISP, ADS, or ARx program refers to this tile.

    str: a string.

- **label** = "*str*";

    Text of the list box's title.

    str: a string.

- **list** = "*str*";

    The default text for the list box (no default).

    str: a string with \n to separate lines.

- **mnemonic** = "*char*";

    List box receives focus when user presses key.

    char: a character in the **label**.

- **multiple_select** = *flag*;

    User is allowed to select more than one item.

    flag: true, false (default).

- **tabs** = "*str*";

    Specifies the tab spacing to create vertical columns.

    str: a string of real or integer numbers, separated by a space.

- **value** = "*str*";

    Indicates which list items are initally selected or highlighted.

    str: a string of zero or more integers, separated by a space.

- **width** = *nbr*;

    Minimum width of tile.

    nbr: any real or integer number in units of character width.

TIPS

■ The **list_box** tile can also be used for a list of **radio_button** tiles.

■ The scroll bar automatically appears when there are more items that the **list_box** can hold.

■ Use the **value** attribute to preselect items in the list box to create a default selection.

RELATED DCL TILES

button	A push button.
edit_box	Enters a single line of text.
image_button	A non-vector image button.
popup_list	A dropbox with a list.
radio_button	A single-choice selector.
slider	A slider.
toggle	A multiple-choice selector.

ok_only

Exit and error handler: Displays only the **OK** button and not the **Cancel** or **Help** buttons (*an external function defined in Base.Dcl*).

Example

```
: ok_only;
```

SYNTAX

```
: ok_only;
```

ATTRIBUTES

none

TIPS

- As a minimum, this one button must appear in every dialog box.
- This tile has a pre-assined **key** of "accept."
- The souce code in Base.Dcl:

```
ok_only : column {
  fixed_width = true;
  alignment = centered;
  : ok_button {
      is_cancel = true;
  }
}
```

RELATED DCL TILES

errtile   Displays a message at the bottom of the dialog box.

ok_cancel   The **OK** and **Cancel** buttons.

ok_cancel_help   The **OK**, **Cancel**, and **Help** buttons.

ok_cancel_help_errtile

                 The **OK**, **Cancel**, and **Help** buttons and an optional message.

ok_cancel_help_info

                 The **OK**, **Cancel**, **Help**, and **Info** buttons.

ok_cancel

Exit and error handler: Displays the **OK** and **Cancel** buttons (*an external function defined in Base.Dcl*).

Example

```
: ok_cancel;
```

SYNTAX

```
: ok_cancel;
```

ATTRIBUTES

none

TIPS

■ Most dialog boxes will have this tile, rather than the **ok_only** tile.

■ These two buttons have a **key** pre-assigned: the **OK** button is "accept" and the **Cancel** button is "cancel".

■ The source code in Base.Dcl:

```
ok_cancel : column {
    : row {
        fixed_width = true;
        alignment = centered;
        ok_button;
        : spacer { width = 2; }
        cancel_button;
    }
}
```

RELATED DCL TILES

errtile   Displays a message at the bottom of the dialog box.

ok_only   The **OK** button.

ok_cancel_help The **OK**, **Cancel**, and **Help** buttons.

ok_cancel_help_errtile

       The **OK**, **Cancel**, and **Help** buttons and an optional message.

ok_cancel_help_info

       The **OK**, **Cancel**, **Help**, and **Info** buttons.

ok_cancel_help

Exit and error handler: Displays the **OK, Cancel,** and **Help** buttons (*an external function defined in Base.Dcl*).

Example

```
: ok_cancel_help;
```

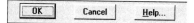

SYNTAX

```
: ok_cancel_help;
```

ATTRIBUTES

none

TIPS

- AutoCAD preassigns a **key** to each othe buttons, as follows:

Button	key
OK	"accept"
Cancel	"Cancel"
Help	"help"

- Have the **Help** button call the **acad_helpdlg** function.
- The souce code in Base.Dcl:

```
ok_cancel_help : column {
    : row {
        fixed_width = true;
        alignment = centered;
        ok_button;
        : spacer { width = 2; }
        cancel_button;
        : spacer { width = 2; }
        help_button;
    }
}
```

RELATED DCL TILES

errtile Displays a message at the bottom of the dialog box.

ok_only The **OK** button.

ok_cancel The **OK** and **Cancel** buttons.

ok_cancel_help_errtile

  The **OK, Cancel,** and **Help** buttons and an optional message.

ok_cancel_help_info

  The **OK, Cancel, Help,** and **Info** buttons.

---

ok_cancel_help_errtile

Exit and error handler: Displays the **OK**, **Cancel**, and **Help** buttons and a text message at the bottom of the dialog box (*an external function defined in Base.Dcl*).

Example

`: ok_cancel_help_errtile;`

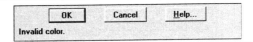

SYNTAX

`: ok_cancel_help_errtile;`

ATTRIBUTES

none

TIPS

■ AutoCAD preassigns a **key** to each othe buttons, as follows:

Button	key
OK	"accept"
Cancel	"Cancel"
Help...	"help"

■ Have the **Help** button call the **acda_helpdlg** function.

■ The souce code in Base.Dcl:

```
ok_cancel_help_errtile : column {
  ok_cancel_help;
  errtile;
}
```

RELATED DCL TILES

errtile   Displays a message at the bottom of the dialog box.

ok_only   The **OK** button.

ok_cancel   The **OK** and **Cancel** buttons.

ok_cancel_help   The **OK**, **Cancel**, and **Help** buttons.

ok_cancel_help_info

                The **OK**, **Cancel**, **Help**, and **Info** buttons.

ok_cancel_help_info

Exit and error handler: Displays the **OK, Cancel, Help,** and info buttons at the bottom of the dialog box (*an external function defined in Base.Dcl*).

Example

: ok_cancel_help_info;

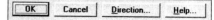

SYNTAX

: ok_cancel_help_info;

ATTRIBUTES

none

TIPS

■ AutoCAD preassigns a **key** to each othe buttons, as follows:

Button	key
OK	"accept"
Cancel	"Cancel"
Help...	"help"
Info...	"info"

■ Have the **Help** button call the **acda_helpdlg** function.

■ The souce code in Base.Dcl:

```
ok_cancel_help_info : column {
    : row {
        fixed_width = true;
        alignment = centered;
        ok_button;
        : spacer { width = 2; }
        cancel_button;
        : spacer { width = 2; }
        help_button;
        : spacer { width = 2; }
        info_button;
    }
}
```

RELATED DCL TILES

errtile   Displays a message at the bottom of the dialog box.

ok_only   The OK button.

ok_cancel   The OK and Cancel buttons.

ok_cancel_help The OK, Cancel, and Help buttons.

ok_cancel_help_errtile

                    The OK, Cancel, and Help buttons and an optional message.

paragraph

Text tile: A vertical cluster of text (*an external function defined in Base.Dcl*).

Example

```
: paragraph {
}
```

> **Linetypes**
> 0 = continuous line
> 1 = ...
> 2 = ----   ----   ----   ----
> 3 = -----   -----   -----   -----
> 4 = ------. ------. ------. ------.
> 5 = ---- - ---- - ---- - ---- -
> 6 = --- - - --- - - --- - - --- - -
>
> **Note: Linetypes 7 thru 12 are valid, adaptive linetypes.**
> **Please see your HP plotter manual**

SYNTAX

```
: paragraph {
    }
```

ATTRIBUTES

none

TIPS

- This function adds a margin around itself.
- The souce code in Base.Dcl:

```
paragraph : cluster {
   layout = vertical;
   fixed_height = true;
}
```

RELATED DCL TILES

concantenation Joins one or more text strings together.

text   A text tile.

text_part   A portion of text.

popup_list

Active tile: A list that pops down when the arrow is clicked.

Example

```
: popup_list{
    action = "(poplist2)";
    edit_wdith = 0;
    key = "poplist2";
    value = "Closed Filled";
}
```

Closed Filled	▼

Closed Filled	▼
None	
Closed	
Dot	
Closed Filled	
Oblique	
Open	
Origin Indication	
Right-Angle	
User Arrow...	

SYNTAX

```
: popup_list {
    action
    alignment
    edit_width
    fixed_height
    fixed_width
    height
    is_enabled
    is_tab_stop
    key
    label
    list
    mnemonic
    tabs
    value
    width }
```

ATTRIBUTES

■ **action** = "(*function*)"

> Callback: executes an AutoLISP function when user clicks on button.
>
> **function**: name of an AutoLISP function (cannot be ADS or ARx).

■ **alignment** = *position*;

> Horizontal alignment.
>
> Column **position**: left (default), right, centered.

■ **edit_width** = *nbr*;

> Width of the edit box in characters.
>
> **nbr**: any real or integer number (default = 0, box stretches to fit available space.)

- **fixed_height** = *flag*;

    Determines whether height fills available space.

    flag: true, false (default).

- **fixed_width** = *flag*;

    Determines whether width fills available space.

    flag: true, false (default).

- **height** = *nbr*;

    Minimum height of tile.

    nbr: any real or integer number in units of character height.

- **is_enabled** = *flag*;

    Determines if button is *not* initially grayed out.

    flag: true (default), false.

- **is_tab_stop** = *flag*;

    Button receives focus when user presses **[Tab]**.

    flag: true (default), false.

- **key** = "*str*";

    The name by which an AutoLISP, ADS, or ARx program refers to this tile.

    str: a string.

- **label** = "*str*";

    Text of the edit box's title.

    str: a string.

- **list** = "*str*";

    The default text for the list box (no default).

    str: a string with \n to separate lines.

- **mnemonic** = "*char*";

    Button receives focus when user presses key.

    char: a character in the **label**.

- **tabs** = "*str*";

    Specifies the tab spacing to create vertical columns.

    str: a string of real or integer numbers, separated by a space.

- **value** = "*str*";

    Indicates which list items are initally selected or highlighted.

    str: a string of zero or more integers, separated by a space.

■ **width** = *nbr*;

Minimum width of tile.

nbr: any real or integer number in units of character width.

TIPS

■ Unlike the **list_box**, the **popup_box** first appears as a single line; the list does not appear until the user clicks on the arrow.

■ Unlike its name, the **popup_box** pops *down*, not up.

■ Use this tile to save on dialog box real estate.

RELATED DCL TILES

button	A push button.
edit_box	Enters a single line of text.
image_button	A non-vector image button.
list_box	A scrollable list.
radio_button	A single-choice selector.
slider	A slider.
toggle	A multiple-choice selector.

radio_button

Active tile: A vertical list of radio buttons.

Example

```
: radio_button {
    action = "(parent)";
    key = "parent";
    label = "Parent";
}
```

```
⊙ Parent
○ Linear
```

SYNTAX

```
: radio_button {
    action
    alignment
    fixed_height
    fixed_width
    height
    is_enabled
    is_tab_stop
    key
    label
    mnemonic
    value
    width }
```

ATTRIBUTES

■ action = "(*function*)"

Callback: executes an AutoLISP function when user clicks on button.

function: name of an AutoLISP function (cannot be ADS or ARx).

■ alignment = *position*;

Horizontal or vertical alignment.

Column **position**: left (default), right, centered.

Row **position**: top, centered (default), bottom.

■ fixed_height = *flag*;

Determines whether height fills available space.

flag: true, false (default).

■ fixed_width = *flag*;

Determines whether width fills available space.

flag: true, false (default).

■ height = *nbr*;

Minimum height of tile.

nbr: any real or integer number in units of character height.

- **is_enabled** = *flag*;

  > Determines if button is *not* initially grayed out.
  >
  > **flag**: true (default), false.

- **is_tab_stop** = *flag*;

  > Button receives focus when user presses **[Tab]**.
  >
  > **flag**: true (default), false.

- **key** = "*str*"; The name by which an AutoLISP, ADS, or ARx program refers to this tile.

  > **str**: a string.

- **label** = "*str*";

  > Text of the button.
  >
  > **str**: a string.

- **mnemonic** = "*char*";

  > Button receives focus when user presses key.
  >
  > **char**: a character in the **label**.

- **value** = "*str*";

  > Determines whether the default of the button is on ("1") or off ("0").
  >
  > **str**: a string; no default.

- **width** = *nbr*;

  > Minimum width of tile.
  >
  > **nbr**: any real or integer number in units of character width.

TIPS

- The user can only select one radio button at a time; use check boxes to select more than one option at a time.

- If you write DCL code that has more than one radio button on, AutoCAD ignores all after the first one it encounters.

- A dot appears when the radio button is on (selected).

- The **radio_button** tile must appear in one of the radio column or row tiles.

RELATED DCL TILES

button	A push button.
edit_box	Enter a single line of text.
image_button	A non-vector image button.
list_box	A scrollable list.
popup_list	A dropbox with a list.
slider	A slider.
toggle	A multiple-choice selector.

radio_column

Tile cluster: A column of radio buttons.

Example

```
: radio_column {
    label = "Parent";
}
```

SYNTAX

```
: radio_column {
    alignment
    children_alignment
    children_fixed_height
    children_fixed_width
    fixed_height
    fixed_width
    height
    label
    width }
```

ATTRIBUTES

■ **alignment** = *position*;

　　　　Vertical alignment.

　　　　position: left (default), right, centered.

■ **children_alignment** = *position*;

　　　　Default alignment of the cluster's children.

　　　　position: left (default), right, centered.

■ **children_fixed_height** = *flag*;

　　　　Default height for all tiles in a cluster.

　　　　flag: true, false (default).

■ **children_fixed_width** = *flag*;

　　　　Default width for all tiles in a cluster.

　　　　flag: true, false (default).

■ **fixed_height** = *flag*;

　　　　Determines whether height fills available space.

　　　　flag: true, false (default).

■ **fixed_width** = *flag*;

　　　　Determines whether width fills available space.

　　　　flag: true, false (default).

- height = *nbr*;

> Minimum height of tile.

> **nbr:** any real or integer number in units of character height.

- label = "*str*";

> The key of the selected radio button.

> **str:** a string of value "1".

- width = *nbr*;

> Minimum width of tile.

> **nbr:** any real or integer number in units of character width.

TIPS

- The user can only select one radio button at a time; use check boxes to select more than one option at a time.

- A dot appears when the radio button is on (selected).

RELATED DCL TILES

dialog The master tile that defines the entire dialog box.

column A vertical column of tiles.

row A horizontal row of tiles.

boxed_column Places a border around a column of tiles.

boxed_row Places a border around a row of tiles.

boxed_radio_column

> Places a border around a column of radio buttons.

boxed_radio_row

> Places a border around a row of radio buttons.

radio_column A radio button.

radio_row A horizontal row of radio buttons.

radio_row

Tile cluster: A row of radio buttons.

Example

```
boxed_column : cluster {
    label = "0";
}
```

| ⊙ **0** | ○ **90** |

SYNTAX

```
: radio_row {
  alignment
  children_alignment
  children_fixed_height
  children_fixed_width
  fixed_height
  fixed_width
  height
  label
  width }
```

ATTRIBUTES

■ **alignment** = *position*;

Horizontal alignment.

Row **position**: top, centered (default), bottom.

■ **children_alignment** = *position*;

Default horizontal alignment of the cluster's children.

Row **position**: top, centered (default), bottom.

■ **children_fixed_height** = *flag*;

Default height for all tiles in a cluster.

flag: true, false (default).

■ **children_fixed_width** = *flag*;

Default width for all tiles in a cluster.

flag: true, false (default).

■ **fixed_height** = *flag*;

Determines whether height fills available space.

flag: true, false (default).

■ **fixed_width** = *flag*;

Determines whether width fills available space.

flag: true, false (default).

- height = *nbr*;

    Minimum height of tile.

    nbr: any real or integer number in units of character height.

- label = "*str*";

    The selected radio button.

    str: a string of format "1".

- width = *nbr*;

    Minimum width of tile.

    nbr: any real or integer number in units of character width.

TIPS

- The user can only select one radio button at a time; use check boxes to select more than one option at a time.

- If you write DCL code that has more than one radio button on, AutoCAD ignores all after the first one it encounters.

- A dot appears when the radio button is on (selected).

RELATED DCL TILES

dialog   The master tile that defines the entire dialog box.

column   A vertical column of tiles.

row   A horizontal row of tiles.

boxed_column   Places a border around a column of tiles.

boxed_row   Places a border around a row of tiles.

boxed_radio_column

    Places a border around a column of radio buttons.

boxed_radio_row

    Places a border around a row of radio buttons.

radio_column   A radio button.

radio_row   A horizontal row of radio buttons.

row

Tile cluster: A row of horizontal tiles.

Example

```
: row {
}
```

Color...	■ BYBLOCK

SYNTAX

```
: row {
    alignment
    children_alignment
    children_fixed_height
    children_fixed_width
    fixed_height
    fixed_width
    height
    label
    width }
```

ATTRIBUTES

■ **alignment** = *position*;

Horizontal alignment.

Row **position**: top, centered (default), bottom.

■ **children_alignment** = *position*;

Default horizontal alignment of the cluster's children.

Row **position**: top, centered (default), bottom.

■ **children_fixed_height** = *flag*;

Default height for all tiles in a cluster.

flag: true, false (default).

■ **children_fixed_width** = *flag*;

Default width for all tiles in a cluster.

flag: true, false (default).

■ **fixed_height** = *flag*;

Determines whether height fills available space.

flag: true, false (default).

■ **fixed_width** = *flag*;

Determines whether width fills available space.

flag: true, false (default).

- **height** = *nbr*;

    Minimum height of tile.

    nbr: any real or integer number in units of character height.

- **label** = "*str*";

    Text displayed with the row of tiles.

    str: a string.

- **width** = *nbr*;

    Minimum width of tile.

    nbr: any real or integer number in units of character width.

RELATED DCL TILES

dialog	The master tile that defines the entire dialog box.
column	A vertical column of tiles.
row	A horizontal row of tiles.
boxed_column	Places a border around a column of tiles.
boxed_row	Places a border around a row of tiles.
boxed_radio_column	

Places a border around a column of radio buttons.

boxed_radio_row

Places a border around a row of radio buttons.

radio_column	A radio button.
radio_row	A horizontal row of radio buttons.

slider

Active tile: A horizontal or vertical slider that returns a 16-bit integer in the range of -32768 to 32767.

Example

```
: slider {
    action = "(slider2)";
    big_increment = 16;
    key = "slider2";
    max_value = 1024;
    small_increment = "1";
    value = "512";
}
```

SYNTAX

```
: slider {
    action
    alignment
    big_increment
    fixed_height
    fixed_width
    height
    key
    label
    Layout
    max_value
    min_value
    mnemonic
    small_increment
    value
    width }
```

ATTRIBUTES

- action = "(*function*)"

    Callback: executes an AutoLISP function when user clicks on button.

    function: name of an AutoLISP function (cannot be ADS or ARx).

- alignment = *position*;

    Horizontal or vertical alignment.

    Column **position**: left (default), right, centered.

    Row **position**: top, centered (default), bottom.

- **big_increment** = *int*;

    The large increment value when user clicks on slider.

    int: an integer in the range of **min_value** and **max_value** (default = $^1/_{10}$ of total range).

- **fixed_height** = *flag*;

    Determines whether height fills available space.

    flag: true, false (default).

- **fixed_width** = *flag*;

    Determines whether width fills available space.

    flag: true, false (default).

- **height** = *nbr*;

    Minimum height of tile.

    nbr: any real or integer number in units of character height.

- **key** = "*str*"; The name by which an AutoLISP, ADS, or ARx program refers to this tile.

    str: a string.

- **label** = "*str*";

    Text of the slider's title.

    str: a string.

- **layout** = "*position*";

    Orientation of the slider.

    position: horizontal (default), vertical.

- **max_value** = *int*;

    Maximum value the slider returns (maximum = 32767).

    int: a 16-bit integer (default = 10000).

- **min_value** = *int*;

    Minimum value the slider returns (minimum = -32768).

    int: a 16-bit integer (default = 0).

- **mnemonic** = "*char*";

    Button receives focus when user presses key.

    char: a character in the **label**.

- **small_increment** = *int*;

    The large increment value when user clicks on slider.

    int: an integer in the range of **min_value** and **max_value** (default = $^1/_{10}$ of total range).

■ value = "*str*";

        The current value of the slider.

        str: a string holding the value of an integer.

■ width = *nbr*;

        Minimum width of tile.

        nbr: any real or integer number in units of character width.

TIP

■ Depending on where the user clicks, the slider moves faster or slower.

RELATED DCL TILES

button	A push button.
edit_box	Enters a single line of text.
image_button	A non-vector image button.
list_box	A scrollable list.
popup_list	A dropbox with a list.
radio_button	A single-choice selector.
toggle	A multiple-choice selector.

spacer

Decorator tile: A blank tile.

Example

```
: spacer {
}
```

Extension	0.0000
Spacing:	0.3800
Color...	■ BYBLOCK

SYNTAX

```
: spacer {
    alignment
    fixed_height
    fixed_width
    height
    width }
```

ATTRIBUTES

- **alignment** = *position*;

    Horizontal or vertical alignment.

    Column **position**: left (default), right, centered.

    Row **position**: top, centered (default), bottom.

- **fixed_width** = *flag*;

    Determines whether width fills available space.

    flag: true, false (default).

- **fixed_width** = *flag*;

    Determines whether width fills available space.

    flag: true, false (default).

- **height** = *nbr*;

    Minimum height of tile.

    nbr: any real or integer number in units of character height.

- **width** = *nbr*;

    Minimum width of tile.

    nbr: any real or integer number in units of character width.

TIPS

■ This (and the other spacer tiles) are not normally needed since AutoCAD often automatically spaces tiles.

■ This tile affects the placement of the next tile.

RELATED DCL TILES

image   Displays a vector image.

spacer_0 Inserts a zero-width space.

spacer_1 Inserts a unit-size space.

spacer_0

Decorator tile: A blank tile of no initial width but can grow dynamically (*an external function defined in Base.Dcl*).

Example

```
: spacer_0;
```

SYNTAX

```
: spacer_0;
```

ATTRIBUTES

none

TIPS

■ This (and the other spacer tiles) are not normally needed since AutoCAD often automatically spaces tiles.

■ Use this function to tell AutoCAD where to automatically put extra space, when needed.

■ This tile affects the placement of the next tile.

■ The source code in Base.Dcl:

```
spacer_0 : spacer {
    height = 0;
    width = 0;
    horizontal_margin = none;
    vertical_margin = none;
}
```

RELATED DCL TILES

image   Displays a vector image.

spacer   Inserts a space.

spacer_1   Inserts a unit-size space.

spacer_1

Decorator tile: A blank tile of width and height equal to 1 (*an external function defined in Base.Dcl*).

Example
```
: spacer_1;
```

SYNTAX
```
: spacer_1;
```

ATTRIBUTES
none

TIPS
■ This (and the other spacer tiles) are not normally needed since AutoCAD often automatically spaces tiles.

■ This tile affects the placement of the next tile.

■ The souce code in Base.Dcl:

```
spacer_1 : spacer {
    height = 1;
    width = 1;
    horizontal_margin = none;
    vertical_margin = none;
}
```

RELATED DCL TILES
image   Displays a vector image.

spacer   Inserts a space.

spacer_0   Inserts a zero-width space.

text

Text tile: Places a string of text.

Example

```
: text {
    key = "subdir2";
    label = "D:\acad13\win";
}
```

D:\acad13\win

SYNTAX

```
: text {
    alignment
    fixed_height
    fixed_width
    height
    is_bold
    key
    label
    value
    width }
```

ATTRIBUTES

- **alignment** = *position*;

    Vertical alignment.

    position: left (default), right, centered.

- **fixed_height** = *flag*;

    Determines whether height fills available space.

    flag: true, false (default).

- **fixed_width** = *flag*;

    Determines whether width fills available space.

    flag: true, false (default).

- **height** = *nbr*;

    Minimum height of tile.

    nbr: any real or integer number in units of character height.

- **is_bold** = *flag*;

    Determines whether text is displayed in boldface style.

    flag: true, false (default).

- **key** = *"str"*;

    A reference name used by the AutoLISP, ADS, or ARx program.

    str: a case-sensitive string.

- **label** = "*str*";

    Text displayed by tile.

    str: a string.

- **value** = "*str*";

    Text displayed by tile.

    str: a string.

- **width** = *nbr*;

    Minimum width of tile.

    nbr: any real or integer number in units of character width.

TIP

- This function is rarely needed since most tiles have their own title.

RELATED DCL TILES

concantenation Joins one or more text strings together.

paragraph   Presents one or more lines of text.

text_part   A portion of text.

text_part

Text tile: A text tile that can be concantenated with other text (*an external function defined in Base.Dcl*).

Example

```
: text_part {
    label = "Min";
}
```

SYNTAX

```
: text {
    label }
```

ATTRIBUTE

■ label = "*str*";

Text displayed by tile.

str: a string.

TIPS

■ Use this tile in conjunction with the **concantenate** tile.

The souce code in Base.Dcl:

```
text_part : text {
    horizontal_margin = none;
    vertical_margin = none;
}
```

RELATED DCL TILES

concantenation Joins one or more text strings together.

paragraph   Presents one of more lines of text.

text   A text tile.

toggle

Active tile: A check box.

Example

```
: toggle {
    action = "(endpt)";
    label = "Endpoint";
    value = "1"
}
```

⊠ Endpoint	☐ Insertion
☐ Midpoint	⊠ Perpendicular

SYNTAX

```
: toggle {
    action
    alignment
    fixed_height
    fixed_width
    height
    is_enabled
    is_tab_stop
    label
    value
    width }
```

ATTRIBUTES

■ action = "(*function*)"

Callback: executes an AutoLISP function when user clicks on button.

function: name of an AutoLISP function (cannot be ADS or ARx).

■ alignment = *position*;

Horizontal or vertical alignment.

Column **position**: left (default), right, centered.

Row **position**: top, centered (default), bottom.

■ fixed_width = *flag*;

Determines whether width fills available space.

flag: true, false (default).

■ fixed_height = *flag*;

Determines whether height fills available space.

flag: true, false (default).

■ height = *nbr*;

Minimum height of tile.

nbr: any real or integer number in units of character height.

- **is_enabled** = *flag*;

    Determines if button is *not* initially grayed out.

    flag: true (default), false.

- **is_tab_stop** = *flag*;

    Button receives focus when user presses **[Tab]**.

    flag: true (default), false.

- **label** = "*str*";

    Text of the check box's title.

    str: a string.

- **value** = "*str*";

    Default value of the check box where the X appears if "1" and is unchecked if "0".

    str: a string (default = "0").

- **width** = *nbr*;

    Minimum width of tile.

    nbr: any real or integer number in units of character width.

RELATED DCL TILES

button	A push button.
edit_box	Enters a single line of text.
image_button	A non-vector image button.
list_box	A scrollable list.
popup_list	A dropbox with a list.
radio_button	A single-choice selector.
slider	A slider.

Introduction to System Variables

AutoCAD stores information about the current state of itself, the drawing and the operating system in *system variables*. The variables help programmers (who often work with menu macros and AutoLISP) determine the state of the AutoCAD system.

Variables

TIPS

■ You get a list of system variables at the Command: prompt with the ? options of the SetVar command:

```
Command: setvar
Variable name or ?: ?
```

■ *Italicized system variables* are not listed by the **SetVar ?** command nor in AutoCAD's *Command Reference*.

■ Some system variables have the same name as a command, such as Area; other variables do not work at the Command: prompt. These are prefixed by the 7 character.

■ **Default Value:** The table lists all known system variables, along with the default values as set in the Acad.Dwg prototype drawing.

■ **Ro:** Some system variables cannot be changed by the user or by programming; these are labeled "R/O" (short for "read only") in the table below.

■ **Loc:** System variables are stored in a variety of places:

■ Acad	AutoCAD executable (hard-coded)
■ Cfg	Acad.Cfg or Acad.XmX files
■ Dwg	Current drawing
■ ...	Not saved

Variable	Default	Ro	Loc	Meaning
_PKSER	117-999999	R/o	Acad	Software package serial number
_SERVER	0	R/o	Cfg	Network authorization code

A

Variable	Default	Ro	Loc	Meaning
ACADPREFIX	"d:\ACAD13\"	R/o	...	Path spec'd by ACAD environment var
ACADVER	"13"	R/o	...	AutoCAD version number
AFLAGS	0	...	...	Attribute display code:
				0 No mode specified
				1 Invisible
				2 Constant
				4 Verify
				8 Preset
ANGBASE	0	...	Dwg	Direction of zero degrees relative to UCS
ANGDIR	0	...	Dwg	Rotation of angles:
				0 Clockwise
				1 Counterclockwise
APERTURE	10	...	Cfg	Object snap aperture in pixels:
				1 Minimum size
				10 Default size
				50 Maximum size
AREA	0.0000	R/o	...	Area measured by Area, List or Dblist
ATTDIA	0	...	Dwg	Attribute entry interface:
				0 Command-line prompts
				1 Dialog box
ATTMODE	1	...	Dwg	Display of attributes:
	0	Off		
				1 Normal
				2 On
ATTREQ	1	...	Dwg	Attribute values during insertion are:
				0 Default values
				1 Prompt for values
AUDITCTL	0	...	Cfg	Determines creation of ADT audit log file:
				0 File not created
				1 ADT file created

Variable	Default	Ro	Loc	Meaning
AUNITS	0	...	Dwg	Mode of angular units:
				0 Decimal degrees
				1 Degrees-minutes-seconds
				2 Grads
				3 Radians
				4 Surveyor's units
AUPREC	0	...	*Dwg*	*Decimals places displayed by angles*
AUXSTAT	*0*	...	*Dwg*	*-32768 Minimum value*
				32767 Maximum value
AXISMODE	*0*	...	*Dwg*	*Obsolete system variable*
AXISUNIT	*0.0000*	...	*Dwg*	*Obsolete system variable*

B

Variable	Default	Ro	Loc	Meaning
BACKZ	0.0000	R/o	Dwg	Back clipping plane offset
⌨ BLIPMODE	1	...	Dwg	Display of blip marks:
				0 Off
				1 On

C

Variable	Default	Ro	Loc	Meaning
CDATE	19950105.15560660	R/o	...	Current date and time in YyyyMmDd.HhMmSsDd format
CECOLOR	"BYLAYER"	...	Dwg	Current entity color
CELTSCALE	1.0000	...	Dwg	Global linetype scale
CELTYPE	"BYLAYER"	...	Dwg	Current layer color
CHAMFERA	0.0000	...	Dwg	First chamfer distance
CHAMFERB	0.0000	...	Dwg	Second chamfer distance
CHAMFERC	0.0000	...	Dwg	Chamfer length
CHAMFERD	0	...	Dwg	Chamfer angle
CHAMMODE	0	...	..	Chamfer input mode:
				0 Chamfer by two lengths
				1 Chamfer by length and angle.
CIRCLERAD	0.0000	...	...	Most-recent circle radius:
				0 No default
CLAYER	"0"	...	Dwg	Current layer name

Variable	Default	Ro	Loc	Meaning
CMDACTIVE	1	R/o	...	Type of current command:
				1 Regular command
				2 Transparent command
				4 Script file
				8 Dialog box
CMDDIA	1	...	Cfg	Plot command interface:
				0 Command line prompts
				1 Dialog box
CMDECHO	1	...	...	AutoLISP command display:
				0 No command echoing
				1 Command echoing
CMDNAMES	"SETVAR"	R/o	...	Current command
CMLJUST	0	...	Cfg	Multiline justification mode:
				0 Top
				1 Middle
				2 Bottom
CMLSCALE	1.0000	...	Cfg	Scales width of multiline:
				-1 Flips offsets of multiline
				0 Collapses to single line
				1 Default
				2 Doubles multiline width
CMLSTYLE	"STANDARD"	Cfg	...	Current multiline style name
COORDS	1	...	Dwg	Coordinate display style:
				0 Updated by screen picks
				1 Continuous display
				2 Polar display upon request
CVPORT	2	...	Dwg	Current viewport number
				2 Minimum (default)

D

Variable	Default	Ro	Loc	Meaning
DATE	2448860.54043252	R/o	...	Current date and fraction in Julian format
DBGLISTALL	*0*	...	...	*Toggle*

Variable	Default	Ro	Loc	Meaning
DBMOD	0	R/o	...	Drawing modified in these areas:
				0 No modification made
				1 Entity database
				2 Symbol table
				4 Database variable
				8 Window
				16 View
DCTCUST	""	...	Cfg	Name of custom spelling dicitonary
DCTMAIN	"enu"	...	Cfg	Code for spelling dictionary:
				ca Catalan
				cs Czech
				da Danish
				de German - sharp 's'
				ded German - double 's'
				ena English - Australian
				ens English - British: 'ise'
				enu English - American
				enz English - British: 'ize'
				es Spanish - unaccented capitals
				esa Spanish - accented captitals
				fi Finish
				fr French - unaccented capitals
				fra French - accented captials
				it Italian
				nl Dutch - primary
				nls Dutch - secondary
				no Norwegian - Bokmal
				non Norwegian - Nynorsk
				pt Portuguese - Iberian
				ptb Portuguese - Brazilian
				ru Russian - infrequent 'io'
				rui Russian - frequent 'io'
				sv Swedish

Variables

Variable	Default	Ro	Loc	Meaning
DELOBJ	1	...	Dwg	Toggle source objects deletion:
				0 Objects deleted
				1 Objects retained
DIASTAT	1	R/o	...	User exited dialog box by clicking on:
				0 Cancel button
				1 OK button

DIMENSION VARIABLES

Variable	Default	Ro	Loc	Meaning
DIMALT	0	...	Dwg	Alternate units selected
DIMALTD	2	...	Dwg	Alternate unit decimal places
DIMALTF	25.4000	...	Dwg	Alternate unit scale factor
DIMALTTD	2	...	Dwg	Tolerance alternate unit decimal places
DIMALTTZ	0	...	Dwg	Alternate tolerance units zeros:
				0 Zeros not suppressed
				1 Zeros suppressed
DIMALTU	2	...	Dwg	Alternate units:
				1 Scientific
				2 Decimal
				3 Engineering
				4 Architectural
				5 Fractional
DIMALTZ	0		Dwg	Zero supresion for alternate units:
				0 Zeros not suppressed
				1 Zeros suppressed
DIMAPOST	""	...	Dwg	Suffix for alternate text
DIMASO	1	...	Dwg	Create associative dimensions
DIMASZ	0.1800	...	Dwg	Arrow size
DIMAUNIT	0	...	Dwg	Angular dimension format:
				0 Decimal degrees
				1 Degrees.Minutes.Seconds
				2 Grad
				3 Radian
				4 Surveyor units
DIMBLK	""	R/o	Dwg	Arrow block name
DIMBLK1	""	R/o	Dwg	First arrow block name

Variable	Default	Ro	Loc	Meaning
DIMBLK2	""	R/o	Dwg	Second arrow block name
DIMCEN	0.0900	...	Dwg	Center mark size
DIMCLRD	0	...	Dwg	Dimension line color
DIMCLRE	0	...	Dwg	Extension line & leader color
DIMCLRT	0	...	Dwg	Dimension text color
DIMDEC	4	...	Dwg	Primary tolerance decimal places.
DIMDLE	0.0000	...	Dwg	Dimension line extension
DIMDLI	0.3800	...	Dwg	Dimension line continuation increment
DIMEXE	0.1800	...	Dwg	Extension above dimension line
DIMEXO	0.0625	...	Dwg	Extension line origin offset
DIMFIT	3	...	Dwg	Placement of text and arrowheads:
				0 Between extension lines if possible
				1 Text has priority over arrowheads
				2 Whichever fits between ext lines
				3 Whatever fits
				4 Place text at end of leader line
DIMGAP	0.0900	...	Dwg	Gap from dimension line to text
DIMJUST	0	...	Dwg	Horizontal text positioning:
				0 Center justify
				1 Next to first extension line
				2 Next to second extension line
				3 Above first extension line
				4 Above second extension line
DIMLFAC	1.0000	...	Dwg	Linear unit scale factor
DIMLIM	0	...	Dwg	Generate dimension limits
DIMPOST	""	...	Dwg	Default suffix for dimension text
DIMRND	0.0000	...	Dwq	Rounding value
DIMSAH	0	...	Dwg	Separate arrow blocks
DIMSCALE	1.0000	...	Dwg	Overall scale factor
DIMSD1	Off	...	Dwg	Suppress first dimension line
DIMSD2	Off	...	Dwg	Suppress second dimension line
DIMSE1	0	...	Dwg	Suppress the first extension line
DIMSE2	0	...	Dwg	Suppress the second extension line
DIMSHO	1	...	Dwg	Update dimensions while dragging

Variables

Variable	Default	Ro	Loc	Meaning
DIMSOXD	0	...	Dwg	Suppress outside extension dimension
DIMSTYLE	"STANDARD"	R/o	Dwg	Current dimension style (read-only)
DIMTAD	0	...	Dwg	Place text above the dimension line
DIMTDEC	4	...	Dwg	Primary tolerance decimal places
DIMTFAC	1.0000	...	Dwg	Tolerance text height scaling factor
DIMTIH	1	...	Dwg	Text inside extensions is horizontal
DIMTIX	0	...	Dwg	Place text inside extensions
DIMTM	0.0000	...	Dwg	Minus tolerance
DIMTOFL	0	...	Dwg	Force line inside extension lines
DIMTOH	1	...	Dwg	Text outside extensions is horizontal
DIMTOL	0	...	Dwg	Generate dimension tolerances
DIMTOLJ	1	...	Dwg	Tolerance vertical justification:
				0 Bottom
				1 Middle
				2 Top
DIMTP	0.0000	...	Dwg	Plus tolerance
DIMTSZ	0.0000	...	Dwg	Tick size
DIMTVP	0.0000	...	Dwg	Text vertical position
DIMTXSTY	"STANDARD"	...	Dwg	Dimension text style
DIMTXT	0.1800	...	Dwg	Text height
DIMTZIN	0	...	Dwg	Tolerance zero suppression
DIMUNIT	2	...	Dwg	Dimension unit format
				1 Scientific
				2 Decimal
				3 Engineering
				4 Architectural
				5 Fractional
DIMUPT	Off	...	Dwg	User-positioned text:
				0 Cursor positions dimension line
				1 Cursor also positions text
DIMZIN	0	...	Dwg	Suppression of zero in feet-inches units:
				0 Suppress 0 feet and 0 inches
				1 Include 0 feet and 0 inches
				2 Include 0 feet; suppress 0 inches
				3 Suppress 0 feet; include 0 inches

Variable	Default	Ro	Loc	Meaning
DISPSILH	0	...	Dwg	Silhouette display of 3D solids:
				0 Off
				1 On
DISTANCE	0.0000	R/o	...	Distance measured by Dist command
DONUTID	0.5000	...	...	Inside radius of donut
DONUTOD	1.0000	...	...	Outside radius of donut
📟 DRAGMODE	2	...	Dwg	Drag mode:
				0 No drag
				1 On if requested
				2 Automatic
DRAGP1	10	...	Cfg	Regen drag display
DRAGP2	25	...	Cfg	Fast drag display
DWGCODEPAGE	"dos850"	Dwg	...	Drawing code page
DWGNAME	"UNNAMED"	R/o	...	Current drawing filename
DWGPREFIX	"d:\"	R/o	...	Drawing's drive and subdirectory
DWGTITLED	0	R/o	...	Drawing has filename:
				0 "Untitled.Dwg"
				1 User-assigned name
DWGWRITE	1	...	...	Drawing read-write status:
				0 Read-only
				1 Read-write

E

Variable	Default	Ro	Loc	Meaning
EDGEMODE	0	...	...	Toggle edge mode for Trim & Extend:
				0 No extension
				1 Extends cutting edge.
ELEVATION	0.0000	...	Dwg	Current elevation relative to current UCS
ENTMODS	*193*	*R/o*	...	
ERRNO	*0*	...	...	*Error number from AutoLISP,ADS,Arx*

Variable	Default	Ro	Loc	Meaning
EXPERT	0	...	...	Controls prompts:
				0 Normal prompts
				1 Supress these messages: "About to regen, proceed?" "Really want to turn the current layer off?"
				2 Also suppress: "Block already defined. Redefine it?" "A block with this name already exists. Overwrite it?"
				3 Also suppress messages related to the Linetype command.
				4 Also suppress messages related to the UCS Save and VPorts Save commands.
				5 Also suppress messages related to the DimStyle Save and DimOverride commands.
EXPLMODE	1	...	Dwg	Toggle whether Explode and Xplode commands explode non-uniformly scaled blocks:
				0 Does not explode.
				1 Does explode
EXTMAX	11.3706,10.0130,0,000	R/o	Dwg	Upper right coordinate of drawing extents
EXTMIN	1.0158,5.6333,0.000	R/o	Dwg	Lower left coordinate of drawing extents

F

Variable	Default	Ro	Loc	Meaning
FACETRES	0.5	...	Dwg	Adjusts smoothness of shaded and hidden-line objects:
				0.01 Minimum value
				0.05 Default value
				10.0 Maximum value

Variable	Default	Ro	Loc	Meaning
FFLIMIT	0	...	Cfg	Maximum number of PostScript and TrueType fonts loaded into memory: 0 No limit 1 One font 100 Maximum value
FILEDIA	1	...	Cfg	User interface: 0 Command-line prompts 1 Dialog boxes (when available)
FILLETRAD	0.0000	...	Dwg	Current fillet radius
FILLMODE	1	...	Dwg	Fill of solid objects: 0 Off 1 On
FLATLAND	*0*	*R/o*	*...*	*Obsolete system variable*
FONTALT	"txt"	...	Cfg	Name for substituted font.
FONTMAP	""	...	Cfg	Name of font mapping file.
FORCE_PAGING	*0*	*...*	*...*	*0 Minimum (default)* *1,410,065,408 Maximum*
FRONTZ	0.0000	R/o	Dwg	Front clipping plane offset

G

Variable	Default	Ro	Loc	Meaning
GLOBCHECK	*0*	*...*	*...*	*Reports statistics on dialog boxes:* *0 Turn off* *1 Warns if larger than 640x400* *2 Also reports size in pixels* *3 Additional info*
GRIDMODE	0	...	Dwg	Display of grid: 0 Off 1 On
GRIDUNIT	0.0000,0.0000	...	Dwg	X,y-spacing of grid
GRIPBLOCK	0	...	...	Display of grips in blocks: 0 At insertion point 1 At all entities within block

Variable	Default	Ro	Loc	Meaning
GRIPCOLOR	5	...	Cfg	Color of unselected grips
				1 Minimum color number
				5 Default color: blue
				255 Maximum color number
GRIPHOT	1	...	Cfg	Color of selected grips
				1 Default: red
				255 Maximum color number
GRIPS	1	...	Cfg	Display of grips:
				0 Off
				1 On
GRIPSIZE	3	...	Cfg	Size of grip box, in pixels
				1 Minimum size
				3 Default size
				255 Maximum size

H

Variable	Default	Ro	Loc	Meaning
▦ HANDLES	1	R/o	...	Obsolete system variable
HIGHLIGHT	1	...	...	Object selection highlighting:
				0 Disabled
				1 Enabled
HPANG	0	...	...	Current hatch pattern angle
HPBOUND	1	...	Dwg	Object created by BHatch and Boundary commands:
				0 Polyline
				1 Region
HPDOUBLE	0	...	...	Double hatching:
				0 Disabled
				1 Enabled
HPNAME	"ANSI31"	...	...	Current hatch pattern name
				"" No default
				. Set no default
HPSCALE	1.0000	...	...	Current hatch pattern scale factor
HPSPACE	1.0000	...	...	Current spacing of user-defined hatching

Variable	Default	Ro	Loc	Meaning
I				
INSBASE	0.0000,0.0000,0.0000	...	Dwg	Insertion base point relative to current UCS
INSNAME	""	...	...	Current block name
				. Set to no default
				"" No default
ISOLINES	4	...	Dwg	Isolines on 3D solids:
				0 Minimum
				4 Default
				16 Good-looking
				2,047 Maximum
L				
LASTANGLE	0	R/o	...	Ending angle of last-drawn arc
LASTPOINT	0.0000,0.0000,0.0000	...	Dwg	Last-entered point
▣ *LAZYLOAD*	*0*	...	...	*Toggle 0 or 1*
LENSLENGTH	50.0000	R/o	Dwg	Perspective view lens length, in mm
LIMCHECK	0	...	Dwg	Drawing limits checking:
				0 Disabled
				1 Enabled
LIMMAX	12.0000,9.0000	...	Dwg	Upper right drawing limits
LIMMIN	0.0000,0.0000	...	Dwg	Lower left drawing limits
LOCALE	"en"	R/o		ISO language code
LOGINNAME	"??"	R/o	Dwg	User's login name
▣ LTSCALE	1.0000	...	Dwg	Current linetype scale factor
LUNITS	2	...	...	Linear units mode:
				1 Scientific
				2 Decimal
				3 Engineering
				4 Architectural
				5 Fractional
LUPREC	4	...	Dwg	Decimal places of linear units

Variables

Variable	Default	Ro	Loc	Meaning
M				
MACROTRACE	*0*	...	...	*Diesel debug mode:*
				0 *Off*
				1 *On*
MAXACTVP	16	...	...	Maximum viewports to regenerate:
				0 Minimum
				16 Default
				32767 Maximum
MAXSORT	200	...	Cfg	Maximum filenames to sort alphabetically:
				0 Minimum
				16 Default
				32767 Maximum
MAXOBJMEM	2,147,483,647	...	...	Maximum number of objects in memory
MENUCTL	1	...	...	Submenu display:
				0 Only with menu picks
				1 Also with keyboard entry
MENUECHO	0	...		Menu and prompt echoing:
				0 All prompts displayed
				1 Suppress menu echoing
				2 Suppress system prompts
				4 Disable ^P toggle
				8 Display all input-output strings
MENUNAME	"acad"	R/o	...	Current menu filename
MIRRTEXT	1	...	Dwg	Text handling during Mirror command:
				0 Mirror text
				1 Retain text orientation
MODEMACRO		""	...	... Invoke Diesel programming language
MTEXTED	""	...	Cfg	External mtext editor
N				
NODENAME	*"AC$"*	*R/o*	*Cfg*	*Name of network node (1 to 3 chars)*

Variable	Default	Ro	Loc	Meaning
O				
OFFSETDIST	-1.0000	...	...	Current offset distance; Through mode, if negative
ORTHOMODE		0	...	Dwg Orthographic mode:
				0 Off
				1 On
OSMODE	0	...	Dwg	Current object snap mode:
				0 NONe
				1 ENDpoint
				2 MIDpoint
				4 CENter
				8 NODe
				16 QUAdrant
				32 INTersection
				64 INSertion
				128 PERpendicular
				256 TANgent
				512 NEARest
				1024 QUIck
				2048 APPint
P				
PDMODE	0	...	Dwg	Point display mode:
				0 Dot
				1 No display
				2 +-symbol
				3 x-symbol
				4 Short line
				32 Circle
				64 Square
PDSIZE	0.0000	...	Dwg	Point display size, in pixels
				-1 Absolute size
				0 5% of drawing area height
				+1 Percentage of viewport size

Variable	Default	Ro	Loc	Meaning
PELLIPSE	0	...	Dwg	Toggle Ellipse creation:
				0 True ellipse
				1 Polyline
PERIMETER	0.0000	R/o	...	Perimeter calculated by Area command
PFACEVMAX	4	R/o	...	Maximum vertices per 3D face
PHANDLE	*0*	...	...	*2,803,348,672 Maximum*
PICKADD	1	...	Cfg	Effect of [Shift] key on selection set:
				0 Adds to selection set
				1 Removes from selection set
PICKAUTO	1	...	Cfg	Selection set mode:
				0 Single pick mode
				1 Automatic windowing and crossing
PICKBOX	3	...	Cfg	Object selection pickbox size, in pixels
PICKDRAG	0	...	Cfg	Selection window mode:
				0 Pick two corners
				1 Pick 1 corner; drag to 2nd corner
PICKFIRST	1	...	Cfg	Command-selection mode:
				0 Enter command first
				1 Select objects first
PICKSTYLE	1	...	Dwg	Included groups and associative hatches in selection:
				0 Neither included
				1 Include groups
				2 Include associative hatches
				3 Include both
PLATFORM	"386 DOS Extender"	R/o	Acad	AutoCAD platform name:
				"386 DOS Extender"
				"DECstation"
				"Microsoft Windows"
				"Silicon Graphics Iris Indego"
				"Sun4/SPARCstation"
PLINEGEN	0	...	Dwg	Polyline linetype generation:
				0 From vertex to vertex
				1 From end to end

Variable	Default	Ro	Loc	Meaning
PLINEWID	0.0000	...	Dwg	Current polyline width
PLOTID	""	...	Cfg	Current plotter
PLOTROTMODE	1	...	Dwg	Orientation of plots:
				0 Lowerleft = 0
				1 Lowerleft plotter area = lowerleft
				of media
PLOTTER	1	...	Cfg	Current plotter configuration number:
				0 No plotter configured
				29 Maximum configurations
POLYSIDES	4	...	...	Current number of polygon sides:
				3 Minimum sides
				4 Default
				1024 Maximum sides
POPUPS	1	R/o	...	Display driver support of AUI:
				0 Not available
				1 Available
PROJMODE	1	...	Cfg	Projection mode for Trim & Extend:
				0 No projection
				1 Project to x,y-plane of current UCS
				2 Project to view plane
PSLTSCALE	1	...	Dwg	Paper space linetype scaling:
				0 Use model space scale factor
				1 Use viewport scale factor
PSPROLOG	""	...	Cfg	PostScript prologue filename
PSQUALITY	75	...	Dwg	Resolution of PostScript display, in pixels:
				$-n$ Display as outlines; no fill
				0 No display
				$+n$ Display filled

Q

Variable	Default	Ro	Loc	Meaning
QAFLAGS	*1*	...	...	*Quality assurance flags*
QTEXTMODE	0	...	Dwg	Quick text mode:
				0 Off
				1 On

Variables

Variable	Default	Ro	Loc	Meaning
R				
RASTERPREVIEW	0	...	Dwg	Preview image:
				0 BMP format
				1 BMP and WMF formats
				2 WMF format
				3 None saved.
REGENMODE	1	...	Dwg	Regeneration mode:
				0 Regen with each new view
				1 Regen only when required
RE-INIT	...	...		Reinitialize I/O devices:
				1 Digitizer port
				2 Plotter port
				4 Digitizer
				8 Plotter
				16 Reload PGP file
RIASPECT	1.0000	...	Rasterin	Raster image aspect ration
RIBACKG	0	...	Rasterin	Raster image background color
				0 Black; default
				7 White
				255 Maximum value
RIEDGE	0	...	Rasterin	Raster image edge detection mode:
				0 Off
				1 On
				255 Maximum value
RIGAMUT	256	...	Rasterin	Raster image gamut of colors
				8 Minimum value
				256 Maximum (default)
RIGREY	0	...	Rasterin	Raster image gray scale conversion:
				0 Off
				1 On
RITHRESH	0	...	Rasterin	Raster image brightness threshold
				0 Off
				255 Maximum threshold value

Variable	Default	Ro	Loc	Meaning
S				
SAVEFILE	"AUTO.SV$"	R/o	Cfg	Automatic save filename
SAVENAME	""	R/o	...	Drawing save-as filename
SAVETIME	120	...	Cfg	Automatic save interval, in minutes
				0 Disable auto save
				120 Default
SCREENBOXES	26	R/o	Cfg	Maximum number of menu items
				0 Screen menu turned off
SCREENMODE	0	R/o	Cfg	State of AutoCAD display screen:
				0 Text screen
				1 Graphics screen
				2 Dual-screen display
SCREENSIZE	575.0000,423.0000	R/o	...	Current viewport size, in pixels
SHADEDGE	3	...	Dwg	Shade style:
				0 Shade faces (256-color shading)
				1 Shade faces; edges background color
				2 Simulate hidden-line removal
				3 16-color shading
SHADEDIF	70	...	Dwg	Percent of diffuse to ambient light
				0 Minimum
				70 Default
				100 Maximum
SHPNAME	""	...	...	Current shape name
				. Set to no default
				"" No default
SKETCHINC	0.1000	...	Dwg	Sketch command's recording increment
SKPOLY	0	...	Dwg	Sketch line mode:
				0 Record as lines
				1 Record as polylines
SNAPANG	0	...	Dwg	Current rotation angle for snap and gird
SNAPBASE	0.0000,0.0000	...	Dwg	Current origin for snap and grid

Variables

Variable	Default	Ro	Loc	Meaning
SNAPISOPAIR	0	...	Dwg	Current isometric drawing plane:
				0 Left isoplane
				1 Top isoplane
				2 Right isoplane
SNAPMODE	0	...	Dwg	Snap mode:
				0 Off
				1 On
SNAPSTYL	0	...	Dwg	Snap style:
				0 Normal
				1 Isometric
SNAPUNIT	1.0000,1.0000	...	Dwg	X,y-spacing for snap
SORTENTS	96	...	Cfg	Entity display sort order:
				0 Off
				1 Object selection
				2 Object snap
				4 Redraw
				8 Slide generation
				16 Regeneration
				32 Plots
				64 PostScript output
SPLFRAME	0	...	Dwg	Polyline and mesh display:
				0 Polyline control frame not displayed; Display polygon fit mesh; 3D faces invisible edges not displayed
				1 Polyline control frame displayed; display polygon defining mesh; 3D faces invisible edges displayed
SPLINESEGS	8	...	Dwg	Number of line segments that define a splined polyline
SPLINETYPE	6	...	Dwg	Spline curve type:
				5 Quadratic bezier spline
				6 Cubic bezier spline

Variable	Default	Ro	Loc	Meaning
SURFTAB1	6	...	Dwg	Density of surfaces and meshes:
				2 Minimum
				6 Default
				32766 Maximum
SURFTAB2	6	...	Dwg	Density of surfaces and meshes
				2 Minimum
				6 Default
				32766 Maximum
SURFTYPE	6	...	Dwg	Pedit surface smoothing:
				5 Quadratic bezier spline
				6 Cubic bezier spline
				8 Bezier surface
SURFU	6	...	Dwg	Surface density in m-direction
				2 Minimum
				6 Default
				200 Maximum
SURFV	6	...	Dwg	Surface density in n-direction
				2 Minimum
				6 Default
				200 Maximum
SYSCODEPAGE	"dos850"	R/o	Dwg	System code page
T				
TABMODE	0	...	...	Tablet mode:
				0 Off
				1 On
TARGET	0.0000,0.0000,0.0000	R/o	Dwg	Target in current viewport
TDCREATE	2448860.54014699	R/o	Dwg	Time and date drawing created
TDINDWG	0.00040625	R/o	Dwg	Duration drawing loaded
TDUPDATE	2448860.54014699	R/o	Dwg	Time and date of last update
TDUSRTIMER	0.00040694	R/o	Dwg	Time elapsed by user-timer
TEMPPREFIX	""	R/o	...	Path for temporary files
TEXTEVAL	0	...	...	Interpretation of text input:
				0 Literal text
				1 Read (and ! as AutoLISP code

Variables

Variable	Default	Ro	Loc	Meaning
TEXTFILL	0	...	Dwg	Toggle fill of PostScript &TrueType fonts:
				0 Outline text
				1 Filled text
TEXTQLTY	50	...	Dwg	Resolution of PostScript &TrueType fonts:
				0 Minimum resolution
				50 Default
				100 Maximum resolution
TEXTSIZE	0.2000	...	Dwg	Current height of text
TEXTSTYLE	"STANDARD"	...	Dwg	Current name of text style
THICKNESS	0.0000	...	Dwg	Current entity thickness
TILEMODE	1	...	Dwg	Viewport mode:
				0 Display tiled viewports
				1 Display overlapping viewports
TOOLTIPS	1	...	Cfg	Display tooltips (in Windows only):
				0 Off
				1 On
TRACEWID	0.0500	...	Dwg	Current width of traces
TREEDEPTH	3020	...	Dwg	Maximum branch depth in xxyy format:
				xx Model-space nodes
				yy Paper-space nodes
				+n 3D drawing
				-n 2D drawing
TREEMAX	10000000	...	Cfg	Limits memory consumption during drawing regeneration
TRIMMODE	1			Trim toggle for Chamfer & Fillet:
				0 Leave selected edges in place
				1 Trim selected edges

Variable	Default	Ro	Loc	Meaning
U				
UCSFOLLOW	0	...	Dwg	New UCS views:
				0 No change
				1 Automatic display of plan view
UCSICON	1	...	Dwg	Display of UCS icon:
				0 Off
				1 On
				2 Display at UCS origin, if possible
UCSNAME	""	R/o	Dwg	Name of current UCS view
				"" Current UCS is unnamed
UCSORG	0.0000,0.0000,0.0000	R/o	Dwg	Origin of current UCS relative to WCS
UCSXDIR	1.0000,0.0000,0.0000	R/o	Dwg	X-dir of current UCS relative to WCS
UCSYDIR	0.0000,1.0000,0.0000	R/o	Dwg	Y-dir of current UCS relative to WCS
UNDOCTL	5	R/o	...	State of undo:
				0 Undo disabled
				1 Undo enabled
				2 Undo limited to one command
				4 Auto-group mode
				8 Group currently active
UNDOMARKS	0	R/o	...	Current number of undo marks
UNITMODE	0	...	Dwg	Units display:
				0 As set by Units command
				1 As entered by user
USERI1–I5	*0*	...	...	*Five user-definable integer variables*
USERR1–R5	*0.0000*	...	...	*Five user-definable real variables*
USERS1–S5	*""*	...	...	*Five user-definable string variables*

Variables

Variable	Default	Ro	Loc	Meaning
V				
VIEWCTR	6.2433,4.5000,0.0000	R/o	Dwg	X,y-coordinate of center of current view
VIEWDIR	0.0000,0.0000,1.0000	R/o	Dwg	Current view direction relative to UCS
VIEWMODE	0	R/o	Dwg	Current view mode:
				0 Normal view
				1 Perspective mode on
				2 Front clipping on
				4 Back clipping on
				8 UCS-follow on
				16 Front clip not at eye
VIEWSIZE	9.0000	R/o	Dwg	Height of current view
VIEWTWIST	0	R/o	Dwg	Twist angle of current view
VISRETAIN	0	...	Dwg	Determination of xref drawing's layers:
				0 Current drawing
				1 Xref drawing
VSMAX	37.4600,27.00,0.00	R/o	Dwg	Upper right corner of virtual screen
VSMIN	-24.9734,-18.00,0.00	R/o	Dwg	Lower left corner of virtual screen
W				
WORLDUCS	1	R/o	...	Matching of WCS with UCS:
				0 Current UCS is not WCS
				1 UCS is WCS
WORLDVIEW	1	...	Dwg	Display during Dview &Vpoint commands:
				0 Display UCS
				1 Display WCS
X				
XREFCTL	0	...	Cfg	Determines creation of XLG xref log files:
				0 File no written
				1 XLG file written

Topical Index

DIALOG BOXES, continued

DISPLAY CONTROL

ERROR HANDLERS

EXTERNAL APPLICATIONS

EXTERNAL APPLICATIONS, continued

FILE FUNCTIONS

FUNCTIONS

LIST MANIPULATION

LOGIC FUNCTIONS

MATH FUNCTIONS

OBJECT HANDLERS, continued

OBSOLETE FUNCTIONS

OUTPUT FUNCTIONS

QUICK STARTS

RESULT BUFFER

STRING MANIPULATION

SYMBOL HANDLERS

TABLES

USER INPUT

NOTES

NOTES

NOTES

NOTES

NOTES

NOTES